BOLLINGEN SERIES V

PAUL RADIN

THE ROAD
OF LIFE AND DEATH

A RITUAL DRAMA

OF THE AMERICAN INDIANS

WITH A FOREWORD BY MARK VAN DOREN

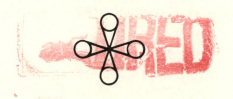

BOLLINGEN SERIES V

PRINCETON UNIVERSITY PRESS

Published by Princeton University Press, 41 William Street,
Princeton, New Jersey 08540
In the United Kingdom: Princeton University Press, Oxford

THIS VOLUME IS THE FIFTH IN A SERIES OF BOOKS
SPONSORED BY THE BOLLINGEN FOUNDATION

Library of Congress Card No. 72-7844
ISBN 0-691-09819-0 (hardback)
ISBN 0-691-01916-9 (paperback)

Fourth printing and first Princeton paperback printing for the
Mythos series, 1991

Princeton University Press books are printed on acid-free paper,
and meet the guidelines for permanence and durability of the
Committee on Production Guidelines for Book Longevity of the
Council on Library Resources

10 9 8 7 6 5 4

Printed in the United States of America
by Princeton University Press,
Princeton, New Jersey

TO MARY MELLON

IN APPRECIATION

THE AUTHOR

EDITOR'S NOTE

In presenting the following ritual-drama to an English-speaking audience presumably unacquainted with the higher aspects of American Indian life, I have had a twofold purpose in view. I wished to make certain first that the translation was accurate and complete and, secondly, to know that it was cast in a form both intelligible and meaningful to readers belonging to a civilization so utterly different from the Winnebago.

I need hardly stress the difficulties attendant upon a translation of Winnebago or, for that matter, of any Indian language into a European tongue. But, in this particular instance, these difficulties were accentuated and augmented by the highly rhetorical and special Winnebago diction, and by the symbolical significance and esoteric meaning attached to so many words and passages. A literal rendering would have been quite meaningless.

Two alternatives, I felt, were open to me. I could either give the literal meanings and provide sufficient notes to explain what the secondary esoteric meanings were, or incorporate, wherever feasible, this secondary meaning into the text itself. I have adopted the latter course and employed it in the following manner. Whenever, to give but one of many instances, the word *announcer* or *messenger* was used with the ritualistic implication of drum or gourd, I have, on the first few occasions of its use, added the words drum or gourd. When, however, the esoteric meaning could not possibly be given in one word, then I have given the literal translation and transferred the esoteric meaning to a note. One example of my procedure will have to suffice. A passage where the literal meaning would be 'Turtle threw himself upon our grandfather, the sacred woman, and life emerged from his navel,' I have rendered as such and then explained its actual significance here in a note.

None of the symbolical or esoteric meanings given, are my own. They were obtained from the Winnebago who dictated the text to me. Nor do they represent my informant's individual interpretations. They are extensions of meaning that have been handed down for many generations and learned by every member of the ceremony who cares to obtain them. They

vii

must be specifically purchased. In a number of cases where my informant failed to give me the meanings, either because he forgot to do so or because he knew that I was acquainted with them, I have provided them myself. In all such cases I had ample confirmatory evidence in my possession.

The notes are of two kinds. The overwhelming number represent the traditional Winnebago exegesis on the text. A few, however, give ethnological information that it was imperative for the reader to possess. These, of course, are exclusively mine and are based on a thirty-year knowledge of the tribe. This knowledge, itself, was acquired not only through personal observation covering many years but also in accounts given to me in Winnebago and embracing some ten thousand pages.

In pursuance of the second purpose I have had in view, namely, of giving an alien reader a better possibility of understanding the ceremony, I have prefixed an introduction to the ceremony which I am calling the prologue, containing a number of narratives pertinent to the ritual-drama itself. They are four in number: snatches from the autobiography of my informant; the account of his invitation to join the ceremony as given by his brother-in-law and mentor, to which I have appended the latter's description of his three reincarnations; the origin myth of the world and of the ceremony obtained in another connection, and, lastly, the description of the ghost's journey to spiritland as it is recounted in the ceremonies for the dead. I have placed the last two narratives in an imaginative setting, but every word in it has been taken from the ritual-drama itself. Needless to say the two narratives, themselves, have not been changed or tampered with in any way. The connections between the various parts of the prologue are, of course, also mine.

My object in having this prologue is primarily to prepare the reader for the actual account of the ritual instead of allowing him to be thrown into it unprepared and, possibly, becoming too bewildered. I had, however, a secondary purpose in mind, namely, of giving him some picture of two vital Winnebago personalities, Jasper Blowsnake who told me the ritual at such a great price to himself, materially and spiritually, and his brother-in-law, Thunder-Cloud, Blowsnake's mentor and one of the great figures of the Winnebago civilization of his time. Besides, I felt it important to let the reader realize, by giving two versions of the same myth, the origin myth and the journey to spiritland, the variations which the same myth may possess.

Those among my readers to whom such things are repugnant, and those

viii

among my anthropological colleagues who regard such things as unwarrantable interferences with an ethnological text, are recommended to begin with the account of the ritual-drama proper.

The text is presented as it was dictated to me. Due to the manner in which it was secured, slight inconsistencies are present. I did not feel justified, however, in correcting them. Those portions that are purely descriptive have been set off in smaller type from the dialogue proper. The songs are not included. Most of the rather complete collection I possessed was destroyed. Owing to technical difficulties it would, however, have been quite impossible to translate them, even had they not been destroyed.

In conclusion, I wish to thank the Bureau of American Ethnology for permitting me to use that part of the material contained in the following pages which was secured under their auspices many years ago.

PAUL RADIN

New York City, August 1944

CONTENTS

FOREWORD

"The problem then resolves itself into finding the native." This sentence from Paul Radin's preface to *Crashing Thunder*, the autobiography of Jasper Blowsnake's younger brother, is relevant to most of what I want to say, or feel capable of saying, about the great document which fills the following pages. Jasper Blowsnake is the name of the Winnebago from whom Mr. Radin secured the text of his Medicine Rite, a text unique in its completeness, and one which I think will long be studied for its revelation of Indian philosophy and religion at their best. I am not competent to speak of what is revealed, but I know Mr. Radin, and I hope I shall be pardoned for becoming personal about him. For his character is at the bottom of his success as an ethnologist.

Jasper Blowsnake and other Winnebago to whom Mr. Radin in 1908 went as one desirous "of obtaining an inside view of their culture from their own lips and by their own initiative" came to the conclusion that he must have been sent by God, since he came at precisely the moment in their history when success was possible. Their old religion was fading, and a new one which promised to take its place had not yet done so to the degree that the Medicine Rite, for instance, was forgotten by those who had known it. Jasper Blowsnake remembered it, but he had just now ceased to respect it as the sole vehicle of truth. He could be induced to repeat it; and he did so, in the manner described hereafter by Mr. Radin.

What Jasper Blowsnake could not have known was that Mr. Radin was extraordinarily, not to say uniquely, equipped for the enterprise. The miraculous thing was not when he came but who he was. "The usual external fashion" of collecting data "which is the pride of scientific procedure among ethnologists" was only the first item in his equipment. The rest of it was human character—the same simple thing that made it possible for *Crashing Thunder* to tell Mr. Radin all he knew about himself, and that on other occasions has made Negroes, Japanese, and Chinese confide their life stories to him, and that makes all of Mr. Radin's friends so much at home with him. He knows a secret which is as old as the world. Other people are both different from you and similar to you. All men have much in common. And the business of telling secrets is mu-

xiii

tual. The white man who would understand the Indian must remember that the Indian wants to understand him also. Mr. Radin both received and gave during those long months when Jasper Blowsnake committed the once mortal sin of repeating the Medicine Rite.

"This, too, remember," ran the ritual at one point. "Never tell anyone about this Rite. Keep it absolutely secret. If you disclose it the world will come to an end. We will all die. . . . Into the very bowels of our grandmother, Earth, must we project this information, so that by no possible chance can it ever emerge into daylight. So secret must this be kept. Forever and ever must this be done." But Jasper Blowsnake went ahead. Nor need we, I take it, feel ashamed of knowing what in consequence we now know concerning the ancient Winnebago way of life. It is a way that has been lost forever, along with the newer way which in 1908 promised to replace it. Winnebago culture is extinct, or is in the last stages of becoming so. Its intense effort to perpetuate itself through centuries of self-contemplation in the manner of this Rite has reached its period, and only Mr. Radin's text remains as evidence of that effort. "Such a highly artificial drama," says Mr. Radin at the conclusion of a passage in *Primitive Religion* which is concerned with the Winnebago Medicine Dance, "can manifestly represent the achievement only of men who have thought deeply on the meaning of life, who possessed the artistic skill to articulate their vision and the leisure in which to do it, not to mention an audience that was willing to accept it." The readers of this book are free to consider themselves an extension of such an audience. And if they are without pride they may hope to learn something they had not previously known about the meaning of life on earth.

New York, 1945   MARK VAN DOREN

xiv

THE ROAD OF LIFE AND DEATH

PROLOGUE

Crashing-Thunder steps forward and speaks:

Nianājinga, Stands-on-the-water, my friend.

What I am about to tell you was told to me by Thunder-Cloud, my brother-in-law, and to no one else. If any other person claims to know the Medicine Rite as given by our band, he is not telling you the truth for to no other man but myself did Thunder-Cloud reveal it.

Up to the present time this ritual was known only to the Winnebago and not again, be assured, will I tell it to a member of your race . . .

I am called Warudjaxega, Crashing-Thunder. It is said that when the thunderbirds come, they approach to the accompaniment of crashes of thunder. Everything, everyone on earth, they deluge with rain—the animals, the plants, human beings and the earth itself. For all of this they have a name, Warudjaxega. That is my name.

When I was a very small child, the first thing that has stayed in my memory is how my father once carried me to a long lodge where I saw many Indians sitting. I remember particularly an old man with very gray hair who was sitting there, singing and drumming. To a seat near him my father carried me and we both sat down. Closely and intently I watched that old man. I remember clearly how I enjoyed his drumming and singing and I wondered whether I, too, when I grew older, would be able to drum and sing and deliver speeches as he did. How I yearned to be able to say what he was saying! This, I remember clearly, was in my mind.

As I grew older, all these yearnings and desires remained steadfast within me, were ever uppermost in my heart. At no time did they stop agitating me. At all times it was my most fervent desire and goal to learn the songs that I had heard the old man sing when I was a child in arms and which I had then enjoyed so keenly: this, and

1

the thorough knowledge of all the old customs so dear and sacred to the tribe. Assuredly, it was the influence of these thoughts and desires that enabled me to kill my first deer and derive so much pleasure from it. Assuredly, it was the influence of these same thoughts and desires which soon brought it about that I was placed in charge of the ceremonial deer-hunts, with the obligation of securing all the deer needed for the feasts. Sometimes twelve, sometimes eight, sometimes only six, were secured, all by me.

My uncles were loud in their approbation of my efforts and encouraged me into believing that, some day, the most coveted of all possessions, the warbundle, would be mine. Indeed it would be mine, that and whatsoever speeches my ancestors delivered in connection with the rites associated with it. 'May we be present when you deliver them!' they prayed.

Moreover, so my uncles assured me, if I continued as I had begun, all the members of my family would think highly of me and place in my hands the means for obtaining a full life. Indeed, at that time, my father turned over to me a right that belonged to him namely, the one of selecting the names for my fellow clansmen.

From the time I was a young child I had had a brother-in-law named Thunder-Cloud. He was living his third life as a human being. Many years ago he had lived on this earth, joined the Medicine Rite and adhered strictly to all its precepts. He had then been a good man, a virtuous man, disliking no one, never stealing and never fighting. Well did he perform all his duties as a member of the Medicine Rite, continually making offerings of tobacco, giving feasts and preparing the sacrificial beverage.

Finally, after reaching a ripe old age, he died. Properly and humbly he had progressed along the Road of the sacred Rite. That now was finished. Up above, where all those go who have heeded the injunctions of the Rite, he went. There, in this new home, he lived and there he married.

After living there some time, he prepared to come back to earth. Once a month he fasted and all the different spirits whom Earthmaker had created, gave him their blessings. And so, in the course of time, he was born again on earth, born as a human being. Here

2

on this earth he fasted again and the spirits above, who dwelt where Earthmaker sits, all bestowed their blessings upon him. Thus he became a holy man, a shaman, in fact the reincarnation of the North-Spirit.

In the course of time he became my brother-in-law and I went along with him when he was on his errands, doctoring.

Once I, myself, fell ill and he treated me. As soon as he came, my father arose with his tobacco and made him an offering, speaking to him as follows:

'Son-in-law, tobacco, here do I offer you, and I shall make offerings to the spirits who blessed you as well. Clearly you have been encouraged in holiness, clearly the spirits have bestowed their powers upon you.' Thus spoke my father as he arose, weeping.

And he, my brother-in-law, for whom tobacco was being poured, accepted what we gave and exerted his powers that I might become well again. Standing above me he then recounted his fasting experience:

'Brother-in-law, this is how I learned to cure human beings. I was carried up to the spirit-village of those who live in the sky, a doctor's village, and there I was instructed as follows. A dead and rotten log, almost completely covered with weeds, was placed in the middle of the lodge. This log I was to treat as though it were a sick human being. I breathed upon the log and the spirits in the lodge breathed with me. Twice, three times, four times, we did the same. Finally the log that had seemed dead was transformed into a young man, who arose and walked away. "Human being," said the spirits, "you are indeed a holy person!"

'Brother-in-law, from the middle of the ocean, the spirits came after me, from a shaman's village situated there. They, too, bestowed their powers upon me and they, too, made me try my powers. They asked me to blow upon waves they had created, all of them as large as the ocean, and I blew upon them and they became as quiet as water in a small saucer. Three times I did this and three times I succeeded. Then the spirits created a choppy ocean, where the waves piled one upon the other furiously and I was told to blow upon it.

3

I did so and that ocean of waves, mighty as it was, subsided and became quiet.

' "Human being," they said, "thus will you always act. There will indeed be nothing that you cannot accomplish. No matter what illness one of your fellowmen may happen to have, you will be able to cure it."

'Brother-in-law, at Blue-Clay-Bank (St. Paul) is the home of the dancing grizzly-bear spirits. From that place they came for me to bestow their blessings upon me, to tell me that should I ever meet with some sudden trouble they would come to my aid. They told me that I could offer them as much tobacco as I thought fit, that they would always accept and smoke it. There they gave me some songs as well as the power of beholding them, a holy sight. Their claws, a holy thing, they gave me. Finally, these grizzly-bear spirits danced, exhibiting their powers as they danced. They would tear open their abdomens, then making themselves holy, heal themselves. Or, again, they would shoot bear-claws at each other and stand there choking with blood. Then, making themselves holy, they would cure themselves.'

Then my brother-in-law sang, breathed upon me and finally squirted some water upon my chest. 'All of this I have told you,' he said to me, 'is quite true and is very holy. Indeed, you will get well.'

My brother-in-law knew all the good medicines that exist and all of them he used in order to cure me. I recovered from my illness and got well. From this I knew that Thunder-Cloud was holy.

On another occasion Thunder-Cloud told me that he had come from the home of Earthmaker and that Earthmaker had told him to bring back with him, in due time, four Indians. They were to be virtuous men—they were not to be quick-tempered and not to be men of changeable ideas. On the contrary, they were to be truly virtuous—men of conservative tendencies. And he led me to believe I might be one of them.

For all these things, I loved my brother-in-law. Never did I show any disrespect toward him. Whatever he told me to do, I did. Never was I angry at him. Zealously and painstakingly did I live up to all the obligations I took upon myself for I felt that if, in return for them,

4

he loved me and bestowed upon me his blessings, I would assuredly be one of the four men he was to take back with him to Earthmaker. Wholeheartily did I wish to be like him. In all my associations with him this was always uppermost in my thoughts. Earnestly and sincerely did I wish to be taken to the presence of Earthmaker and, since I saw my brother-in-law very scrupulous and careful in his dealings with him, so I, too, behaved accordingly.

I was about thirteen years and over, when they told me that they would make me a member of the Medicine Rite. I liked the idea very much. Some people do not like it at all when they are asked to join. But I did. I knew my parents desired me to accept and I was happy to do it for their sake. But, apart from that, I knew that it was the only way in which I could hope to attain to a holy life.

When everything was in readiness for my initiation, we moved to the place where the ceremony was to take place. That night they were to begin the singing at the Medicine Rite and I knew my relatives were to participate. When night came they preached to me and told me how sacred a ceremony it was into which I was now to be initiated. Never had there been so perfect a life, I was told, as the one I was about to lead as a member of this Rite. In fact, so they assured me, I could not possibly visualize such a life, if I tried, nor the prestige and love I would derive from membership.

All this I liked. Nor was I one of those who thought that when, during the initiation, I was shot with the sacred shell, I would be killed as some believed and feared.

The time had now arrived for me to be taken to the Brush-Lodge where I was to be told about the sacred shell and where I was to be initiated into the meaning of the shooting ceremony. I knew that I was to be shot with the sacred shell after the elders had first preached to me. At no time did the prospect of being shot frighten me nor was I in the least bit worried about it, nor did I think to myself, 'I wonder how it's going to be,' as many people do.

Then those who were old-time members of the Medicine Rite, those whom I had had uppermost in my mind throughout my childhood, shot me with the shell. When they shot me I did not die. It is true that such a thought had actually entered my mind for a moment. However, I did not lose consciousness, even for a second. It did not take me long to learn how to shoot properly and the older Medicine Rite members were pleased and delighted with my proficiency.

After the Brush-Ceremony was over I entered the lodge proper. Not in any direction did I glance. Not once did I speak nor move about nor change my position. I remained sitting just where they put me, immobile and uninquisitive as to who was in the lodge or how many. Not once did I permit my glance to wander from side to side.

Thereafter, whenever a performance of the Rite was given, I attended it and stayed in the lodge throughout the night without leaving it. Throughout the Day-Ceremony, too, I stayed without once leaving the lodge. At no time did I permit my glance to stray outside; at no time did I permit myself to lie down from fatigue. Thus had I been told to behave in the midst of sacred things. This was a sacred ceremony and I was bashful in its presence.

This ceremony molded me. I paid the most careful attention to it. I worshipped it as best I knew how. I was careful about everything I did. I never drank. A holy way of life I was seeking. Most earnestly did I pray to obtain the reward for a holy life in the Medicine Rite, to become reincarnated. This it is for which my heart yearned. The members of the Medicine Rite had told me that if, properly and reverently, I obeyed all the things the ceremony enjoined, I would return to Earthmaker. I was considerate to everyone and everyone loved me. This ritual was made with love! . . .

Thunder-Cloud steps forward and speaks:

Crashing-Thunder, Brother-in-law, I have come to speak to you about your ancestors and what they, those Winnebago of yore, were accustomed to say to one who was about to be honored with the request to join this sacred Rite of ours.

I have come to you to speak about their ancient ways and their manner of behavior, about their actions and words that have been handed down to us to the present time.

6

I have come to you with a request from these ancestors and their descendants, that you join this sacred Rite, Earthmaker's way of life. Be assured, only thus can you attain to a true and full life. They have come to you humbly asking that you take pity upon them by joining. Needless it is to recall to you their ancient ways and how, naked and without modern apparel, they nevertheless attained a fuller measure of happiness than today, attained a fuller life. This it is they now offer you.

Needless it is to recall to you the burdens they put upon themselves to attain this full measure of life; how they fasted, how they exposed themselves to cold and sufferings to accomplish their purpose. Is it too much to ask that you take cognizance of these, their humble endeavors, and accede to their entreaty by having compassion upon them? I beg of you, brother-in-law, do not refuse them or me.

This that you will attain is the only true and full life that exists. By accepting you will also bestow this life upon your fellow members, even upon your ancestors. Give them this life!

I wait for your reply. Did I hear you say, 'Yes?' How happy they will be at your acceptance! And you, too, assuredly must be filled with happiness just as am I. I say to you, you have brought them joy and filled them with pride and confidence.

It is I, Thunder-Cloud, who speak, I who am now on earth for the third time, I who am now repeating experiences that I well remember from my previous existences.

Once, many, many years ago I lived with a people who had twenty camps. When I was but a young boy, not large enough to handle a gun, our village was attacked by an enemy warparty and we were all killed, killed to the last man. I did not know, however, that I had been killed. All I knew and felt was that I was running about just as I had been accustomed to do. Not until I saw a heap of bodies piled upon the ground, mine among them, did I realize that I was really dead. No one was present to bury us.

There on the ground we lay and rotted.

Then I was taken to the place where the sun sets and I lived happily for some time with an old couple. In this particular village of spirit-

7

land the inhabitants have the best of times. Whenever you wish to go anywhere, all that you have to do is to wish yourself there and you reach your destination immediately. And so it was that, after a few years, the thought ran through my mind that I would like to return to the earth. Immediately the old man with whom I was staying turned to me and said, 'My son, did you not just say something about wanting to return to the earth again?' Now, as a matter of fact, I had not uttered a word. I had merely thought about it. Yet the old man knew of my thought and of what I wanted. Then, again, he addressed me and said, 'I know you can go but, nevertheless, you must first ask permission from the chief of the village.'

So I went to the chief and I told him of my desire. He listened and then answered me, 'Go, my son, and obtain your full revenge upon those who killed all your relatives and you.'

Thus was I brought back to the earth again. Now it did not seem to me that I entered a woman's womb. Indeed I felt that I had somehow been brought into a room, a room where I remained sitting continuously. Never, throughout all this period, did I lose consciousness. Always, I was keenly aware of what was happening outside. Indeed, it was because of the noise made by some little children which came to my ears that I decided to go outside. And then, it seemed to me, that I was making my way through a door into the open. I stumbled through, and a sudden rush of cold air struck me so bitterly that I began to cry. So, in fact, it appeared. Actually, of course, I was being born from a woman's womb.

In the new village into which I was born, I was taught to fast in order to prepare myself adequately and completely for warfare, for my purpose in returning to this earth. In due course of time I went on the warpath. I did so repeatedly until I had taken full revenge for the death of myself and my dear relatives.

Until old age I stayed in that village, living a full life and taking my revenge. I finally died of old age. My bones became unjointed and my ribs caved in.

This was the second time that I had known death. I felt no more pain then, lost no more awareness of things then, than I had done the first time.

8

When they buried me it was not as they do now. Sticks were first placed in the grave and upon them was laid my body wrapped in a blanket. Throughout it all, I was conscious and watched the people at their various tasks.

There in the grave I lay and rotted.

As I was lying there, rotting, I heard someone speak to me saying, 'Come, we must leave now!' Obediently I arose and we walked, the two of us, in the direction of the sun where lies the village of the dead. There all the people are gay and enjoy themselves, giving dance after dance, joyful, riotous dances. Four nights I was told I would have to stay at this village, but they meant four years.

When my stay was about over I was taken up to the home of Earthmaker. There, at his own home, I saw him and talked to him, face to face, even as now I speak to you. The spirits, too, I saw. In fact I was one of them.

Then I came back again to this world. Here I am.

So let me recall to you, brother-in-law, how all this came about and describe for you that memorable occasion when I myself was initiated many generations ago. Here it is . . .

A summer night just before dawn. An opening in a forest leading to a small secluded thicket. A few old men and women are standing near the entrance to this thicket. One of them is looking intently toward the east. As soon as he notices the first faint streaks of dawn he whispers to the others and they disappear in the brush. He remains standing, ears strained, as if listening for something.

Suddenly a single drumbeat resounds in the distance. Then silence. Another drumbeat, this time nearer. Then a third and a fourth. The old man stands with head slightly bent, peering into the semi-darkness.

In the distance a line of men and women can now be discerned walking slowly, in single file, toward the entrance of the thicket. An old man dressed in full ceremonial garb leads. On each of his cheeks is painted a blue circle. In his right hand he carries a pouch made of a whole otter-skin. The paws of the animal and its tail are encased in wrappings made of porcupine quills. To the end of the pouch are attached a number of small metal bells. His moccasins are likewise covered with porcupine quill decorations. Anklets made of buckskin, to which small pieces of copper are attached, knock against one another as he walks. He is the giver of the ceremony, the Ancestor-Host or Source. Behind him walks a young man very simply dressed and looking somewhat frightened.

9

He is the person to be initiated, the Candidate. *His ceremonial name is* Nephew *or* He-for-whom-we-seek-life. *Then follow four old men all dressed like the leader but with different decorations painted on their faces. They, too, carry pouches made of the whole skin of an otter. The first man is the guest of honor, the Leader of the East Band, the second is the Leader of the North Band, the third the Leader of the West Band and the fourth the Leader of the South Band. Behind the Leader of the South Band walk twelve comparatively young men, in single file, each one carrying a gourd-rattle in his right hand. The first one has a small wooden drum tied to his belt. These are the assistants to the leaders. The rear of the procession is brought up by a dozen or more men and women all carrying otter-skin pouches.*

Slowly the procession wends its way across the opening and then disappears in the thicket. Within the thicket a space can be seen where the grass and the underbrush have been cleared and burnt off in such fashion as to form the outline of a long oval lodge, facing east and west. Before entering this lodge-outline, the Ancestor-Host takes his otter-skin pouch and holding it firmly in both hands, jerks it forward, ejaculating as he does 'dje-ha-hi, dje-ha-hi, e-ho-ho-o-o-o.' Then he enters and, in short dance-like steps, followed by the others, moves along the enclosure, proceeding from right to left. He stops at the places where the leaders of the East, North, West and South Bands are to sit and repeats the same ceremony he did when he entered. Finally he comes to a space directly to the left of the supposed entrance to the enclosure and there, after pointing the otter-skin pouch at it and ejaculating 'dje-ha-hi, dje-ha-hi, e-ho-ho-o-o-o,' he sits down. The Candidate sits down to his left. His two assistants will eventually sit to his right and so will the others belonging to his Band. The leaders of the East, North, West and South Bands continue around the outlined enclosure until they come to their respective seats, East just to the right of the entrance, North some distance to his right, West exactly opposite the entrance and South, some distance to the left of Ancestor-Host.

When they are all seated Ancestor-Host rises and addresses East.

A N C E S T O R - H O S T :   O you who sit in the east where-the-sun-comes-from, you who impersonate the spirit who first sat in that position when He-whom-we-call-our-nephew, Hare, first established this Rite, this holy way of life, I greet you, I welcome you!

You have had pity on me. Good it is you have come and granted me so fully all that I have asked. You have filled my heart with thankfulness and gratitude. Yet what can I give in return? Little indeed. I greet you and welcome you!

He extends the sacred greeting to the East Leader. When he has finished his greeting, Ancestor-Host with some of the members of his Band sing four songs, dancing at Ancestor-Host's place. When they have concluded they sit down and the leader of the East Band rises and addresses the Ancestor-Host.

E A S T :   O you who sit in the seat of our dead ancestors, the source from which we all have sprung, you who impersonate the first created human being, I greet you, I welcome you!

Kind it has been of you to have me here, to condescend to invite me and give me this seat of honor. And who am I that you should have treated me thus? A poor man, indeed, a pitiable man. But you overlooked my mean condition and, in your kindness, thought of me as a person of prominence, a Medicine Rite man. Assuredly I shall now obtain from you the knowledge of the true way of life, the meaning of life. In my ignorance I deceived myself at times into thinking that I actually possessed it. Yet, within my heart I recognized only too well my lack of wisdom and my self-deception. I greet you, I welcome you!

He extends the sacred greeting to Ancestor-Host. Then he and some of his Band sing four songs, dancing in their places. When they are finished they sit down and Ancestor-Host rises again and addresses North.

A N C E S T O R - H O S T :   O you who sit in the North, where-the-cold-comes-from you, who impersonate the spirit who sat in that place at the first initiation, I greet you, I welcome you!

You have had pity on me. Good it is you have come and granted me so fully all that I have asked. You have filled my heart with thankfulness and gratitude. Yet what can I give in return? Little indeed. I greet you, I welcome you!

Greeting, singing and dancing as before.

N O R T H :   O you who sit in the seat of our dead ancestors, the source from which we all have sprung, you who impersonate the first created human being, I greet you, I welcome you!

Greeting, singing and dancing as before.

A N C E S T O R - H O S T :   O you who impersonate the place where-the-sun-comes-from; O you who impersonate the place where-the-cold-comes-from; O you who impersonate the place where-the-sun-sets; O you who impersonate the place where-the-sun-straightens; O you who impersonate our Nephew, He-for-whom-we-seek-life, I greet you all, I greet you all!

E A S T :   Hāho, I greet you!

N O R T H :   Hāho, I greet you!

W E S T :   Hāho, I greet you!

S O U T H :   Hāho, I greet you!

A N C E S T O R - H O S T :   O ancestors, we greet you! In the far distant past, those who have long since left this life, whose bones lie mixed and mingled with the dust, they all performed this Rite with love and utter humility. In no way let us depart from what they laid down and established, from the manner in which they performed it so many years ago. What these beloved and revered ancestors of ours, whose bones lie mixed and mingled with the dust, what they so earnestly desired and prayed for, that let us, too, desire and pray for.

O you who are sitting in the place of the spirits, I greet you all, I greet you all! May you have compassion upon us and help us to accomplish what we so earnestly and reverently desire.

He now turns to the Candidate and addresses him.

You-for-whom-we-seek-life and light, nephew, just as our ancestors told it, exactly as they did, so He-who-sits-in-the-east will now describe to you the Road you are to travel, the Road of life, of death and of rebirth. He-whom-we-call-our-nephew, Hare, founded this Medicine Rite, obtained this life-ensuring ceremony for us. This is the only way of life. No other exists. Try, O nephew, with all your

12

strength and all your power, to follow in the footsteps of your ancestors, to walk along their road. Try to adhere to the teachings of this, their holy Rite, their way of life. I know that you are intent upon what I am telling you. I know that you are listening carefully. By hearkening to my words you will help, and be of benefit to yourself and you will attain to that true life all real men desire.

Thus it is the old people, our ancestors, whose bones have long been mixed and mingled with the dust, thus it is they told us to act. My nephew, if you perform this Rite correctly, you will obtain the life we all so earnestly desire for you. Let me again beseech you to try with all your power and all your strength to master that which you are about to witness, to learn of the journey that has to be taken by the ghost of the departed member whose seat you are about to occupy, and to learn of the journey that all members of the Medicine Rite must, likewise, take.

Ancestor-Host sits down and East now rises to speak.

E A S T : My nephew, when at the Four Nights' Wake, we bade farewell to the ghost of him whose seat you are about to take, I, because I have that right, was asked to tell him of the route he would have to take and the requests he was to make at the lodge of the old woman where doors face both the rising and the setting sun. This is what I said to the departing ghost:

'Hähä, are you ready, my dear grandson? Indeed, though we do not see each other, we cannot be far away.

'Here is the tobacco and here is the pipe which you must keep ever in front of you as you walk along the path. Here also is the fire, and the food which your relatives have prepared for your journey.

'In the morning when the sun rises you must start. You will not have gone very far before you come to a wide road. This is the road you are to take. As you go along it you will notice something barring your way. Take your club, strike it, and throw it behind you. Then proceed but never look back. As you proceed farther you will come across another object barring your way. This, too, you must strike and throw behind you. Never look back. Farther on you will come across some animals that will attempt to impede your advance. These,

13

likewise, you must strike and throw behind you. Then you must proceed, but never look back.

'These objects and obstacles on your path which you have struck and thrown behind you, will find their way to the relatives you have left behind you on earth. They represent victory in war, riches, and animals for food.

'Only a short distance from the place where you encountered the animals, you will come to a round lodge. One of its doors faces the rising sun, the other the setting sun. Enter it and you will find a very old woman on your right. Go and sit down directly opposite her. Then our great-grandmother will speak to you and say:

' "My great-grandchild, my dear one, when you were leaving, when your life was over, what is it your relatives said to you?"

'Then you must answer and say:

' "My dear great-grandmother, as I listened to my beloved relatives, they said very little indeed. They did say, however, that I was breaking their hearts in leaving them and that they hoped that no one would follow me soon. Four requests I was to make of you:

' "I was to ask for life, that the flames from the lodge fires might rise straight upward. Yet they would be content, they said, if, at my departure, the flames only swayed to and fro.

' "I was to ask that whatever fruits had been predestined for me to eat had I lived my allotted term of years and which I did not taste, that my relatives not be deprived of them.

' "I was to ask that whatever nuts, whatever herbs, whatever hides and skins, whatever medicinal roots and grasses, had been allotted to me and which I had not used, that my relatives not be deprived of them.

' "I was to ask that the weapons of my beloved relatives' friends have a keen edge on one side.

' "These are the four requests I was to make. They told me, in addition, dear great-grandmother, to follow the four steps that would be imprinted with blue marks."

'Then our dear great-grandmother will answer you and say:

' "Though you are young, beloved great-grandchild, you are wise.

14

This, now, I must tell you. My lodge is a place where all who enter must pass an examination. Earthmaker looks upon it as a keen-edged instrument. No clouds of ill omen ever pass over this lodge.

' "Your four requests will be granted. Of no part of the food predestined for you and which you did not eat, will your relatives be deprived. They shall have the fruits and nuts and herbs, the hides and the skins. If they have friends their weapons shall be keen on one side. All that they have requested through you will be given them. But, now, you must be hungry. Here is some food I set before you in this wooden bowl."

'Now, be sure, grandson, that you take just a taste of what is set before you and then push the bowl away. When your great-grandmother sees that she will say to you, "Dear great-grandchild, what you have left behind you in that bowl represents the vegetables of the earth. Many older than you have eaten all that I set before them. You have indeed a wise head on young shoulders. All that you have left in that bowl shall grow on the face of the earth.

' "But now you must proceed onwards. Earthmaker is waiting for you in great expectation. The road lies there through the door of the setting sun. On the road you will encounter those who have been sent to escort you to your home, the souls of warriors. They will touch you when you meet. At the place where you will meet them, the road branches to the right. On that branch road you will see the footprints of light on the blue sky before you. These are the footprints of those who have passed into life again. Step into the places where they have stepped and plant your feet into their footprints. Be careful, however, that you do not miss any.

' "Before you have gone very far you will come to a forest of trees broken, here and there, by open prairies. Here, in this beautiful country, those souls, whose duty it is to gather other souls, will come to meet you. Walking on each side of you they will conduct you safely to your home. As you enter the lodge of Earthmaker you must hand him the tobacco you have brought. Earthmaker will accept it and then address you:

' " 'My dear grandson, when you were leaving, when your life was over, what is it your relatives said to you?'

' "Then you must answer and say:

' " 'As I listened to my beloved relatives, they said very little indeed. They did, however, say that I was breaking their hearts in leaving them and that they hoped that no one would follow me soon. Four requests I was to make of you.

' " 'I was to ask for life, that the flames from the lodge fires might rise straight upward. Yet they would be content, they said, if, at my departure, the flames only swayed to and fro.

' " 'I was to ask that whatever fruits had been predestined for me to eat had I lived my allotted term of years and which I did not taste, that my relatives not be deprived of them.

' " 'I was to ask that whatever nuts, whatever herbs, whatever hides and skins, whatever medicinal roots and grasses, had been allotted to me and which I had not used, that my relatives not be deprived of them.

' " 'I was to ask that the weapons of my beloved relatives' friends have a keen edge on one side.'

' "Then he will answer:

' " 'All that you asked your great-grandmother will be granted. But, now, you must go for your relatives are waiting for you in great expectation. Your home awaits you. Its door faces the midday sun. Here you will find your relatives gathered, awaiting you. . . .'

' "Then you will be escorted to the long lodge in which your relatives who belonged to the Medicine Rite lived. As you enter the lodge, grown-up man that you are, you will be passed from one person's lap to the other.

' "After you have stayed in this lodge for a little time the attendants of Earthmaker will come for you and bring you to his presence again. Again, you will see him face to face. He will speak to you and he will tell you that you have done well and that, as recompense, he will permit you to be born into the world of men again, whenever and wherever you wish."

'Inasmuch, then, as our ruler will nod assent and express his approval by word of mouth, so shall we now do the same. Are you ready?'

16

A L L :　Ho-ha, ho-ha!

A N C E S T O R - H O S T :　But now we cannot pause, for He-who-sits-in-the-place-where-the-sun-sets, West, will begin the story of how the world was created and the Medicine Rite was established . . .

W E S T :　What it was our father, Earthmaker, lay upon as he came to consciousness, we do not know. Tears flowed from his eyes and fell below him. He lay there motionless. He saw nothing. Nothing existed in the world. Now he began to move, his right arm first, then his left, then his right foot and then his left. His eyes were open and he turned on his side and looked below him, far down from where he lay. There, far below him, he noticed something bright and shining. Those were his tears and they had formed the waters of the earth. As he lay there stretched out, he kept thinking and thinking. 'Unbeknown to me, without my intention, my tears as they fell below, formed bodies of water. Perhaps now, if I really intend something, if I really wish something, it will come into existence just as the waters were formed from my tears, by themselves.'

Thereupon he stretched out his hand and seized a portion of that upon which he was lying and sent it hurtling down below him. Then he turned his head to see what he had done. There it lay. The something he had thrown down, slowly assumed the appearance of this earth of ours. But nothing grew upon it. It was without a covering of any kind. Moreover it kept spinning around continuously. Never was it quiet.

Suddenly he thought of another expedient. 'Perhaps if I do this it will become quiet and stop.' He decided to make a covering, to put some hair upon it. He took a weedlike object from that on which he lay, changed it to grass and sent it hurtling down toward the earth. Thus he did, and then looked below to see what he had created. Yet the earth kept spinning around and was not quiet. Then he thought to himself, 'I must try to do some other thing to make it stop spinning around.' So he took a tree and sent it hurtling toward

17

the earth. Again he looked at what he had created. It was the same, it was still spinning around.

Then he thought to himself, 'I must try something else.' So he sent four male-beings, brothers, and placed one in the east, one in the north, one in the south and one in the west. Again he looked at what he had created. Yet it was still spinning around.

Then he thought to himself for a long time and said, 'Perhaps if I do the following it will become quiet.' With his own hands he made four beings, those that we call waterspirits, and placed them under the earth. For that reason they are also called *Island-Anchorers*. Finally, he scattered a female being over the whole earth. By female being we mean stones and rocks. After he had done all this, he again looked at what he had created and he saw that the earth had at last become quiet.

Now he had made the rocks go right through the earth, from one end to the other. But their tops, their heads, he permitted to obtrude, to remain uncovered.

Again and again he looked at what he had created and he saw that the earth had indeed become quiet. No clouds were visible anywhere. Even the shimmering of light that one always sees in the daytime, even these had ceased. And the heat vibrations seemed like spiderwebs as they floated past.

All the birds that were destined to roam over the skies, all the four-footed animals who were to wander over the surface of the earth and all the animals who were to live in the sea and below the surface of the waters, all these he placed in lodges specially provided for them. After that, he made the various insects that were to live on the earth.

And then, at the very end of his thoughts, he made us, man. We were not even equal in strength to a fly. Indeed we were the very weakest of all things Earthmaker created.

When he was finished Earthmaker looked at all the things he had created and he liked what he had done and lay there, filled with happy thoughts.

Of us he was proud and he gazed, again and again, at the human beings he had created. But alas! not equal in strength to any of the

18

other beings that lived on the earth had he made us and we were on the point of being destroyed by evil ones. So he formed a being,[1] just like ourselves, and when he had finished him, he called him, Trickster, Foolish-One. 'O, Foolish-One,' he said, 'you are going to be sent to the earth. Weak and pitiable in every respect I have created the human beings, for I made them as the last of my thoughts. And now this last creation of mine is being attacked on all sides by evil spirits. Evil spirits are indeed destroying them, the human beings. So do you, Foolish-One, go to earth and put things aright.'

Thus was Foolish-One sent to the earth, with this purpose. Yet when he came to the earth he did not do what he had been told. He just roamed around and accomplished absolutely nothing. No good did he accomplish. In fact he injured some of the creations of Earthmaker. So Earthmaker made him come back and made him sit near him, to the right of his seat.

Then Earthmaker formed another being like man and when he had finished him, he called him, Turtle. And he spoke to Turtle and said, 'O, Turtle, the two-legged-walkers, the human beings, those that I created as the last of my thoughts, are about to be exterminated by evil beings. Do you go and help them and set the earth aright.'

Thus was Turtle sent to the earth, with this purpose. He came here bringing with him a knife that he had received as a present. But after he came he did nothing but lead people on the warpath. He took no interest in setting things aright. He did not look after the welfare of Earthmaker's last creation as he had been told to do. So Earthmaker had this second person also brought back and he placed him to the left of his seat.

Then Earthmaker made a third being like us and, when he finished him, he called him, Bladder. And he spoke to him and said, 'O, Bladder, you are to go to the earth. As the last of my thoughts I created the two-legged-walkers and their lot is pitiable in the extreme. Indeed, evil spirits are about to exterminate them. You are being sent to save and rescue them. Try with all your strength to accomplish this for which I am sending you.'

Thus was Bladder sent to the earth, with this purpose. When he arrived on the earth he immediately built a long lodge and, himself,

19

created twenty other men. Thus he had many younger brothers. Then they all started to go around this island world of ours and thus all his younger brothers were killed. Bladder, too, failed completely in his mission. What our father, Earthmaker, had sent him to accomplish, in that he failed utterly.

Then Earthmaker formed another being and he called him He-who-wears-human-heads-as-earrings. He sent him to the earth but he, too, failed.[2]

Then Earthmaker formed another being, the last one, his body exactly like ours.[3] He called him Hare. And he spoke to him and said, 'O, Hare, you are the last one I am going to create for this task of rescuing the two-legged-walkers from the evil ones, so try with all your strength to do what I tell you.' Now, Hare, nephew, was the last being that Earthmaker, our father, desired to create. He created him entirely by the force of his thoughts.[4]

Earthmaker continued exhorting Hare and giving him courage for his mission. 'Hare, what I am doing, that, too, you ought to be able to accomplish. Exert all your strength! If the evil spirits destroy or injure my creation, it will not be good, life will not be good. So try and overcome these evil spirits.'

Thus was Hare sent to earth. When he came here he said to himself, 'My brothers acted in a certain manner and failed. I must act differently.' As he walked along he came to an oval lodge and out of this lodge there came, at the same time, a young woman with a little pail. She was going to the river. 'Indeed,' said Hare to himself, 'neither Foolish-One, nor Turtle, nor Bladder, nor He-who-wears-human-heads-as-earrings, could have done what I am now going to do.' [5] Thereupon, he entered the body of the young woman so that he could become born as a human being.

There he sat in the womb of the young woman. And, sitting there, he heard the piteous cries of the human beings who were being killed by the evil spirits. He heard them crying and crying and he said to himself, 'My father sent me to give them advice and, for a long, long time I have been merely sitting and sitting here.' Outside he heard the piteous shrieks and cries of the human beings. 'O my, O my,' thought Hare as he sat in the woman's womb, 'I have been sitting here too long. If I stay any longer, the evil spirits will, in the end, destroy my uncles and my aunts.'[6] Seven months had he been waiting there when he said this. Finally, when the proper time had elapsed, he walked out through an opening. Four days after, the young woman died.

From then on he lived with his grandmother. Now, in the daytime, he always stayed at home but at night he would roam all about the world. Whenever he walked inside the lodge, light would radiate from him.[7] As soon as daylight came he became quiet and rested. It was his custom to sit thinking throughout the day and plan the work he had to do to rescue his uncles and his aunts.

He started out at sunset of the third day and traveled over half of the earth, and all the evil spirits who were growing wild throughout the world, he killed and put an end to. 'Not again will they live, these evil ones; not, for a second time, will they kill or annoy my uncles and my aunts.' Just before daylight appeared, he began walking toward his home and as he approached it, his heart felt good. Then he entered the lodge and all day he sat there wrapped in thought.

When the sun went down he continued his travels. But this time he covered the whole of the world, as large as it is; to the very edge of the island did he go. And all the evil spirits he encountered, he killed and put an end to. Just about daylight he went up into the heavens. Tremendous was the noise as he pursued the evil birds living up there and killed them. Then, very early in the morning, he walked toward the lodge, thinking pleasant thoughts. 'The work my father sent me to do, that I have accomplished. The life of my uncles and aunts will be like mine from now on.'[8]

As he sat there in the lodge he spoke to his grandmother. 'Grandmother, the work, my father, Earthmaker, sent me to do, that I have now accomplished. He sent me to set his creation aright, to put it in order. That I have now accomplished. Hereafter the lives of my uncles and my aunts will be the same as my own.' 'But, grandson, how can that be,' his grandmother replied, 'how can the lives of your uncles and your aunts be like yours? It is not so. The world and all about it must remain the way our father created it. It cannot be changed.' Then Hare murmured to himself, 'That old woman, she must be related to these beings that I killed [9] and that is why she does not like what I say and what I have done.' 'No,' she answered, 'that is not so. Our father has ordained that my body shall fall to pieces. I am the earth. Our father ordained that there should be death, lest otherwise there be too many people and not enough food for them. Indeed, if death did not exist, people would crowd each other too much on this earth. For that reason it was arranged that men should die and that a place be reserved for them to go to after death.'

But Hare did not like what his grandmother had said. 'Surely, grandmother does not like what I have done because she is related to the evil spirits I have killed. She is just taking their part.' So did he think. 'But it is not so,' his grandmother answered, 'you speak in this way because your heart feels sore. Your uncles and your aunts will obtain enough of life; they will live to a ripe old age.

'However, grandson, if you do what I now ask of you, they will become immortal. Get up and follow me. Your uncles and your aunts will follow you in time to come. Try with all your strength to do what I am going to tell you. Be a man now, a real man, and, under no circumstances, turn around to look back [10] as we walk along the road.'

They started to go around the world. 'I was not to look back, grandmother said. I wonder why she said it?' Thus he thought. But just the least little bit, so he thought to himself, he would look back, for he was suspicious of his grandmother. And as he peeped, the place from which he had started, caved in completely and instantaneously.

'O grandson, O grandson, what have you done? I thought you were a man, a person of real prominence! And I encouraged you so greatly! But now, my grandson, it is done. Decay, death, can in no way be taken back!'

And then around the world the two continued until they came to the edge of the fire that encircles it. Thus far they traveled, so it is said. There they united the fire [11] so that Hare's uncles and aunts would attain to old age. This was grandmother's purpose.

Yet Hare was not satisfied. 'To look back, she forbade me. But I have already made up my mind that my uncles and aunts are to be immortal. Indeed, when they become like me, only then will I be satisfied and be happy. That is my thought.'

Then he went to where-the-sun-rises, to the east.[12] In that direction he went and, after a while, entered a lodge. He sat himself opposite the occupants and did not say a word. But what he had come for the occupants knew. 'Hare,' said the one in charge, 'there is nothing I can say to you. If the one ahead wishes to say anything to you, let him do so.' So Hare greeted the man and went out.

Then, to the place where-the-cold-comes-from, the north, he went, and entered the lodge. 'There is nothing I can say to you,' said the one in charge. 'If the one ahead of me wishes to say something, he will undoubtedly do so.' Then Hare greeted him and left.

Then Hare traveled to the place where-the-sun-sets, the west. In spite of what the first two old men had said, he still had but the one thought in his mind: 'I can do it!' When he arrived at the lodge, he entered and sat himself opposite the one in charge. 'Hare, what you have come for I know, but I will not tell you anything. It is the one ahead, he alone is the one who can tell you something.' Then Hare greeted him and left.

Finally, to the lodge of the fourth one, to the place where-the-sun-straightens, the south, there he went. He entered and sat himself opposite the one in charge. 'Hare, what you have come for, that I know. But if even those ahead of me could not say anything, how can I, the very last and least in importance, say anything?' Then greeting him Hare went out.

Hare started for his lodge and arrived there crying, shrieking, 'My uncles and my aunts must not die!' And then the thought assailed him, 'To all things death will come!' He cast his thoughts upon the precipices and they began to fall and crumble. Upon the rocks he cast his thoughts and they became shattered. Under the earth he cast his thoughts and all the beings living there stopped moving and their limbs stiffened in death. Up above, towards the skies, he cast his thoughts and the birds flying there suddenly fell to the earth and were dead.

After he entered his lodge he took his blanket and, wrapping it

23

around him, lay down crying. 'Not the whole earth will suffice for all those who will die! Indeed, there will not be enough earth for them in many places!'

There he lay in his corner wrapped up in his blanket, silent.[13] After a while the news reached our father, Earthmaker. And the people on the earth were crying, 'Now, truly, the evil spirits will try to destroy us utterly!' The news reached our father that Hare was not feeling very well. As soon as he heard it he spoke to Foolish-One, the first of the four beings he had created after man. 'Foolish-One, Hare is not feeling well. You must go after him and bring him back to me.' So toward the earth, Foolish-One came and he said to Hare, 'Hare I have come to take you back to Earthmaker.' But Hare did not answer him. He did not even move his blanket to acknowledge his presence. So Foolish-One returned.

Then Earthmaker said to the second one, Turtle, 'You are to go after Hare and bring him back here to me. He is not feeling well. Try very hard to do what I say.' When he arrived on earth he said, 'Hare, I have come to take you back to Earthmaker.' But Hare made no reply and did not move his blanket. So Turtle returned and told Earthmaker, 'Hare would not even answer me.' Then Earthmaker spoke to Bladder and said, 'You are to go after Hare for he is not feeling well.' When he came to earth he said to Hare, 'Hare, I have come here to take you back to Earthmaker.' But Hare made no reply. Indeed, Hare was not feeling well at all.

Then Earthmaker spoke to the fourth, He-who-wears-human-heads-as-earrings. 'You are to go after Hare and bring him back here. Be sure and bring him. Try with all your strength and power!' And the fourth one replied, 'No matter how difficult it will be I shall bring him back to you!' So he started for the earth and when he got there he went directly to Hare and said, 'Hare, for a long time, indeed, has your heart been sore. But now it is time for us to go home. Come, get up!' And Hare arose and went back with him to Earthmaker.

Yet not directly to Earthmaker's lodge did he take him, but to that opposite, to the lodge of the chief of the Thunderbird spirits.[14] Now, in front of the lodge of the Thunderbird chief, there was a mound and, on one side, a little warclub, painted red. The chief of the thunderbirds took hold of the little warclub and, handling it, shook it lightly, ever so gently. The noise that it made was terrific and Hare was so frightened that he almost ran away. Yet, in this manner, did they free him of the sad and bitter thoughts that he had on earth and, thus, did they restore his spirits to their normal condition.

Shortly after he was taken to Earthmaker. Earthmaker spoke to him and said, 'Hare, sad must your heart have been there on earth. Sore indeed must have been your heart, worrying about your uncles and your aunts. But I shall give you some solace, something by which their lives may be benefited. A sacred teaching you are to take back to them. But, before I say more, I want you to look at something. Come, look!' As he spoke, he pointed toward the south. There a long lodge stood revealed. As he looked at it he saw old people in it, their hair white with age.

And Earthmaker spoke. 'Thus will your uncles and aunts live. In this ceremony there will be very much noise made. But now look down again. Some help is to be given them. Within that lodge not one evil spirit will I place.' Then pointing toward the earth, Earthmaker said, 'You are to return from where you came, Hare, and establish this ceremony for your uncles and your aunts. But not, alone, are you to do it. You must do it with the aid of your own friends, Foolish-One, Turtle, Bladder and He-who-wears-human-heads-as-earrings.' Thus Earthmaker spoke and that is what he meant. 'But another one will help you, too, your grandmother, Earth.

'This, too, remember, that if any one of your uncles and aunts performs this ceremony and everything connected with it properly, he will have more than one life. I will always keep the door through which he may return to earth open to him. When he becomes reincarnated he can live wherever he wishes. He can return to the earth as a human being or he can join one of the various bands of spirits or, again, if he wants to, he can become one of the beings who live under the earth.'

All this did our father, Earthmaker, arrange for us.

But now nephew, I will sit down and let my friend in the south finish and tell you how the Medicine Rite was established on earth . . .

S O U T H :   O you who sit in the seat of our dead ancestors, the source from which we all have sprung, you who impersonate the first created human being, I greet you, I welcome you.

O you who sit in the east where-the-sun-comes-from, you who impersonate the spirit who first sat in that position when He-whom-we-call-our-nephew, Hare, first established this Rite, I greet you, I welcome you.

O you who sit in the north, where-the-cold-comes-from, you who impersonate the spirit who first sat there when He-whom-we-call-our-nephew, Hare, first established this Rite, I greet you, I welcome you.

O you who sit in the south, where-the-road-straightens, you who impersonate the spirit who first sat there when He-whom-we-call-our-nephew, Hare, first established this Rite, I greet you, I welcome you.

A N C E S T O R - H O S T :   Hāho, I greet you!

E A S T :   Hāho, I greet you!

N O R T H :   Hāho, I greet you!

W E S T :   Hāho, I greet you!

South now rises to finish the origin myth.

S O U T H :   So Hare returned to the earth and to his grandmother. And he spoke to her, 'Grandmother, what I tried to obtain for my uncles and aunts, that now I am bringing back with me.' 'But, no, grandson, how was it possible for you to make them immortal like yourself and me? As the world was created so must it remain.' 'But I tell you, grandmother, my uncles and aunts are to choose their lives for themselves and you are to help me.' 'Well, it is good, grandson, that which you say. I thank you.'

'When the time comes my friend, Foolish-One, will arrive,' he thought to himself. Then he struck his drum and started two songs.

26

Then suddenly Foolish-One was there. 'I thought that you would come, my friend, and here you have arrived already.' 'Indeed, my friend, I knew your thoughts and, for that reason, I came.' Then they walked out together and, outside the village, they sat down and discussed what they were to do. All day they discussed this matter sitting there on the outskirts of the village.

When they were finished they returned to the lodge and sat down. 'My friend, Turtle, will come,' thought Hare. And almost immediately Turtle was there. 'My friend,' said Hare, 'I knew you would come and now you have arrived.' 'Yes, indeed, I knew your thought and, for that reason, I came.' Shortly after Bladder arrived, for Hare had thought of him and thus brought about his immediate appearance. Then Hare concentrated his thoughts upon He-who-wears-human-heads-as-earrings and, by the power of his thought, he caused him to arrive.

All this time our grandmother, Earth, sat there listening. She was quiet and she did not quite understand what was happening. But then Hare turned to her and said, 'Grandmother, you know that what I tried to accomplish for my uncles and aunts I have obtained. About that I am going to tell you now. Come here to the fireplace and sit down and listen to what I have to say. I know that you are anxious to help us.' 'Truly I know that it is good,' said grandmother and she arose and, taking her work, sat down near the five men. Then she laid her hands upon their heads in turn. She had placed her work in front of our nephew, Hare. 'If you get this Medicine Rite for your uncles and your aunts, Hare, they will live happily thereafter. This ceremony they must continue to perform for all time. I thank our father, Earthmaker, for this work of his.' Then she returned and took her seat.

Again our grandmother, Earth, arose and said, 'Did you wish to know how I was to help you, grandson? Well, look at me. Earthmaker had me bring what I shall now show you so that the human beings will have something with which to ask for life.' Then she opened her body where her heart was and, suddenly, very green leaves were to be seen there, the shape of an ear. It was tobacco. It was as white as a blossom. Then she opened her body on the right side and, again, she spoke, 'Grandson, look at me!' There, unexpectedly, ears of corn were to be seen. 'These, Earthmaker had me bring for your uncles and your aunts.' Soon a stalk became visible whose leaves were very green and whose tassels were white. It was the corn which was to become our food.

'Let us greet our grandmother,' said Hare. And the five of them walked toward her. They walked up to her and laid their hands upon her head, each in turn. They made the circuit of the enclosure once again and greeted her, the five of them, Foolish-One, Turtle, Bladder, He-who-wears-human-heads-as-earrings and Hare. 'It is good,' said Hare. 'Grandmother, this is what I meant when I said you were to help my uncles and my aunts. You may now close up your body.'

Then Hare walked toward the east and stopped there. Then he turned toward the west.

In the meantime grandmother had closed her body. 'I have done what was asked of me, grandson,' she said. 'Yes, it is good,' said Hare.

Then he walked toward the entrance, stopped there and was wrapped in thought. 'This is the way it will be,' he said. And immediately, there from where he was standing, eight yellow snakes he threw around the enclosure. They became the sidepoles of the lodge. He turned their heads toward the east and he turned their tails toward the west. To tie them together, he used strings made of rattlesnakes. The two posts at the doorway he also constructed out of snakes, placing a black female snake at the left and a white male snake at the right. For the doorway in the west, he constructed posts out of two blue snakes. Then he took some reed-grass which he had brought with him from above and threw it over the enclosure.

The lodge was now entirely wrapped in darkness. Under this covering we were to dwell. Then he took another piece of reed-grass and threw it along the right side of the lodge, the whole length of it. It became transformed into white mats. Then he threw another piece of reed-grass along the left side of the lodge, the whole length of it. And this became transformed into white deerhide. Then he took still another piece of reed-grass and threw it along the right side of the lodge, the whole length of it, and it became transformed into long bearskins. Now he constructed a doorway for the east entrance. He

28

made it of a real, living mountain-lion. The mountain-lion was to prevent evil spirits from entering the lodge. The doorway at the west he made of a real bull buffalo. When this was all finished he peeped into the lodge. The animals were bellowing and roaring. Inside the lodge there was light.

Then he started to prepare himself for entering the lodge formally. First he went for his friends. 'Well, my friends, I am through,' he said to them. 'The lodge is finished.' Then he spoke to his grandmother, 'Grandmother, get up, for we are going to follow you.' So toward the lodge they walked, grandmother first, and the others behind. When they came to the door, the fear-inspiring mountain-lion who guarded it, snapped his teeth at them. But they marched right in and making the circuit of the lodge, stopped right near the entrance and sat down to the left of it.

Thus did grandmother and Hare enter the first lodge.

Now Hare sent public-criers all over the world to invite the spirits to attend. The bear and wolf he sent to traverse the entire length of the earth and two crows, the common crow and the shrieking crow, he sent to traverse the skies.

When the bear and wolf returned, their bodies were old and they were quite without hair.[15] They had to support themselves on staffs. When the two birds returned their wings were worn out, their eyebrows fell over their eyes and they were very old, exceedingly old. They entered the lodge and stopped in front of Hare's seat. 'O Hare, when your uncles and aunts speak of you in time to come, they will forever intone your praise. We, too, have brought something. We place these life-giving objects within the lodge.' 'Well, my friends, it is good. This is what I meant you to do. I thank you in the name of my uncles and my aunts.'

All the messengers, the public-criers that Hare had sent out, had now returned.

It was now time for the first four beings Earthmaker had created after man, to enter. They were already standing at the door. The oldest one started to enter first but he turned back for he was afraid of the animals within. The second and the third they, too, started to enter but they likewise were frightened by the animals within.

Finally the youngest, He-who-wears-human-heads-as-earrings, opened the door and went in and the others followed. After they entered, they made the circuit of the lodge and when they came to the entrance, Hare again rose up and, leading the oldest one, walked to the east. 'My elder brother, this is your seat.' Then he took the second one and they stopped at the north seat. 'My elder brother, this is your seat,' he told him. And then he sat the third one in the west seat and the fourth one in the south seat. After that he walked on and took his own seat.

The spirits who had been invited now began entering the lodge. Then came the human beings. Four belonging to the bird clan were made to sit in the east seat, four belonging to the bear clan were made to sit in the north seat, four belonging to the wolf clan were made to sit in the west seat and four belonging to the snake clan were made to sit in the south seat. Those in the fourth seat, the south, were the ones to be initiated.[16]

Hare now arose and spoke to those present in the following words: 'My friends, I have had you come together here for the sake of my uncles and my aunts. They were living a most pitiable life. You are now to teach them the kind of life which they are to live in the future and which they are to hand down from generation to generation. That is what I am asking of you. You now know what it is I would like to have you do. Do try with all your strength to achieve it! But now I pass on what is to be done and spoken to my friend in the east.'

Then the one in the east arose and spoke: 'I greet you all. We are to teach the uncles and the aunts of Hare, the meaning of life so that they may hand it down from one generation to the other. Today, for the first time, have we discussed this thing of happiness for them. From now on they shall lead the true life and obtain all that we mean by life—happiness, honor, wealth, spiritual and material.'

After East had finished, the other three, North, West and South arose in turn and repeated what East had said. And when they had all spoken they arose, made the circuit of the lodge, and returned to their seats, greeting them before they sat down.

Hare now arose again and said, 'You friends who are sitting here,

I greet you. This that you all have said is what I wished for my uncles and my aunts. This council-lodge that I have made for them is theirs and, as long as they follow the precepts taught in the Creation-Lodge, they will be happy and invulnerable. For that reason have these seats been created for them, that whosoever desires may sit in them and gain life.'

All day long the spirits taught those who were to be initiated what they were to do. And when the sun was on the treetops and it was time to stop, the spirits dispersed and, as they left, half of the light within the lodge went with them. As they went out they rubbed their bodies against the doorposts and pushed them in deeper and more firmly so that they would never fall over.

After they had left, Hare arose and spoke: 'Grandmother, look at me! Here I will be sitting forever, waiting for all those of my uncles and my aunts who correctly perform this ceremony we have taught them. Weeping, their eyes filled with tears, they will come to me and my heart will feel sore for them. I will go up above and sit down there and, if any one of my uncles and my aunts who has correctly performed this ceremony, this holy Rite we have taught him, comes to me, he will be as I am.

'Come now, look at me, grandmother! Behold my body!' And grandmother looked at him and, behold! he was a small child.[17] 'If anyone repeats what we have done here, grandmother, this is the way he will look.'

'Come now, look at me, grandmother!' Thus Hare spoke for the second time. There he stood, a full-grown man.

'Come now, look at me again, grandmother!' There he stood, a man of middle age, his hair interspersed with white, half black and half gray.

'Come now, look at me, grandmother!' said Hare for the fourth time. And there he stood, the hair covering his head looking as if he were wearing a swan as a headdress. There he stood in the east, leaning, tremblingly, on his staff. 'Thus shall it be, grandmother, if any of my uncles and aunts perform this ceremony properly and live up to its precepts and its teaching.'

'Come look at me, grandson,' grandmother now said in her turn.

31

And when Hare looked, there he saw a very young woman, her hair as smooth as a shawl.[18] 'It is good, grandmother. I thank you in the name of my aunts.'

'Come look at me, grandson!' said grandmother, the second time. He looked at her and there she stood, a full-grown woman. 'It is good, grandmother. I thank you in the name of my aunts.'

'Come look at me, grandson!' said grandmother, a third time. He looked at her and there stood a woman in middle age, her hair almost gray. 'It is good, grandmother. That is what I meant you to be.'

'Come look at me, grandson!' she said again. He looked at her as she stood there. Her hair was entirely dried up. There was a hollow in the nape of her neck and she looked like a duck staring at the sun. Her chin was like a wooden poker, burnt short. There she stood, trembling with age.

'Well, grandmother, this is indeed what I meant when I asked you to help me. This is what I desired for my uncles and my aunts.'

It is finished. I greet you all . . .

A N C E S T O R - H O S T :   It is finished, O nephew, the path you are to take and the story of its origin. I greet you.

O you who sit in the east, where-the-sun-comes-from, you who impersonate the spirit who sat there in the Creation-Lodge when He-whom-we-call-our-nephew first established this holy Rite, I greet you and thank you.

O you who sit in the north, where-the-cold-comes-from, you who impersonate the spirit who sat in that seat in the Creation-Lodge when He-whom-we-call-our-nephew first established this holy Rite, I greet and thank you.

O you who sit in the west, where-the-sun-goes-down, you who impersonate the spirit who first sat in that place when He-whom-we-call-our-nephew first established this holy Rite, I greet you and thank you.

O you who sit in the south, where-the-sun-straightens, you who impersonate the spirit who first sat in that place when He-whom-we-call-our-nephew first established this holy Rite, I greet you and thank you.

32

Good it is you have come to partake with me in this Rite and to help me conduct it correctly, to help me perform it exactly as our ancestors did in the far distant past.

You have taken pity on me and have come to my poor feast knowing that I am of no value or importance and that I cannot feed you properly.

Good it is you have come, you who impersonate our ancestors whose bones long since lie mingled and mixed with the earth. I greet and thank you.

Tomorrow we shall begin our ceremonies. Tomorrow we shall pour out our tears, weeping for the spirit of our fellow member who has died. For him we shall all mourn in speech and song. O let the mourning song we intone come from the depths of our heart, let it be sung with deep sincerity. And, then, when our tears flow and our cries break out in music, let us be careful that our voices are always clear and unbroken and that there is no quaver. Let us be careful for, often, it has been said, the voice of one whose grief and crying is insincere will falter and break and quaver.

Good it is you have come. Tomorrow when we pour out our tears for the spirit of our departed fellow member, by your presence you will help him obtain the request we always put to the ghost of the deceased. We humbly pray that he ask the spirits to bestow upon us all the years he left behind, the years that were his due but which he did not live; that he obtain for us the food he would have eaten and the good and prestige-bringing acts he would have performed, had he lived the normal number of years. This is what we shall ask of him tomorrow as we pour out our tears in grief for his death. For thus it has always been and thus may it ever be!

E A S T :   Hãho, it is well; it is finished.

N O R T H :   Hãho, it is well; it is finished.

W E S T :   Hãho, it is well; it is finished.

S O U T H :   Hãho, it is well; it is finished.

33

I. The Recording of the Medicine Rite

He who secures a narrative from an aboriginal tribe owes his readers some account of the conditions under which he obtained it. Since this is true of the simplest myth or song, I need not stress its importance where one is dealing with a secret and sacred ritual such as that presented in the following pages. That must be my excuse for going into the details of my personal relations with the Winnebago Indians in the year 1908-1909. Needless to say, only such incidents will be emphasized that bear directly or indirectly on the securing of the text of the ritual.

The summer of 1908 was of more than usual significance to those Winnebago who still adhered to their old manner of living. Most of them did so adhere, even the division of the tribe residing in Nebraska which had the reputation for not being conservative. In that year, a new religion, compounded of Christian and Indian elements, first began its triumphant sweep through the reservation. The adherents of the new faith called themselves peyote-eaters because of the fact that the cardinal purpose of the new cult was to partake of the peyote, a small cactus to be found in northern Mexico. The peyote is a mild narcotic that produces fairly intense hallucinations and extraordinarily vivid color visions.

It had been brought to the Winnebago some years before, but the individual who introduced it, a very remarkable man named John Rave, had had little success with his proselytizing until the summer of 1908. The new cult had been brought to the Winnebago from the south, from Oklahoma, and should have constituted only a very partial threat to the older ceremonies and beliefs. The Winnebago had not infrequently borrowed ceremonies from neighboring tribes without disturbing the old order of things. But here the case

35

was different, and in John Rave's hands the cult he introduced developed into a religion that categorically denied the validity and efficacy of the whole older religious structure of the tribe. To accept it, therefore, meant the complete rejection of their former mode of life.

Why 1908 proved to be so propitious for Rave's propaganda it is difficult to say. But it did prove so, and the Nebraska division of the Winnebago soon found itself split into two contending camps, the peyote-eaters and the so called pagans.

It was into this atmosphere of conflicts and dissensions, where all men's minds were unusually disturbed and perturbed and where feelings and emotions ran high, that I unwittingly stepped on my ethnological field-trip. Nor was I in the least aware that my coming at that particular time meant more than it would have meant five years before. As it was my first anthropological field-trip, I was both bewildered and ill at ease.

I arrived with a letter of introduction to Oliver Lamere from his cousin, a thoroughly westernized Winnebago woman teaching at Carlisle. Lamere was a quarterblood who spoke perfect English and perfect Winnebago but knew very little indeed about the older customs of his tribe. He had, until a short interval before my arrival, been a completely demoralized man and a hopeless drunkard. The peyote had cured him and he was filled with the glories and the wonders of the new dispensation. He insisted repeatedly that it had given him the first real feeling of internal well-being that had ever come to him, and he was humble and grateful. The force of his conversion was still upon him when I presented my letter, and, for a few days after my arrival, he could talk about little else.

Lamere was only mildly interested in my proposal that he become my interpreter and help in my work of making a record of the customs and beliefs of the tribe. As already stated, he had but a passing acquaintance with them and regarded their perpetuation as something ridiculous and, at that moment, possibly sinful. Yet the prospect of semipermanent employment and the prestige he might acquire induced him to accept, although with some misgivings, for he was properly suspicious of a white stranger who had come to his

36

people on what looked, on the face of it, to be a foolish and strange mission.

My first task, of course, was to learn a little of the language and then to take down some texts phonetically. The recording of the texts had some important consequences for my work. It must be remembered that, with the exception of a missionary stationed at Black River Falls, Wisconsin, who was interested only in translating the Bible into Winnebago, and the very casual visit of the famous ethnologist J. O. Dorsey in the early nineties of the last century, no white man had ever been among the Winnebago for the purpose of studying their customs. Very few, if any, of the white people living in the neighborhood, even when they could speak a little Winnebago, could pronounce any of the unusual sounds in their language correctly. That a complete stranger like myself should immediately, and without any difficulty, not only pronounce these sounds but be able to write down a whole story and then read it back to them—that partook of the unusual, and seemed to the highly excited imaginations of the peyote-eaters an omen that had to be properly interpreted. They were given to making such interpretations in connection with their new cult. Assuredly, it was suggested, this newcomer had been sent to them for this particular purpose. Indeed Lamere's father, a blind old man who was a member of the peyote-eaters and who enjoyed considerable standing in the community at large, pagan and peyote, was of the opinion that since I had come at this very opportune time and seemed to possess such unusual gifts, I must have been sent by God. Some such theory the elder Lamere unquestionably spread and it was of considerable importance both in making my purpose more intelligible to the peyote-eaters and in quieting their fears that I might possibly be a secret government agent. It also advertised my presence to the pagans, increasing both their dislike for and their fear of me.

The elder Lamere who had now taken me under his wing was particularly interested in my securing an account of the greatest and most secret of all Winnebago ceremonies, the Medicine Rite. Never having been a member of it himself he was probably somewhat curi-

37

ous as to what it really was like. Yet, undoubtedly, he was also interested in dealing a deadly blow to the members of this society who were, naturally, the most bitter foes of the peyote-eaters. To induce a member to divulge the secrets of their Rite would, he felt, constitute such a blow. But the task was extremely difficult and the elder Lamere was unable to persuade any of its former members who had subsequently become peyote-eaters to do it. Whether this was due to indifference, laziness, or fear on their part, it would be impossible to say. It was probably a mixture of all three. Yet he did succeed in persuading three old ex-members to agree to recount to me the most sacred of all the myths in the tribe and one that only members of the Rite knew, namely the Origin Myth of the World, of the Indians and of the Medicine Rite.

Very dramatic circumstances attended the securing of this famous myth. The three old men who had agreed to tell it insisted that it would be too dangerous to do so on the reservation with so many of the pagans about and suggested that we all go to Sioux City, Iowa, about twenty-five miles away. Of the three men, only two were personally known to me. Of these two, one was famous throughout the Winnebago area for his sense of humor. He was not a truly religious man, according to some of the stories told about him, but he had, nevertheless, been a prominent member of the Medicine Rite. The other was a quiet, self-contained individual who had joined the new religion essentially because he felt that the older religion had lost its meaning. He was a deeply religious person. His name was John Walker and we shall hear of him afterwards.

As soon as we arrived in Sioux City we took rooms at the top floor of a little hotel. Although it was only early evening when we got there, the old men refused to make their preparations for the recounting of the myth until eleven-thirty. Then we all went to the room occupied by the Indians. Great care was taken to see there were no unwanted Indians about. When everyone was satisfied on that score the windows were firmly closed, the shades pulled down and the shutters fastened securely. The door was then locked and bolted. There was no interpreter, in fact no one who knew any English. The question of an interpreter had not even come up and it is very diffi-

38

cult for me to decide whether they thought I knew enough Winnebago to understand what was being said or whether they realized that I would at some future time read the account I had received in Winnebago to my interpreter, Oliver Lamere, who would then translate it for me.

Precisely at midnight one of the three began the story. When it was about half finished, a second one continued it to the end. The third person said nothing except when some special point was discussed during the pauses. It had been agreed that, although they would not repeat anything, they would speak reasonably slowly so that I would have ample time to write down everything. The narration, including the interruptions, took five hours in all. The interruptions seemed to be concerned with discussions about discrepancies in the various ways in which the myth was told. This was but natural, since the three belonged to different bands of the Rite. When it was finished, well after dawn, they shook hands with each other and then with me, and all retired to snatch some sleep before returning to the reservation.

In spite of the highly artificial circumstances under which the myth was told, no distortions seem to have been introduced, for it is essentially identical with the official version as recounted in the full version of the Medicine Rite.

News spreads with amazing rapidity on an Indian reservation and, in spite of all the precautions that had seemingly been taken, by the next afternoon everyone knew about the trip of the three exMedicine Rite members to Sioux City. The younger peyote-eaters and the older ones who had not belonged to the Medicine Rite soon began pressing me to read to them the text of the Origin Myth. There seemed to me no reason for refusing, and, after discussing the matter with the older men, it was arranged that if those interested would gather at the elder Lamere's house there would be a public reading. An audience of something over forty appeared. Not a word was said throughout the reading, and very little afterward. Yet there was no question of the awe and respect that this assemblage of unbelievers and renegades to the old beliefs paid to this first public narration of what they had always been taught to regard as the great secret which members of the Medicine Rite alone possessed. Part of this awe and respect, mixed with amazement at my supposed courage, was passed on to me. So, at least, the elder Lamere assured me.

The securing of the sacred myth was an exceedingly fortunate thing for me, but, of course, it carried its own dangers. It stirred up the wholly justifiable antagonism of the pagans. Even among some of the peyote-eaters there was, in fact, a difference of opinion as to whether the sacred myth should have been given. There was no point, they contended, in hurting the feelings of the pagans, nor did it help in making them more amenable to peyote propaganda. I had, however, one outstanding person behind me, the leader of the peyote cult himself, John Rave. Rave shared something of the elder Lamere's theory of the semimiraculous nature of my presence at this time among the Winnebago, and he felt that the publicizing of the contents of the Origin Myth would do much toward disclosing its wholly ridiculous character.

It was rather fortunate that I had to return to New York at the end of the summer of 1908, as time was thereby allowed for some of the antagonism toward my work to abate before I returned the following summer. It so happened that it did not. Yet, even so, during the nine months of my absence, the peyote cult had made great inroads on the reservation, and thus the chances of getting someone who would be willing to describe the ceremonies of the Medicine Rite were markedly enhanced. As soon, therefore, as I returned to the reservation, I immediately began an intensive search for such an individual. The method I adopted was simple enough. I told all my numerous and friendly peyote acquaintances exactly what I wanted and exhorted them to be on the alert for any Medicine Rite member who had recently joined the peyote-eaters. The ideal informant would naturally be one who had performed the ceremony but a short time ago.

How they set to work I do not precisely know, but from reports that came to me I discovered that at least three of those to whom I spoke took their task seriously, overzealously in fact. They used two types of argument: first, that a real peyote-man would be doing the new religion a distinct favor if he divulged the secrets of the Medicine

40

Rite and thus showed how ridiculous it was to believe in its teachings; and, second, that such a one could prove his actual respect for the ways of his ancestors that were now rapidly becoming a thing of the past, by helping to record the Rite and thus preserve it for posterity. For the second argument I was largely responsible.

The elder Lamere, too, was quite in favor of recording the Rite, and Rave gave his approval although he thought the matter highly unimportant except in so far as it advanced the peyote cause. As a final argument, the three individuals who felt themselves my emissaries pointed out that since, after all, the most sacred and most secret object which the Medicine Rite contained, the Origin Myth, was now generally known, there was little reason in withholding the rest.

Barely a month after my arrival I was told that a well-known middle-aged member of the Medicine Rite had joined the peyote-eaters. His name was Jasper Blowsnake and he belonged to the Wisconsin division of the tribe. About his competence there could be no question for he was the leader of one of the five groups of which the Rite was formed and, consequently, would know all the five rituals perfectly. The three emissaries were not certain, however, that he could be persuaded to talk. In fact, they were not too confident about the completeness of his conversion to the new faith.

In this they proved to be wrong, although their doubts were justified since Blowsnake apparently did not at first identify himself too closely with the cult. He had, until recently, been a bitter and uncompromising opponent of everything connected with the peyote. Had I known, at the time, the nature and circumstances of Blowsnake's conversion, much delay would possibly have been avoided. However, I knew nothing about him and had no other recourse therefore than to press my friends to redouble their efforts at persuading the new convert to talk. At first they met rebuff after rebuff. Then, suddenly, without any apparent reason, Blowsnake consented and was brought to me. He told me he was prepared to tell, in detail, the complete ceremony, that he wanted no remuneration, and that he wanted Oliver Lamere to be my interpreter. There was nothing left to do but to arrange the time and place. Although he would

41

accept no remuneration, he was willing to move into the small cottage I had rented and be my guest. His wife naturally accompanied him, and later on he was joined by his brother and his wife. His brother was a peyote-eater and his presence gave Jasper much needed moral support.

Jasper began his account of the Rite the following day. He would allow no one to be present except Oliver Lamere. Before he started he told Oliver to inform me of all the dangers that, according to native belief, surrounded the divulging of the secrets of the Rite. Someone would die. While he had himself given up such beliefs, nevertheless he felt it his duty to call attention to this one. I assured him that I was willing to take the risk if he was. Why he gave this warning I did not know at the time, for I had been told nothing of Blowsnake's personality beyond his reputation for great knowledge and probity, and I did not think it advisable to ask any questions.

The account was taken down in phonetic script. Blowsnake was asked to speak moderately slowly, but it soon developed that by the use of a few shorthand devices I could take down the narrative more rapidly than I thought. As a result Blowsnake, finally, was dictating the text at approximately the same speed that he would have used if speaking at the Rite itself. It was, of course, important to obtain the Rite with as few distortions as possible, and the fewer the breaks and interruptions, the fewer distortions that were likely to creep in.

The one real danger lay in the highly artificial conditions under which the account was given. I had great misgivings about this and could only hope for the best. I had succeeded in getting permission to attend two meetings of the Medicine Rite, and thus had some knowledge of the ceremony, but that was, necessarily, very superficial. Yet I had reason to believe that there were few distortions, first, because Blowsnake revised the text; second, because Blowsnake was in such a state of mind that he was more than meticulous in his rendition; and, third, because he apparently tried to visualize Oliver and myself as though we constituted the regular audience of the Rite. This last remark is not a mere surmise on my part but is based on a statement he made to me subsequently.

The recording took about two months, working six hours a day

42

and including Sundays. Although Oliver was present throughout, the translation was begun or, at least, was intended to have been begun, only when the complete text had been secured. To have attempted any translation before that would have unquestionably led to all sorts of distortions and unnecessary recapitulations.

When Blowsnake had finished his dictation we all decided to take a much needed rest for a few days and then begin on the translation. Fate willed it otherwise and the contemplated rest of a few days lengthened into eight months. The day after we finished, I received a telegram from New York telling me that my father had become seriously ill and was not expected to live. I hurried home immediately. My father died within a few days and all thought of the Medicine Rite had to be indefinitely postponed. The very worst thing possible had happened. I had a text of unusual significance, one that it would never be possible to obtain again, but no translation.

Fortunately, soon after my father's death, I received an appointment to the Bureau of American Ethnology and this enabled me to obtain a running translation of the text from an Indian who happened to be visiting Washington. This translation at least proved one thing, that a man might know the literal meaning of every word of the Rite and yet not understand its true significance. Frequently, indeed, a passage would be quite unintelligible. The translator would insist that he understood every word and yet have to confess it made very little sense to him. To understand the Rite, it was thus clear, a man would have to know not only the special and strange extensions of meaning words had in the Rite but also all the secondary esoteric interpretations. In fact two translations were really needed, a literal one and an esoteric one. The literal, the essentially meaningless one, I now possessed. But the prospects of getting the only significant one, the esoteric, seemed remote, for it required little intuition to realize how difficult it would be to persuade Blowsnake to continue.

After an eight months' absence I returned to the Winnebago reservation hoping for the best but expecting the worst—at least as far as securing Blowsnake's services again was concerned. I had written my interpreter, Oliver Lamere, that I was coming. At the station Oliver met me and told me, almost before I got off the train, that

43

Jasper had been informed of my coming and had left in great fear and trepidation, saying that he did not wish to have anything more to do with an undertaking which had already led to such tragic consequences. Since he had only left that afternoon, and the general direction in which he had gone was known, there was nothing left for me to do but to pursue him. After resting a very short time, a buggy with two white horses was secured and the pursuit began. If Blowsnake really wanted to hide, I realized that I would have difficulty in finding him. But even if I found him, what would happen then? If he refused to continue no one could have made him do so. The case still looked fairly hopeless.

Just about dawn I reached a farmhouse and as I got out to make some inquiries about him I saw a face pressed against the window-pane. It was Jasper. The suspense was over. But it was still not clear what would happen. Jasper settled that question immediately and in a fashion that no one could possibly have anticipated. He was at the door before I was, and insisted in his broken English that he would return at once and continue with the Rite, that he knew now that this was his mission in life and he could not hope to evade it. 'When after the dictation had been finished,' so he continued, 'your father died, I realized that this telling of the Rite was too dangerous and was not right. I was sorry, and when Oliver told me that you were coming back again to finish it I made up my mind that I would not help you. The day you were to come I left. I was terribly worried but I was quite well. After a few hours' driving I became ill. I could hardly move. So I stopped here with these friends and before I could turn around you were here driving a buggy with white horses. Let us return and begin the translation immediately. There is no sense in my resisting any longer. I will continue with it now until it is entirely finished no matter what happens.'

Tired as I was, I preferred to drive back immediately and begin at once. I was of course overjoyed, although quite puzzled about this unbelievable piece of good luck.

The next day the translation was to have been begun, but Blowsnake insisted that he had not been as accurate as he should have been in some passages of the text and suggested we do it all over

44

again. Now revision is always welcome, but this one was not as welcome as it might otherwise have been because it again postponed the translation. However, since there was clearly no alternative, we immediately began on the revision. That took at least a month. Blowsnake made very few corrections that seemed to me important, but he insisted they were necessary and that the description would not have been accurate otherwise. He explained that he had made these slips originally because he did not really know when we started what was actually wanted. This was only partially true. It is far more likely that he was at first indifferent to the various nuances because, presumably, it made no difference when relating them to a white man. But now, of course, the case was different. Absolute accuracy was imperatively demanded, first, because it was his mission to record the Medicine Rite, and secondly, because there might otherwise be danger.

After a month or so the translation was finally taken up again and continued without interruption until finished. The translation itself, as already indicated, presented difficulties. Not only did the Rite contain obsolete words which the interpreter did not know and which had to be explained to him carefully by Blowsnake, but many of the ordinary words had unusual extensions of meaning. Nor was it always easy to find the right word in English. The symbolical interpretations and the esoteric meanings, on the other hand, presented no problem because Blowsnake realized that the interpreter could not possibly know them. He stopped, therefore, to explain them at great length, even without being asked to do so.

It took exactly two and a half months, working six hours a day seven days a week to obtain the full translation. When it was completed I returned to Washington. Blowsnake was ostracized for half a year by the pagan members of the tribe, many of whom were his relatives and his former colleagues in the old rituals. It was not a pleasant experience but the opinions of the pagans had come to mean very little to him by that time and he was steeled to any fate.

The account given in the preceding pages represents, of course, my viewpoint and experiences exclusively. It leaves certain questions unexplained, however. For, granting that the circumstances existing on the Nebraska reservation in 1908 and 1909 were unusually propitious for finding someone who knew and would dictate the ceremonies performed in the Medicine Rite, the chances that such a person would be found were not very good. That one person, out of at least a dozen qualified ones, should have consented when the others refused or evaded, requires some explanation. Clearly the pressure upon Blowsnake to dictate the ceremony was great. But so was the counter pressure. The abrupt breaking down of his resistance puzzled me. Its explanation lay in factors unknown to me at the time. It lay in certain harrowing personal experiences through which he had but recently passed and which made him unusually amenable to suggestions, particularly to suggestions from people whom he had but recently learned to love and respect deeply. This I would never have known had he not, subsequently, dictated to me some personal reminiscences in which, among other matters, his account of the events that transpired during the momentous months before he agreed to record the Rite was given in some detail. Perhaps I had better give the account in his own words:

I was at the old agency. There they were to try me for murder. At night, as I sat in jail, certain people came to me and told me that they had a gallon jug of whisky and that if I was free that night I should come and drink with them. They would wait for me. That same night there was a peyote meeting at John Rave's house and my brother Sam invited me to go there. Sam stood around waiting for me. He was in low spirits for he knew of the other invitation which I had received. He said he would go with me wherever I went. I wanted very badly to go to the place where they had the liquor and should, of course, have done so if Sam had given me the least chance. However, since I could not get rid of him, I decided to go to the peyote meeting. When we arrived there we found just enough room in the center for myself and Sam. Sam sat at the right of me and John Bear at the left. In front of me was some peyote infusion, and some peyote proper, ground up and dampened.

As we sat there Sam began to cry and I began to think. I knew why Sam was crying: he wanted me to take some of the peyote. After a while I began to think of some of my own troubles. But I thought this wasn't the proper way of taking it just because I was in trouble. Then I thought of

46

the other peyote-eaters, how much they must be wanting me to eat the peyote. After a while I spoke to Sam and said, 'I am going to eat this medicine, but . . .' Then I began to cry. After a while he tried to get me to say the balance, but I couldn't. I drank some of the infusion. As the others saw that I was willing to take it they gave me a big ball of dampened peyote. However, I didn't like that and I asked for some more peyote in the dry state. I sat there asking for more and more peyote. This I kept up all night.

When morning came I stopped. Just then Harry Rave got up to speak, and no sooner did he get up than I knew exactly what he was going to say. This must be the way of all peyote-eaters, I thought. I looked around me and, suddenly, I realized that all those within the room knew my thoughts and that I knew the thoughts of all the others. Harry Rave spoke and finished his speech, but I had known it all before he said a word. Then A. Priest, who was leading the meeting, arose and asked the rest to get up so that they might turn themselves over to Christ. I also rose but, when I got up, I was seized with a choking sensation. I couldn't breathe. I wanted to grab hold of Bear and Sam, but I didn't, thinking that I was going to stand whatever was coming to me. When I made up my mind to that, I felt relieved. Then I knew what the real meaning of turning one's self over to Christ was.

In the morning they stopped the meeting and everyone seemed happy and glad. I, however, was very serious and wondered why they were laughing. Every once in a while they would come and talk to me. I wondered why they did it when they knew what was going on within me. For that reason I wouldn't answer them.

That week there were four meetings and I went to all of them and ate great quantities of peyote. The fourth meeting was at the usual place, John Rave's house. I sat with Sam as usual. At night I became filled with the peyote. *All at once I heard a voice saying, 'You are the one who is to tell of the Medicine Rite.' I thought that Sam was speaking to me so I turned around and looked at him, but he hadn't said a word. Soon I realized that nobody near me had said anything and I began to think, 'Why should it be I? Why not one of the others?' I rather pushed the idea from me; but no sooner had I done so than I began to have a tired and depressed sensation. This passed all over me. I knew that if I got up with the sincere purpose of giving in to the power that was wanting me to speak of the Medicine Rite, I should be relieved. However, for some reason or other, I know not why, I felt like resisting.*

The next morning I asked to be baptized and said that I would thereafter have nothing to do with offerings to the spirits; that I would not give any more feasts and that I would not have any more to do with the Medicine Rite. From that day to this I quit all my old beliefs. I did not feel like saying all this for, indeed, my heart was turned just the other way, but I couldn't help it for I was filled with the peyote.

From that time on, at every meeting that I attended, I could not rid myself of the idea that I must tell of the Medicine Rite. At all such times a feeling of heaviness would come over me. There I would be with but one thing on my mind; should I, or should I not, tell of it? I did not want to and thought of all sorts of excuses—that I was not a member of the Nebraska division, etc.

I was in this frame of mind while living with John Walker. There I received word that I would be wanted to tell of the Medicine Rite. From that moment I could not rest. My mind was very much distressed. I went to the barn and prayed and wept, asking that God might direct me. I walked from one place to another. I simply could not find any rest or quiet. My wife stayed with me crying. As I stood there, restless, someone with a white team, drove up. Then I thought of all the unhappiness I would cause to members of the Medicine Rite if I told the secrets of the Rite and I asked myself if it really would not be a sin to cause so much misery. The man who was driving the white team was John Baptiste and he told me that I was wanted to tell about the Medicine Rite. I got ready and entered the buggy. I was still crying and praying. Then it occurred to me that I would like to see John Rave. No sooner had I thought of this than John Rave appeared in the road. I got out of the buggy and shook hands with him and told him where I was going and for what purpose, and asked him what he thought of the matter. He began to thank me for the work I was going to do and said, 'This is what we should try to do, to help one another and to work for the Creator.' Then he thanked me again. Perfect happiness now came over me and I went to Sioux City and got married legally. From then on I was entirely filled with the desire to tell all that I knew about the Medicine Rite. 'This must be the work assigned to me by the Creator,' I thought, 'and yet I have rejected the idea all the time.'

On Paul's last trip, although I had not finished the translation, I didn't care to have any more to do with it and said that somebody else should finish the work, my excuse being that I was too busy. So, as soon as I heard that Paul was coming, I packed up my belongings and hurried out west as quickly as possible for I knew that he would bother the life out of me

48

if he found me. However, no sooner had I reached the home of my friend than I was seized with an attack of rheumatism with which I had never been afflicted before and the next morning Paul appeared with a wagon to take me back to Winnebago. *Now I know that the telling and the translation of the Medicine Rite is my mission in life and I am willing to tell all to the full extent of my knowledge.*

There is much to comment upon in Blowsnake's account. The reader, in passing, will notice for himself the discrepancies between some of his statements and mine. It is easy to see what Blowsnake omitted and to guess at the reasons. Nor would it be difficult to show how he secondarily reinterpreted most of his life after he had become a peyote-eater, so that it fitted into his new role, that of the divinely delegated person to record the Medicine Rite. However, into all these fascinating psychological questions I shall not enter here. The only important thing which we have to remember is that a multitude of factors were involved in his final acquiescence to do something fundamentally quite repugnant to him.

We must regard this acquiescence, in short, as in the nature of a conversion of the same type as his conversion to the peyote. Only through the chance combination of such an extraordinary series of external happenings as actually took place, plus a conversion, can Blowsnake's willingness to speak really be explained. The conversion, likewise, will explain the extraordinary vividness and completeness of the account and, let us hope, also explain why it appears so accurate and undistorted, in spite of the artificial conditions under which it had to be obtained.

II. Winnebago Civilization and the Medicine Rite

1. INTRODUCTORY

The Winnebago are a Siouan-speaking people belonging to a group of tribes that are today spread from Wisconsin to Montana and from Oklahoma to Saskatchewan and Alberta. At the time of the discovery of America some members of this stock extended as far south as southern Louisiana and as far east as Virginia and South Carolina. Then, however, their northern and western extension had taken them no farther than North Dakota.

Apart from the Winnebago, the best known members of this far-flung stock are the Dakota, Omaha, Osage, Iowa and Oto.

With negligible exceptions, the civilization of all these tribes was essentially the same and many of its traits were shared by other tribes contiguous to the Siouan, speaking distinct languages such as the Pawnee, Arikara, Creek, Choctaw, etc. All were agricultural, possessed, by and large, the same general type of social organization, religion, mythology and ritualism. The center of this civilization lay presumably, somewhere along the lower Mississippi from which it must have spread north, east and west along its main affluents, the Arkansas, Missouri and Ohio, rivers. I, for one, am of the opinion that not a few of its distinctive characteristics, particularly in religion, ritualism and mythology, it owes to influences that came ultimately from Mexico, possibly no earlier than the twelfth century A.D.

Although the Winnebago were first encountered by the French far to the north, at Green Bay in northeastern Wisconsin, completely cut off from their nearest kinsmen, the Iowa and Oto, they belong definitely further south and west, probably in eastern Iowa.

To understand Winnebago civilization and, incidentally, the history and significance of the Medicine Rite, it is necessary to keep in mind two historical facts, first, that the Winnebago belong to the highly complex widespread general civilization we have just mentioned and, secondly, that they were completely cut off from this civilization by simpler tribes with whom they were almost continuously at war. As a result of this peculiar situation they were able to keep much of their older culture intact, particularly their whole social, religious and ritualistic systems. Entirely uninfluenced by these simpler tribes they did not remain but what they borrowed was not important. During the eighteenth and early nineteenth centuries they were at times drawn into more intimate contact with some of these tribes, during the intervals when they were not fighting them, and it is from one of them, the Fox, that they probably adopted the specific shooting ritual today practiced in the Medicine Rite.

It is just this contrast between the manner in which the basic older structure remained intact and yet new elements were freely adopted that is so characteristic of the Winnebago civilization. The explanation for their ability to do both these things lies in the fact that, like the Iroquois and Navajo, they have always quickly transformed and reinterpreted the influences which they absorbed from the outside. We shall shortly see how the history and analysis of the Medicine Rite illustrates all these three tendencies, the marked conservatism of old patterns, the receptivity to new ideas and the capacity for making new integrations. Before turning to this history, it will be best, first, to give a brief sketch of the Winnebago civilization as a whole, particularly those phases of the social organization, religion, ritualism and mythology, which can throw light on the Medicine Rite.

2. SOCIAL ORGANIZATION

The Winnebago social organization contains two structural patterns characteristic of many North American Indian tribes, first, the division of the tribe into two halves and, second, the clan. Every clan belongs to either one or the other of these two halves or phratries, called respectively, those-from-above or upper people and those-from-the-earth or lower people.

The phratries possess, or rather possessed at one time, a number of distinctive and fundamental functions, lay and religious. Marriage within the same phratry, for instance, was forbidden. Each phratry had different burial customs. In the ceremonial lacrosse game one was always pitted against the other.

Nowhere were these contrasting duties and functions more fundamental, however, than in the political-social realm. In the upper phratry are centered, in the person of the tribal chief, all the peace and humanitarian functions of the tribe. He is selected from the clan generally regarded as the most important one in the tribe, the thunderbird. He is the representative of peace, par excellence. He cannot go to war or have anything to do with the many war ceremonies of the tribe. Be it remembered that victory on the warpath is the highest honor a Winnebago can attain. He must succour the needy and plead for clemency in all cases of infractions of tribal law and custom, even in case of murder. His lodge is a sacred asylum and absolutely inviolate. Not only is a prisoner of war safe if he manages to take refuge there, but even a dog, about to be sacrificed, must be spared, should he manage to run into it. Naturally all the other male members of the thunderbird clan as well as all the male members of the other clans in the upper phratry, go on the warpath and seek prestige through war. But, after all, this warfare is waged against people who have no status within the tribe. Acquiescence in it does not constitute approval of violence nor is it regarded as a resort to violence. And it is this condemnation of violence for which the tribal chief and his phratry stands.

In contrast to this is the attitude of the chief of the lower division, who always belongs to the bear clan. In him are centered preeminently the police, the disciplinary and the war functions. He and his associates police and guard the village, inflict punishment for transgressions of law and custom, take charge of the whole tribe when it is on a communal warpath or engaged in hunting, etc. It is in the official lodge of the bear chief that prisoners are confined before being killed and it is in the same lodge where the sacred warbundles are stored and guarded against contamination.

We are dealing here with a very old and persistent classification of the two opposing forces in society and one which reflects the answer to a question asked repeatedly, namely, how are we to meet the two aspects of life and of reality with which we are being continually confronted, the protective, constructive and positive, and the repelling, destructive and negative? Winnebago thinkers seemed to have been particularly fond of posing this problem.

It is not strange then, that they should have felt the contrast between the functions of the two phratries to lie, fundamentally, in their attitude toward evil. For the tribal chief evil was to be warded off before it came and always by passive methods. If that did not

52

succeed and evil was already upon the tribe, then his attention was directed toward alleviating the suffering caused by it and toward preventing any violence that might come in its wake. His function was to be protective and constructive. As one Winnebago told me, 'The chief of the tribe is like a motherbird feeding its young ones.'

The chief of the lower division, by contrast, went out to meet evil, attacked it ferociously when encountered, and paid little attention to the violent mood it developed among the defender-assailants. The important thing was to attack, fight and gain the victory.

The two opposing approaches to the problem can best be illustrated by the attitudes of the two chiefs toward sickness and murder. The tribal chief meets the first by giving a feast of conciliation and making direct appeals to Earthmaker. The chief of the lower division, on the other hand, immediately starts in pursuit of it. With his assistants he makes the circuit of the village four times to look for its cause. He is on the warpath and should a dog cross his path, he is immediately killed. Then he pays a visit to the sick people, dances before them and lays his hands upon them.

If a murder has been committed, the tribal chief not only intercedes for the life of the murderer but actually, if need be, offers to take the place of the malefactor. The chief of the lower division, on the other hand, seizes the murderer and conducts him to the family of the murdered person to be punished.

The objects associated with the two chiefs are typical and symbolical of their activities. For the first it is the peace-pipe, the emblem of conciliation and humility; for the second, a curiously formed baton, the emblem of punishment and pain, with which, when need be, he strikes those who transgress.

The recognition of these two aspects of social life and reality, contradictory, colliding, complementary, had its counterpart in the Winnebago analysis of human nature. There too, they insisted, good and evil, the spiritual and the material, the sacred and the profane, seemed forever at strife and forever striving for reconciliation, neutralization or fusion. This philosophy, we shall now see, is reflected, particularly, in mythology, religion and ritualism.

3 . MYTHOLOGY

Running through the whole of Winnebago mythology-literature, is the distinction between two types of narrative, the worak and the waikā. The first, literally translated, means what-is-recounted, and the second what-is-sacred. The worak belongs to the realm of what is regarded as true and humanly possible and attainable, as pertaining to the present workaday world as we know it. The hero must be a human being and the plot must end tragically. The waikā, on the other hand, belongs to the past that is irretrievably gone, to the realm of things no longer possible or attainable by man. It pertains to the world of spirits and deities, to the world of wish fulfillment. The hero must be a divine personage and immortal and the end can never be tragic. A waikā can become a worak by the simple device of bringing the plot into relationship with the contemporary human scene. The divine being has then become, for the time being, a human one. But there is no tragic dénouement. A worak, however, can never become a waikā.

As an example of the change from waikā to worak, let me take the cycle concerning the favorite heroes of the Winnebago, the Twins. Their adventures constitute real happenings and not, what one might have supposed far-off divine events, for one simple reason, namely, their resting-place is on earth and they, and this resting-place, have actually been seen by the fathers of present-day Indians.

It seems to have been one of the persistent endeavors of those Winnebago who reflected on such matters, to emphasize not only the distinctions mentioned above but, likewise, for them to link together the various adventures of their more important heroes into reasonably well-integrated epics, each one possessing its own developmental scheme. There are four such major cycles, that of Trickster, that of Hare, that of the battles of the good deities against the evil ones, and that of the Twins.

The theme of the Trickster epic is the unconscious, yet purposive, evolution of the hero from a grotesque, chaotic figure knowing neither good nor evil, to one with the lineaments of man. He symbolizes the gradual evolution from irresponsibility to responsibility.

54

Where Trickster stops Hare begins. He is a combination of a trickster and a culture-hero. His benefactions, for instance, are all accidental. But from the start, he possesses the lineaments of a human being and his orientation is toward man. He is no longer the supreme egoist that Trickster was. At the end of his adventures the earth has been transformed into a place where human beings can live and operate.

It is the function of the heroes of the third cycle to prevent this order which Hare has established from being again disrupted and returning to chaos. The function of the Twins is to continue the struggles of the heroes of the third cycle and to attempt to stabilize this order for all time.

Now although the theme of all these epics is the struggle against chaos and the introduction of order, each one of the great heroes of the last three epics, attempts to disrupt the order he has himself established. Hare brings death into the universe, Storms-as-he-walks, one of the heroes of the third cycle, kills wantonly and unnecessarily and the Twins kill one of the deities who hold our earth in place. In the case of the Twins it is important to stress the fact that, as we shall see, their attack on the world order is the result of exuberance of energy which is, in itself, constructive.

This same theme of the necessity for intelligent order and the establishment of stability runs, like a guiding thread, through the Origin Myth given on pages 17 ff. and pages 252 ff. There, the first problem of Earthmaker after he has, so to say, given himself a fixed orientation in the universe at large and brought about order within himself, is to stop the earth he has created from continuing its ceaseless motion. This he achieves by anchoring it at the four cardinal points and then weighing it down by means of vegetation and mountains. The anchorage, significantly enough, is brought about by pinning the island-earth down by four waterspirits and four snakes. Now snakes are the specifically sacred animals of the Winnebago, the intermediaries between the deities and man. Waterspirits, on the other hand, are, essentially, the most productively evil and dangerous of all the deities for man, fascinating him, confusing him, and placing in his hands the means for his own destruction and the destruction of his fellowmen. By giving to the waterspirits the positive and constructive function of helping to stop the earth from spinning around and then holding it in place, part of their primary and ancient danger has thus been neutralized. Yet it can, at best—in fact, it must—only be neutralized. To destroy it completely would be equivalent to saying that man has ceased to err, overcome all temptation and become one of the deities. Such a condition, the Winnebago insist, neither the deities nor man desire.

According to the esoteric view, the ambivalent but fundamentally evil and disruptive nature of the blessings of the waterspirit have never ceased. It is one of the subtle and symbolic features of the final adventure of the Twins, namely, the destruction of one of the waterspirits, the anchorers of the earth, that they are, after all, only doing in a human fashion what Earthmaker himself found it necessary to do, prevent the waterspirits from harming man. They kill the waterspirit and feed on its body. They do not understand that disruption and disintegration represent one half of the process of living and can, at best, be neutralized and delayed, never eliminated and destroyed. It is the symbol for motion and change without which life not only ceases to exist but is indeed inconceivable. Earthmaker, of course, recognizes this and he must, therefore, put a stop to the activities of the Twins and he punishes them. Their punishment is a symbol for the error they have committed. They became fixed, motionless and permanent, both of them traits that, according to Winnebago beliefs, are forms of death. In the puberty vision-quest one of the signs that foreshadows death is to dream of rocks or stones.

I cannot think of a closer parallel to what has here happened to the waterspirits than that of the transformation, in the Oresteia of Aeschylus, of the Furies into beneficent creatures.

But to continue with the Origin Myth. Having created order within himself and established it for the stage on which man is to play, Earthmaker proceeds to create the first beings who are to people the universe, the spirits and deities. To each one he assigns a fixed and specific amount of power, to some more, to some less. In a nature religion like that of the Winnebago, this is, of course, only another way of giving the objects and forces of nature their

56

various attributes. A definite gradation of power is thus established with no one spirit possessing powers even measurably comparable to those which Earthmaker has reserved for himself.

This principle of gradation and subordination is part of the order that Earthmaker is represented as introducing into the universe so that it can advantageously function. The instant it is changed there is danger and the threat of disruption. This is the theme of the first part of the Twin cycle, for instance. The plot is clear. The hero, one of the eight great Winnebago deities, Morning Star, has been decapitated by his enemy, a waterspirit. The body of the hero still remains alive and is being taken care of by his sister. The waterspirit, by keeping the head of Morning Star, has added the latter's power to his own. So formidable is this combination of powers that none of the deities, individually or in combination, are a match for him now. In fact only Earthmaker is his equal. Here is a threat of the first magnitude to the order ordained by Earthmaker and it must be met lest destruction overtake the world. Manifestly, the only manner of coping with the situation is to find some hero who can conquer the waterspirit, deprive him of the head of Morning Star and restore it to its owner.

But where is such a hero to be found? Nowhere. Consequently he must be newly created. This can be accomplished either by Earthmaker creating him directly as he has already done others or by his being born of some spirit. The days of special creation, however, are over. He must, therefore, be born as all creatures are now born, divine or human. But how can it be arranged that the hero, so born, has the requisite powers to achieve victory? The answer must be by such a hero being endowed for the task with enough power by all the deities, including Earthmaker.

This is accordingly done and these powers which will make its possessor greater than all the deities in existence and the equal of Earthmaker are delivered to the Sun with instructions that he impregnate the sister of Morning Star. The children born of Sun and the sister of Morning Star, who is herself a deity, are the Twins. They vanquish the waterspirit and restore the head of their uncle to his body. Thus the original order ordained by Earthmaker has been

57

reestablished. Earthmaker, however, faced with the necessity of reestablishing it, has laid the seeds for further disruption by contravening the basic principle of limited and graded powers. The danger entering in such an act makes itself felt immediately; for the Twins, after completing their proper mission of destroying whatever evil spirits still exist on earth, or at least neutralizing them, destroy, as we have seen, one of the foundations of the earth. They do so in conformity with the Winnebago realistic conception that the possession of power necessitates its exercise.

Earthmaker, however, has no powers, within himself, to stop them. If, in the end, he does succeed, it is by a device which, on first blush, must strike us as puerile yet which is actually quite profound. He frightens them. The unafraid are made to be afraid, something that comes from within themselves. They try to hide and seek shelter, without success because, of course, they cannot hide from themselves. Finally, in desperation, they flee for protection to Earthmaker. This is, of course, what he is seeking. The moment they are in his possession and have come as suppliants, he has gained contact with them and thereby attained ascendancy over them. He can then speak to them and point out the nature of their transgression as well as its dangers. They recognize both and acquiesce cheerfully in the punishment meted out. Thus, for the time being, order and responsibility have again been reestablished in their rights.

We have so far dealt with the problem of order and disorder in its general, cosmological aspects. We must now take it up in its relation to man.

It is only after the spirits and deities have been created and endowed with the powers they are to have that Earthmaker, according to the Origin Myth, creates man. As the Winnebago say this happened at the end of Earthmaker's thoughts. Man is thus in the position of the orphan of Winnebago story: he possesses nothing. Earthmaker has nothing to give him. Accordingly, man is both weak and defenseless.

This depiction of man as completely unprovided for the vicissitudes of life, has a number of important implications. First of all, it is a well-recognized literary device, indeed almost a cliché, to have

58

the last and least qualified of the personages in a myth or tale, become the true hero. Secondly, it is the cardinal ethical principle of the Winnebago that the lowly shall be raised to high estate. That is the reward for humility. Thirdly, a hero or a virtuous man must show a development, must bring about order within himself. We have seen that hold true for Trickster, for Hare and for Earthmaker himself.

In both versions of the Origin Myth, man is projected naked into an atmosphere over which he has no control whatsoever and where he is immediately attacked by evil spirits. This is in flat contradiction with the accounts of his original state in the exoteric myths. There he is almost immediately placed in possession of tobacco, the intermediary between man and the deities, as well as of flint, corn, etc.

If this is not mentioned in the Origin Myth that is because he is not to save himself or receive the wherewithal of life through the accidental benefactions of culture-heroes. On the contrary, he is to be in dire straits and saved. Earthmaker is represented as withholding tobacco from the spirits in order to present it to man and as endowing these same spirits with an overpowering craving for it. In short, it is to be the mechanism for an exchange between man and the deities. He will give them tobacco; they will give him powers to meet life and overcome obstacles. Yet the deities cannot, by themselves, save him. They are at strife with one another. This can only be done by Earthmaker. For this purpose he dispatches the great primordial culture-heroes, Trickster, Bladder, Turtle and Hare to the earth.

This is a completely new role for all three. Naturally they do not succeed. They cannot be saviours. Their antecedents are against them. Trickster is the supreme egoist, the chaotic buffoon hero, a kind of Priapus, without any sense of responsibility and without purpose as far as man is concerned. His most positive contribution is to point out the stupidity, the cupidity, the vanities and foibles of creatures. He cannot help anyone. With man he has never had any connection. Turtle is not much better. He is the embodiment of cowardice, braggadocio and unabashed sensualism. The best he can do is to participate in warfare and, then, never as a hero.

If Hare succeeds, it is because all his antecedents fit him better for the task. In the original Hare cycle he is born of a human woman and brought up by grandmother Earth herself. Although, at the beginning, his benefactions to mankind are all accidental, they do, at the end, give man the complete quota of his needs. It was comparatively easy to transform him into a hero without blemish. His one fault is demanding too much for man.

It is at this point that the problem of order versus disorder again presents itself. Not content with destroying evil on earth Hare demands immortality for his uncles and his nieces. Thus, like the Twins, he disrupts the world order through excess of constructive powers. But the difference between the Twins and Hare is that the former do it out of a kind of power drive while Hare does it in the supposed interests of man.

According to the story Hare, of course, fails. So obstinately, however, does he refuse to accept the inevitable that Earthmaker consents to an apparent revision of the world order in one respect. He will grant man the possibility of transcending death, by means of successive reincarnations, on condition that he agrees to face life and its vicissitudes in accordance with a specific ethical code. This is, of course, the theme of the Medicine Rite. For man, then, an exception to the law of birth, growth and death is permitted to this extent—he can repeat the cycle of birth, growth and decay an indefinite number of times.

But it is naturally in religion and ritualism that we must expect to find the best illustrations of the basic principles we have so far discussed in connection with social organization and mythology and to these we shall now turn.

4. RELIGION

Because of the highly complex character of Winnebago religion I shall confine myself primarily to an analysis of the nature of the powers the spirits and deities are supposed to possess, the relationship postulated between them and man, and the requests man makes to them. To understand properly these three problems we must, at the outset, try to distinguish between the layman's and the priest's conception, between the exoteric and the esoteric viewpoint although, to be sure, the two are never mutually exclusive.

For the ordinary man, the lay Winnebago, the primary powers of the vast majority of the deities have always inhered in the deities themselves. They are their own possessions and have not been bestowed upon them from without. Moreover these powers relate to the actual natural functions these deities perform. The prayers of man to the Sun, the Moon, the Stars, the Night-spirits, the Thunderbirds, etc. are, primarily, that they continue their functions and do not deviate from them. But man recognizes that they also have secondary functions, that, for instance, the sun, the morning and evenings stars, the thunderbirds, the night-spirits, all possess the power to give man long life and victory on the warpath; that the grizzly bear spirits have curative powers to bestow upon him and the waterspirits have special powers in connection with death-dealing medicines, etc. This socialization of the spirits and deities brings them that much closer to man. By bringing them this much closer to man they are deprived, however, of something of their independence and freedom of action. They have now become more specifically oriented toward mankind than toward their functioning in the universe at large. This change in orientation did not come about mechanically or accidentally. It represents the priest-thinker's conception, his attempt to establish linkages and meaningful relationships between men and the world of spirits. This attempt, from the nature of things, can never completely succeed for the simple reason that the primary functions of most of the nature gods—and they are the important ones—cannot be eliminated, must, in fact, not be eliminated. In the case, however, of animal deities, their older primary functions can be attenuated to a very marked extent and deities can be developed who never possessed functions other than those we have designated as secondary, that is, deities who function only in relation to man.

Since the nature gods, however, were the great gods, they served as patterns for all the others and the marked split in their orientation became, more or less, the characteristic of all spirits and deities. The older condition, where the god concerned himself with his primary functioning and where relations to man were strictly neutral, was set off against his later condition where he was specifically enmeshed in man and man in him. These older deities—the waterspirits, for instance, belong here—never bestowed upon man either good or evil blessings. Like the waterspirits, they gave man the materials out of which he could prepare his own good or evil. That, I think, was always the lay point of view. Manifestly this led at times, to extreme individualism and clearly did not make for organization. The priest-thinker in seeking to bring more order into the various functions of the deities introduced new evaluations and new distinctions. For example, the earlier functioning of most of the deities was now interpreted as essentially evil or at least of no positive relation to man. In their later status, on the contrary, they generously brought man good blessings and they themselves became beneficent and friendly deities.

This socialization of the deities was entirely the work of the priest-thinkers. It succeeded completely, only in the case of Earthmaker and in their masterpiece, the Medicine Rite. In all other instances the lay interpretation was still largely dominant: man could never be certain what he would receive from the spirit to whom he was praying and making offerings, nor feel that he could always guard himself adequately against the dangers inherent in the approach to the supernatural. This uncertainty was expressed in a number of ways. One of them is very typical for the Winnebago. Every youth, during his puberty vision-quest, was warned by his elders against accepting too generous a gift of power from the deities. This was the matter-of-fact parent's euphemistic way of saying, 'Do not let them deceive you or work evil upon you.' The thinker, of course, interpreted this in an entirely different fashion. For him, a faster who accepted more from the gods than he could fulfill was the victim of his own overreaching and lack of that sense of proportion which, alone, can save man from destruction.

This recognition, then, of the ambivalent or, at least, veiled nature of the deity's attitude toward him is something that man must learn to accept and which he must also learn to meet in such fashion that

62

the spirit or deity will be constrained, willingly or otherwise, to grant him his request. How can this be done? The answer will depend upon who is speaking, a Winnebago layman or a Winnebago priest-thinker. The layman's view is embodied in the myth of the origin and function of tobacco. There the deities are mechanically constrained to give the powers they possess to any human being who comes with an offering of tobacco. Here the human suppliant theoretically determines what he is to receive and how he is to employ it. In actual practice, of course, the situation is never so simple even in the case of the most matter-of-fact individual or the most-matter-of-fact deity. Both are swayed by contradictory and conflicting emotions. Man wishes a maximum of power but is held back from making the maximum request for fear that it will be too dangerous for him to do so. The deities wish to be sustained by the tobacco for which they have an almost uncontrolled craving but dread the loss of power it entails. As a result man is prone to ask too little or too much and the deities to give too little or too much. Both lead to disorder and result in evil.

To restore order in such a situation where, on the one hand, you are dealing with human nature with its ceaseless changes, its impermanence and its inability to foresee the future and the consequences of its demands and, on the other, with divine nature, with its unchangeability, its permanence and its foreknowledge, was a problem of extreme difficulty and delicacy. The added fact that, according to the universally accepted Winnebago belief, the spirits and deities depended for their happiness and much of their functioning upon the sustenance they obtained from man, further complicated it. The problem, of course, existed primarily for the priest-thinker.

To a large degree it was of the latter's own making. To the matter-of-fact man, the man of action, the relationship between the deities and man was, as has already been pointed out, direct, mechanical and constraining for both. It was but an extension of the theory of exchange of goods which prevailed on earth between men, to the world of spirits. That theory of exchange insisted that the receiver of a gift should always make a return gift of greater value than that which he had received. Of the spirits who had so much, man could at least, demand an equal exchange. The crux of the question then was, who is to evaluate the human gift? The answer of the matter-of-fact man was both, the spirits and man. For that reason, he contended, risk and danger must always inhere in the human-god relationship and there was little that could be done about it except to take every precaution one could. This must be accepted. Such was life. Suffering and tragedy loomed large there and the relationship between the deities and man was part of it. The gods could, at best, only help man to keep his balance and maintain his sense of proportion. It had always been a human problem and always would remain one. A whole class of literature, the *worak*, dealt with this theme. The picture it painted was not too optimistic.

It was the priest-thinker who was the optimist. He attempted a time-honored solution of philosophers, that of giving man some of the attributes of divinity, in other words, a greater sense of fixity and security, a greater degree of permanence, and some possibility of foreknowledge.

Winnebago philosophers seem to have attacked this problem repeatedly and suggested a number of solutions. According to one theory, gods and men had been equal in the beginning. At that time all existent beings could transform themselves at will into the one or the other *ad infinitum*. When, however, the world was to take its present shape, all the beings had to transform themselves permanently into the one or the other, into gods or into human beings.

Thus, at one time, man had actually partaken of the divine. This was, of course, only divinity in retrospect, and was not of great importance in developing divine stature for man now. Winnebago thinkers, instead, fell back upon two universally accepted folkloristic beliefs, that in the immortality of the soul and that in reincarnation. The first, however, implied a complete and irretrievable separation from the earth and human beings. To be of any value in the task of developing divine traits for man, the soul, the permanent component of man which left him at death had to be bound, in some way, to the earth. This could best be done by reinterpreting the nature of death. This was done by having it merely imply no loss of personal consciousness at all but simply a temporary stumbling.

64

There existed an unbroken continuum. No more, however, could be done in the way of reinterpretation. The philosopher could not do away with the palpable fact that the body of a deceased person remained motionless and decayed. The ghost, conscious though he remained and fully aware of what was going on around him, was unable to establish contact with the living or they with him and he always remained jealous of the living and not too kindly disposed to them. The continuum predicated was, consequently, reduced to a mere shadow.

With the belief in reincarnation, the priest-thinker could do much more. Here a kind of continuum already existed. The priest-thinker had merely to develop the concept of a continuing consciousness. Thus the first attribute of divinity, permanence, was on its way to accomplishment. This permanence was further enhanced and fixed by having an individual born again into the very same family and reliving, in every detail, his previous existence.

In the myth giving the origin of the Four Nights' Wake over the body of the dead, this is the main and insistent theme. Thus the second attribute of divinity, unchangeability, was on its way to accomplishment. The two other traits of divinity, foreknowledge and omnipresence, presented greater difficulties for their attainment. The latter, however, was not of great significance in the Winnebago concept of divinity. The former was. Here the belief in reincarnation offered little help. Recourse had therefore to be made to shamanistic practices and magic proper where both beliefs were quite common. On the whole the Winnebago priest-thinker, particularly in his greatest triumph, the Medicine Rite, eschewed magical practices and that is why little really is ever said about foretelling events. Yet it is significant that the very first story in the Medicine Rite and the one which purports to be the account of how the Rite was begun by a man, makes this foreknowledge of the future, the basic gift that a prospective member received. How fundamental it remained is proved by the fact that when the Peyote Cult was introduced among the Winnebago, the two gifts the peyote bestowed were the foretelling of the future and the ability to transport oneself anywhere by mere thought.

The priest-thinker thus contended that man could be made to approximate to the deities by simply manipulating powers and attributes which some individuals, at least, already possessed. Was it, however, wise to leave it to the individual himself to attempt this approximation? There had always been individuals in the community who essayed it but the net results of their attempts had spelled misfortune for them and misfortune for the community. They were generally the practitioners of evil magic, the poisoners. The Medicine Rite is replete with stories about them. Apparently, then, this was not a matter to be left to the discretion of an individual or for that matter to human beings at all. Man was to be educated to divinity by the deities themselves. For this purpose both were to be transformed into more disciplined, more responsible, more ethical and more profoundly realistic beings. Just as in the attainment of the goods of life, so now in the attainment of the benefits flowing from divinity, he was to face the problem bravely and realistically and endure stoically and understandingly the hardships and sufferings involved. In short, divinity had to be achieved. It could not be thrust upon one. The deities, likewise, had to be educated and be made to realize that nothing was due them as such and that they could expect no sustenance from man unless their own way of life was organized and ethically ordered and unless their blessings were given in good faith and in gratitude.

The poet-philosophers composed many a *worak* to bring out just these points. To give an example. A child is fasting and refuses one gift after another from the deities. Perturbed, they turn to the father and ask him to discover what the boy wants that has not already been granted him. In answer to his father's question, the boy says he does not wish to die. Neither the entreaties of the father or the spirits avail. And so the boy must die although he is rewarded by being transformed into a pine tree.

Now this is actually a completely transformed version of a well-known story, *The Child Who Fasted Too Long*. In the original version he dies because he has overreached himself. In such stories the spirits are neutral, that is, where they are not actually inciting

66

the young faster to overreach and destroy himself. Thus we see along what lines the reinterpretations of the priest-thinker were made.

This was the theory that the priest-thinker tried to impress upon his fellowmen in order to introduce a greater sense of confidence and security in the relationship between man and the deities. Because of the very high demands it made upon the worshipper, it remained largely a philosophical-ethical ideal and the fairly sharp line of demarcation between human beings and the spirits continued in force as the popular theory. Some there were who even insisted that it was, not only the courageous, but the morally justifiable thing to do, to coerce the deities into acquiescing in man's demands. That was the proper way to meet divinity, to challenge the gods, accept what they granted and, then, to attempt to fulfill the conditions imposed even if they meant death. Few individuals in the community, for instance, had greater prestige than the few who had secured a blessing from the much dreaded deity, *Disease-giver*. He had two faces, one dealing life and the other death. No suppliant knew which side would be turned toward him when he made his offerings, at noon, in the full blaze of day, contrary to what held for all the other deities, namely, that they must be approached at night.

This, of course, is the warrior's creed and, in a civilization like that of the Winnebago where the highest ambition as a man was to achieve distinction on the warpath, it naturally was very important. Yet to this, the chief of the tribe might well retort: such courage and such risks have their moral justification only when one is fighting the enemy or avenging the death of a kinsman. They are inapplicable when approaching a god. The taking of great risks concerns not only oneself but the whole community and must be subject to the sanctions of the community. A person must be carefully and properly educated before he dare take them. To exhibit fearlessness and heroic courage is, in itself, no virtue. Indeed, in the wrong place or on the wrong occasion, they can and do lead to death and destruction.

And so, in the realm of religion as in that of social organization and mythology, the problem to be faced is depicted as being the same. How are we to resolve the differences between the 'earth' interpre-

67

tation with its insistence upon warding off evil by force and obtaining good by force, and the 'sky' interpretation, with its emphasis on conciliation and appeasement and its attempts at the resolution of the opposites? The rituals take up the same question.

5. RITUALISM

There are two fundamental types of ritualistic organization among the Winnebago, those based on clan membership and those based on blessings from the same spirits. In other words, the bond is either a social one, membership in the same clan, or a spiritual one, a common religious experience. The clan rituals have one major extension, a ceremony where those members of each clan who are the guardians of the warbundle of that particular clan, gather together in a feast for all the main deities. At this ceremony they ask for the renewal of the powers of these warbundles and for the promise of success on the warpath. Set off, apparently, from these two types of ritual there is a third, the Medicine Rite, with but one example, where membership is based upon personal conduct and achievement other than war and where, usually, one can only enter when there is a vacancy caused by death. In those cases where a person became a member through personal achievement he was, in the old days, generally, a man in middle age because of the rigorous and difficult entrance requirements. When taking the place of a deceased member a person could, however, even be under twenty.

An individual is consequently either born with the right of membership in a ceremony, like the clan feasts and the warbundle feasts, or he has to achieve it, as in the ritual societies based on blessings from the same spirits and the Medicine Rite.

The clan feasts which are in honor of the ancestral clan animals need not detain us here. Nor do we have to dwell upon the ritual societies based on common supernatural experiences. For membership in the latter there are really no requirements except willingness to endure the comparatively light hardships of fasting. The spirits or deities rarely, if ever, failed to grant the suppliant a vision. Formerly,

68

so many Winnebago informed me, the most sacred and important of the ritual societies of this type was the Night-spirit one. It was practically gone when I first visited the tribe in 1909. In none of these rituals was there any control of membership or insistence upon a special code of conduct either before or after admission.

The warbundle ceremonies require a few words. Each performance is divided into two parts, the first presided over by the Thunderbird spirits and the second by the Night-spirits. However, all the great spirits of the Winnebago pantheon have their place in it and, to all, offerings are made. Although in the eyes of the Winnebago, the warbundle ritual is devoted entirely to the glorification of war, it is interesting and significant to see that, besides the great patrons of war, the Thunderbird spirits, Night-spirits, Sun, Morning Star, Evening Star, Disease-giver, Eagle, Black Hawk, specific peace deities like Earthmaker, Earth, Moon and Water are also included and, at times, even the hero-deities, Trickster, Turtle and Hare. From this we can infer that even in a ceremony devoted preeminently to the enhancement of the importance of the warrior and of warfare, deities symbolizing peace and the antithesis of violence and force, could not be entirely left out. Admittedly their inclusion had little effect upon the one and insistent prayer of the participants, war. Even Earthmaker is represented as bestowing success on the warpath, something completely new. Yet the mere fact that Earthmaker was included did act as a reminder that the pursuit of war was not everything.

The warbundle rituals represent the classic and most complete expression of the war spirit, the glorification of the viewpoint of the chief of the lower division of the tribe, namely, that one goes out to combat evil, militantly and with violence. In fact, you must preenact the enemy's attack, your method of coping with it, and the manner in which the enemy is to be defeated and overwhelmed. Even orgies, where all self-control is abandoned, are permitted, something that was always abhorrent to the normal Winnebago and greatly dreaded. The remark made to me by the Indian who translated the text, relative to such orgies is quite illuminating here. 'It is good to have one Indian work himself into a paroxysm of enthusiasm but it must never be more than one!'

69

But to come now to the Medicine Rite. It is only superficially that its organization is really unique, for both in the snake clan feast and in the Night-spirit ritual society there are four positions just as in the Medicine Rite. The resemblances between the latter two are, in fact, so marked that we can well understand why some Winnebago regarded the Night-spirit society as the model for the Medicine Rite. In a sense it is true that the Medicine Rite could be interpreted as the society of those who have been blessed by Earthmaker. Yet, in spite of these similarities, it was regarded as something *sui generis*. What is, then, the specific character of its organization that gives it this unique position in the Winnebago ritualistic system?

The answer is simple—two traits, the method of admission and the fact that a large part of the tribe belongs to it. While the size of the membership at the beginning of the nineteenth century was unquestionably larger than a hundred years before, still it must always have been very large. Moreover, there were no restrictions as to sex. Compared to any of the other ceremonies, the Medicine Rite thus stood out as a completely democratic organization where, theoretically, the only requirement was membership in the tribe.

This uniqueness in certain fundamental traits of its organization was matched by its purpose and much of its content. Its avowed purpose was, not only, to ensure man a long and happy life on earth but to ensure his return to it after death. Of course all ceremonies were concerned with the first of these two purposes. And the belief in reincarnation had always, as we have pointed out, been well-known and accepted. The uniqueness lay in the method of attaining it. That method had two parts, a magical-symbolical and an ethical-philosophical. Admission to the Rite entailed being shot and 'killed' by a missile and coming to life again. This is the magical-symbolical part. The ethical-philosophical part consisted in strict adherence to a high code of behavior laid down for you and enforced by the older members of the Rite. Only by adherence to it can you surmount death.

Yet admission is only a preliminary to your real task. It only sets your feet, so to speak, in the proper road. You must steel yourself to being shot and 'killed' innumerable times and you must obtain

70

mastery over death by shooting and 'killing' others innumerable times, so that death, when it finally comes, will be as familiar to you as life. Then, when full of years, you actually die, the passage from life to death will become a mere incident and, being born again will, for yourself, constitute no break with your former existence.

It is quite clear that we are dealing here with the vision of a poet-philosopher and this will become more evident when we recognize the original nature and meaning of the shooting ritual. Shooting missiles into a person was an old and well-recognized shamanistic device. The missiles were generally animal claws and they were meant to kill. Your only protection was to provide yourself with magical counter measures or, to obtain some specific blessing from a spirit. That you could convert what was meant to be a death-dealing missile into a life-giving one by leading a virtuous life was something new when applied, for instance, on the grand scale to be seen in the reinterpretation of the myth of the *Journey to Spiritland* as found in the Medicine Rite (cf. pages 257 ff.). To express it, required a particular language, with new extensions of meaning for words and in which metaphor, symbolism and mysticism ruled supreme, in short, the language of a poet and a philosopher. Myths were reinterpreted in an entirely new fashion and put to entirely new uses. To understand and comprehend it a special and difficult kind of education and training was needed.

Yet, in spite of its esoteric character, one thing was never forgotten, that the ceremony was to serve concrete purposes. It was not the vision of a Road of Perfection to be rewarded by eternal peace and happiness in heaven but, on the contrary, the vision of a Road of Perfection which was to be rewarded by a return to earth and to the vicissitudes of living. It was life that was to be faced, with all its imperfections, trials, and with all the comedies and tragedies that often played such havoc with ideals of perfection.

Indeed the imperfections of life intruded themselves into the poet-philosopher's vision, despite his attempts to exclude them. It was impossible, for instance, for individuals to forget that they were not only members of the Medicine Rite but, likewise, warriors and often shaman. Thunder, as the idealists might well do against the presence of shamanistic practices in the Rite, they could never quite exclude them and the only answer they possessed was to condemn them and show how they led to dishonor, death and destruction.

This interweaving of the concrete and the symbolic and mystical led to a double, at times even a triple, set of significances for every action and word and which, occasionally, reached incredible heights of complication, intricacy and subtlety.

Since no other ceremony resembles the Medicine Rite in the respects just mentioned, we may well stop and ask ourselves what could have led to its creation? What is the cultural meaning of this new mode of expression, this new type of reinterpretation of ancient beliefs and attitudes? Allowing for the natural creative impulses of our Winnebago poet-philosophers, it is not unreasonable to suspect that some particular circumstance or circumstances must have called them forth.

Ordinarily, any attempt to determine such a matter among the American Indians, in the absence of an authentic historic record, would mean mere speculation. Fortunately this does not hold true for the case in point. There are indications within the text of the Rite itself and some historical evidence which proves pretty conclusively that, in its present form, the Medicine Rite is a development late in Winnebago history and after the coming of the French in 1632. We can, in fact, date it more precisely. The otterskin pouch and the shell used in the shooting ceremony come from the *midewiwin* ceremony of the Ojibwa. The Winnebago obtained them from the Fox and this could not possibly have been before 1680-1690.

Now, the Winnebago between 1650-1900 were passing through a very serious crisis. Their numbers had been seriously decimated by ferocious struggles between them and the Illinois and Fox and by the diseases introduced by the Europeans. The influence of the French, as well as the new conditions resulting from French encroachment, were playing havoc with the old order of things. Nor must we underrate the influence of the French missionaries.

That a new type of ceremony should have appeared among the Winnebago just then cannot be ascribed to mere chance. It must bear some relation to the crisis. The moment we put the two together much that would otherwise remain inexplicable about the Medicine Rite becomes clear—its nostalgia for the past, the idealistic and idyllic setting, the absence of any reference to war, the insistent condemnation of shamanistic practices. We can then see it for what it is, the attempt of the priest-poet-philosopher to meet the new and hitherto unknown threats to the old way of life by demonstrating, first, what merit and virtue inhered in the Winnebago civilization of the past and, secondly, by showing how it could be recovered and safeguarded against all outside attacks. The creators of this ritual-drama were concerned only with the description of the Road of Perfection, a road that was to lead the Winnebago back to the past and then forward again. Only if we fully realize that we are not dealing here simply with the inward vision of some poet-philosopher but with the spiritual crisis of a people will we be able to explain the burning intensity that animates the participants.

But, let us forget for the moment the fact that the Medicine Rite is of late appearance in Winnebago history and let us forget the crisis that gave it birth and try to assign it its proper place in Winnebago thought.

We saw before how the warrior ideal received its glorification in the warbundle ceremonies. Nothing comparable to such a eulogy of war and of the warrior's viewpoint existed for the other half of Winnebago life, for the arts of peace. Indications that it was attempted are innumerable but these attempts seem never to have succeeded to any marked degree.

And so the Winnebago, apparently, had to wait until late in their history, until a crisis of major proportions was threatening to disrupt their whole culture, before the ideal which had always been expressed in the symbol of the chief of the tribe could find its full and adequate expression in the present Medicine Rite. That this expression came so late in their history must not obscure the fact that it represents part of a very old struggle between two aspects of Winnebago life that had always been seeking a resolution. It is not only in Winnebago history that a philosophical-ethical ideal has received its highest expression in the midst of a social-economic crisis, as I need hardly point out.

73

Whether, before the coming of the Whites, other crises of equal intensity had ever threatened the security of Winnebago life we do not, of course, know. What we do know, however, is that before Winnebago civilization finally broke up and disintegrated completely, about twenty years ago, a religion of a new type essayed the same task that the Medicine Rite had undertaken and developed a ritual of considerable beauty with a quality all its own. I am, of course, referring to the Peyote Cult.

6. THE HISTORY OF THE MEDICINE RITE

The Medicine Rite is clearly the product of a long development. For proof of this we have not only direct historical evidence but fairly convincing internal evidence. I have already called attention to the fact that the otterskin pouch, the shell and, in fact, much of the whole present shooting ritual stems originally from the *midewiwin* ceremony of the Ojibwa. We know that they are the originators of it and that it spread from them to the Pottawattomie, Menominee and Fox and then to the eastern Dakota and Iowa. The eastern Dakota already had it in 1765. The Winnebago were brought into contact with it by the Fox and the Iowa. We must assume that this could not possibly have been earlier than 1690 and, far more likely, it was later, anywhere between 1710 and 1730. To judge from its present form and content, nothing else was borrowed than the shooting ritual and its appurtenances, apart from a number of songs, at least, from the linguistically and culturally distinct Fox. More was probably borrowed from the linguistically and culturally closely related Iowa.

Two introductory narratives (pages 92 f. and 94 f.) profess to tell how some of the pouches were obtained but they can hardly be accepted as too accurate. In so far as any credence can be placed on what they say, it would appear that they were presented to two Winnebago, whose names are given. No mention, however, is made by the givers of these gifts, one an Iowa and the other a Fox Indian, of their be-

74

longing to the *midewiwin*. Nor do the two Winnebago say anything about their having been incorporated into a ceremony of their own. Yet some connection there must once have been between these gifts and the beginnings of our Medicine Rite, for otherwise there would have been no conceivable reason for their inclusion.

Since everything else in the Medicine Rite of today, apart from the shooting ritual, is so completely different from the Ojibwa and Menominee *midewiwin*, the only two we know reasonably well, we must assume either that a new ceremony was created then and there with the shooting ritual as its nucleus or that the shooting ritual was incorporated into an older Winnebago ceremony. All the evidence at our disposal points to the latter alternative. We have also to assume that this older ceremony contained shamanistic practices of the type that were characteristic of the Night-spirits' Rite.

That it was not the Night-spirits' Rite itself upon which the Ojibwa shooting ritual was grafted, of that there can be little doubt. Fortunately, we have a clue from a very unexpected source, the Pawnee. These Indians have a ceremony called *The Ceremony of the Medicine Men*, where we find the following remarkable resemblances to the Medicine Rite: a shooting ritual which causes the individuals shot to fall prostrate to the ground as if dead and then rise again; the conception that the framework of the lodge consists of snakes; a figure called the sacred woman; the importance of Turtle; a membership possessing occult powers strictly guarded and kept secret from the outside world; a highly elaborate symbolism, etc. Chance must be ruled out here. The only thing we have to decide is how the Winnebago happen to possess a ceremony so similar to that of the distant Pawnee with whom they had practically no contact. Direct borrowing is out of the question.

To me there seems to be only one possible explanation, namely, that the Winnebago and the Pawnee, the Winnebago to a smaller extent, were members of that larger civilization which we mentioned before and which had its roots in Mexico, and of which the Pawnee have preserved the essential traits whereas the Winnebago have preserved only vague memories of it and some special survivals.

Assuming then that the older ceremony upon which the Ojibwa

shooting ritual, plus its appurtenances, the otterskin pouch and the shell, were grafted, was in content very much like the present *Pawnee Ceremony of the Medicine Men* and, organizationally, like the Night-spirits Society; let us see now what changes were necessary to have this older ceremony approximate to the present Medicine Rite.

First, of course, the meaning of the missile shot into the individual being initiated and into the members of the Rite had to be reinterpreted and its overt shamanistic implications removed. The stimulus for that unquestionably came from the Ojibwa shooting ritual. The linkage of the shooting ritual with the doctrine of reincarnation is, however, something entirely new.

The second transformation came about when the Tear-Pouring ritual was grafted upon this older rite. This last named ritual, apparently, was part of the very elaborate ceremonies connected with the dead although, today, it is not found in the official Four Nights' Wake. What is, however, found there is the myth of the *Journey to Spiritland* which has been taken over *in toto* into the Medicine Rite and subjected to a complete and fundamental reinterpretation. I feel that it is the linkage of these elements from the funeral rites with the older form of the Medicine Rite that brought about its basic transformation and gave us the Rite of today, with its stress on reincarnation and on the doctrine of the Road.

The third new trait requiring an explanation is the role of Earthmaker. He is a very old Winnebago deity and was evidently regarded as the supreme deity before the coming of the Europeans. He seems, in fact, to be the counterpart of the well-known Pawnee supreme deity *Tirawa*. Nevertheless, the influence of Christianity in, at least, unifying his characteristics and functions and accentuating his supremacy over the other deities, as well as the theory that he is the creator of all things, must not be excluded. The association of the two crossed lines with him cannot be accidental, even although the symbol itself is very old and is more specifically connected with the cardinal points.

There is, besides, some semihistorical evidence for indirect Christian influence. In a narrative purporting to be an account of the origin of a well-known French half-breed family among the Winnebago, named Decora, a statement is made that the son of the French founder of the family by the daughter of the tribal chief, introduced the figure of Earthmaker into the Medicine Rite. Such an individual would, indeed, have been the ideal person to have done just this. According to the narrative, he was taken, while still a very young child, to France and brought up there for a number of years. He was still only a boy when his excessive homesickness forced his father to send him back to Wisconsin and there he was rigorously subjected to the old Winnebago education for youths.

Thus he was almost made to order to symbolize the meeting of the two civilizations and to become one of individuals best qualified to understand the nature of the crisis threatening his people and the need for a new religious and philosophical synthesis to surmount it, at least, spiritually . . .

It is in some such fashion that we must visualize the growth and development of the Medicine Rite. Only if we bear in mind the various strands that have gone into its making and only, when we realize that in its final integrated form, it is a work of art sprung out of the poignant needs of a people facing a soul-trying ordeal, only then, can it be properly understood, evaluated and appreciated.

THE MEDICINE RITE

PART ONE

THE RITUAL OF TEARS

I. The Preliminary Ceremonies

1. FIRST PRELIMINARY NIGHT

As soon as the poles for the ritual lodge have been cut they are carried to the specially purified ground where the lodge is to be erected. The framework of the lodge is then set up and the canvas-covering stretched over it from east to west. The small bundles of tobacco that are to be given those invited to the performance of the Rite are then prepared and tied up. As soon as it gets dark, those who are to participate, Ancestor-Host, the members of his band, and the initiate, enter. In this particular case Warudjaxega was, himself, the initiate. They discuss the songs they are to sing and extend greetings to one another until all have responded in turn. Then he who is the leader on this particular night rises and speaks.

L E A D E R :   Ancestors, we extend our greetings to you. This is the true religion, this is the way of Earthmaker. To the earth, at the beginning of things, he dispatched four great spirits in succession. Only the last one, Hare, succeeded in accomplishing the mission for which he had been sent. If we could do as he did we, too, could attain to the full life.

Our ancestors, our relatives of the past, they worked for this objective for many years, ceaselessly and untiringly. Whenever parents had a child, one they loved in particular, in order to obtain a full life for it, they always thought of this Rite and what they must do to have this child become a member. Deep into the bowels of the earth they sent their secret desires and hopes; never did they permit them to become manifest to anyone. Yet, when the time was ripe, and a parent appeared at a performance of the Rite, the members had no difficulty in discerning what was in his mind.

81

There he would stand and address them: 'Pitiable and compassion-inspiring, my way of living has always been and yet, despite this humble condition, the means of attaining a full and complete life have been placed before me. What I am to do, I have already been told. It was indeed pleasurable to hear it. I am filled with pride at the thought!

'This it is that makes me, a father, feel that what I had achieved in life, my deeds, my honors, will not all have been in vain, that when I die, that they will not disappear and perish from the face of things.'

Truly this parent had in mind the request the ghosts of all recently departed men make of the spirits. Assuredly, of this, was he thinking. That the sacred Rite alone enables one to attain to the full life, have not Winnebago always been agreed on this? How they might so contrive as to obtain long life for their children, their best beloved, was this not always uppermost in their minds and hearts?

It was in such honor that they always held this sacred Rite and the full measure of life it contained. And they would speak to one another and to their child, that it, too, would feel that way. Indeed, it is good and pleasurable to have such thoughts, such intentions.

Members of the Medicine Rite, you who occupy the four positions that our spirit ancestors once held, we ask pity and compassion of you and of them, and since we know that both you and they are kind and gracious, we know that this compassion will be forthcoming . . .

When our Rite was to be performed for the first time, He-whom-we-call-our-nephew, Hare, went forth to gather the spirits into the sacred lodge. With him he took the offerings we always extend to the spirits when we desire their presence, that with which we ask for the opportunity to lead a full life—tanned buckskins [19] and tobacco. He-whom-we-call-our-nephew carefully prepared the invitations. The tobacco was split in four portions and then each portion tied up securely. Thus did he wrap up for us the means-of-acquiring-life, the full life. From the great spirits he was to ask compassion for us. Now these were the spirits he sent with invitations:

A young white-faced wolf, a very white one. The Island-Anchorers, the great ones, they who, every day, throw their breath upon us,[20] these he would have to pass.

A walker-on-life-and-light,[21] an extremely white one, one whom the good spirit had placed up above.

A shrieking-swan, one of the color of snow.

A young black-furred messenger, he of the very fleet feet, he who wears, girt around him, a basswood bark belt.

All these Earthmaker had put in charge of life-securing powers for human beings.

Then to the spirits Earthmaker had stationed below, to them, the messengers went; upon them they trod.

Now after all were assembled in the lodge, the first messenger who had gone forth, the very young white-faced wolf, returned. Just as the Rite members do today, so did he make the circuit of the lodge: four times he pressed into that road. Then he returned and stood in the middle of the lodge, scattering the earth with his paws in the four directions—the east, the north, the west, the south. 'Hoho, hoho!' he said and shook himself. As young as he had been when he started on his errand so he became again, the very white-faced one. Then he spoke:

'Most beloved of Hares, for this that I have just completed, will your uncles and your aunts always remember me. For this demonstration of the rewards meted out to the members of the Rite and which you are about to teach your uncles and your aunts, for this, I say, they will always remember me. All that will be required of any Rite members, in the days to come, be he man or woman, is just this—that he reverently and meticulously go through the preparations for the Rite itself. Then, indeed, he cannot fail.'

Now it was about time for the walker-on-light to return. When he arrived he immediately set his steps in the road of the lodge. Four times he made the circuit. His head resembled a worn-down moccasin without soles and along his back there stuck out a few scattered hairs. Such was his appearance before he made the circuit, before he stepped into the middle of the lodge. There in the middle of the lodge he now stood, scattering the earth with his feet, toward the

83

east, toward the north, toward the west and toward the south. Then he shook himself thoroughly. And lo! just as young as he had been when he started so, again, he now appeared. And thus he spoke to Hare:

'Most beloved of Hares, for this that I have just completed, will your uncles and your aunts always remember me. For this demonstration of the rewards meted out to the members of the Rite and which you are about to teach your uncles and your aunts, for this, I say, they will always remember me. All that will be required of any Rite member, in the days to come, be he man or woman, is just this— that he reverently and meticulously go through the preparations for the Rite itself. Then, indeed, he cannot fail.'

Now, from below, the black-furred one had returned. A very young man he had been when he left, but when he entered the lodge to step into this sacred Road of ours, his head resembled a worn-down moccasin without soles and along his back there stuck out a few scattered hairs. Then, finally, he stood in the middle of the lodge. After scratching and scattering the earth in the four directions, he shook himself repeatedly and behold! He took on his former youthful appearance. There, in the middle of the lodge, he stood and spoke:

'Most beloved of Hares, for this that I have just completed, will your uncles and your aunts always remember me. For this demonstration of the rewards meted out to the members of the Rite and which you are about to teach your uncles and your aunts, for this, I say, they will always remember me. All that will be required of any Rite member, in the days to come, be he man or woman, is just this—that he reverently and meticulously go through the preparations for the Rite itself. Then indeed he cannot fail.'

When the leader has finished his address, then those in the lodge begin to intone their songs. First they sing a mourning song for the one who has died and, when they have finished this song, they stop their life-beseeching requests for the present. They now turn to the discussion of whom they are to invite to the Rite, to whom they are to offer tobacco. This being agreed upon, four more songs are sung and they file out of the lodge to get some sleep.

84

2 . SECOND PRELIMINARY NIGHT

This takes place in the round private lodge of Ancestor-Host. Present are Ancestor-Host, the members of his band and the initiate.

A N C E S T O R - H O S T :   To you sitting there, my nephew, greetings; to you, my niece, greetings; to you, my friend, greetings; to you, my daughter, greetings; to you, my grandmother, greetings; to you, my grandfather, greetings; to you, my uncle, greetings; to all of you, my ancestors, greetings! . . .

Years ago there lived a man who had acquired a specific kind of knowledge and wisdom.[22] So pleased was he with it that he felt he had to tell someone else about his good fortune. Selecting another man, he acquainted him with the knowledge that he had acquired. He, too, like the first person was able to accomplish all he desired through the knowledge thus obtained. Both soon realized that they were able to foretell events that were going to happen. First, one day, then two, then four and, finally, twenty days, they could foretell. 'Assuredly,' they said to themselves, 'we have acquired powers, true and powerful.' And this common knowledge drew them together and they became good friends.

Then the two decided to ask a third Winnebago to share their knowledge with them. So they selected another person, one who was virtuous, one who was kind-hearted, one who was very wise, indeed, one who was accustomed to wisdom and slightly beyond middle age. To this man the same thing happened as to the other two. First, he was able to foresee one day ahead, then two, then four, then twenty. He was pleased and happy. He realized that what he had obtained was true knowledge. And this knowledge drew all together and they became good friends.

Then the three decided to select a fourth Winnebago to whom they could teach this knowledge, he, too, a virtuous, a righteous, a wise, man. Not once did they think of a young man but always of one slightly over middle age. The new member liked it and to him, too, the same thing happened that had happened to the others. First, he was able to foretell events one day ahead, then two, then four and,

85

finally, twenty. The new member was pleased and happy. He realized that what he had attained was true knowledge.

And so there were four men who now had this knowledge in common, four virtuous men, four righteous men, four wise men. Only with each other did they commune, only with each other did they associate.

From that time on the Rite began to grow. Soon there were nine for whom the Rite meant a full and wise life, a happy life. Never will it come to an end, this Rite of Earthmaker, never, indeed, will it pass out of existence, so they assured one another . . .

From generation to generation, from one person to another, our compassion-seeking ancestors passed on this knowledge. Pitiable in one another's sight they were. And so, even to me, there was brought some slight knowledge of the truth. At least, so I presume to believe. I know it is true; I know it is good.

3. THE SENDING OF INVITATIONS

When they are ready to take the invitations to those who are to attend the Medicine Rite, the official messenger starts out and soon he is speeding along in the footsteps made by the spirits. When he comes to the lodge of the one he is seeking, he calls him secretly and leads him away to some secluded place. There both sit down. Immediately the messenger arises, and greeting him, makes the circuit of the lodge. At the end of the last circuit he greets him again and speaks:

M E S S E N G E R : Ancestors, we greet you. Your ancestors, too, and mine, whose bones long since have mingled with the earth, I greet these all.

Would that they might have compassion upon us!

My ancestors, my relatives, would that tomorrow I might behold your faces as we perform, in our pitiable manner, this compassion-inspiring Rite! This, too, we ask of you—that you place at our disposal the life that you have accumulated through your prayers and

86

those life-giving instruments, the sacred utterances, which your ancestors left you as their heritage when they departed.

Ancestors, we greet you.

Then, in his turn, the one who has been invited arises, greets the messenger and makes the circuit of the lodge. Four times he does it, and at the end of each circuit, he repeats the greeting. Then he sits down and thanks the one who had brought the invitation, speaking as follows:

T H E   I N V I T E D   O N E :   I greet you. It is good. Now I am conscious of really having lived. You and all your fellow members of the Rite have indeed had compassion upon me, have made me cognizant of myself and my possessions. It is good.

You have made me aware that I am to impersonate one of those great Island-Anchorers, the ones that lie-stretched-out-at-the-corners-of-our-island, the ones to whom tomorrow you shall offer your tobacco. It is good.

I know, everyone knows, that the members of the Rite do not really look forward to these performances as though they had anything to obtain from them for themselves. If they take part in the Rite it is rather for us they do it, that they might have compassion upon us. It is good.

I cannot indeed think of anything of significance that I and mine will be able to tell you. However, we can possibly bring enough of the sacred greetings to you to make our presence of some value. And so, with these life-begetting greetings, I salute you. Ancestors, we greet you. (song)

Then tobacco is offered to the spirits.

M E S S E N G E R :   As soon as the time comes, you are to begin your own Preparatory Four Nights, with its speeches and its songs so as to be ready for the fifth night when the Rite itself will be given.

II. The Preparatory Four Nights of Ancestor-Host's Band

1. THE FIRST NIGHT

ANCESTOR-HOST: You who sit over there, my nephew, greeting; you, my niece, greeting; you, my friend, greeting; you, my grandmother, greeting; you, my daughter, greeting; you, my uncle, greeting; you my aunt, greeting; you, my grandfather, greeting; you, my ancestors, greeting.

All our many ancestors are waiting for us to perform this Rite, so that they might bestow upon us their compassion and that we might return it in kind. And you, my nephew, you must listen to me with care as I point out to you the road you must take, as I describe for you the full measure of life that He-whom-we-call-our-nephew, Hare, obtained for us. This, alone, is true living. There is no other. He who is placed upon this road must try hard to stay in it. He must listen to what his ancestors, dead and living, counseled him to do, not merely because he is thereby helping them, but because he is also helping himself, and performing a virtuous and pleasurable act. He will be experiencing life.

Do nothing evil.[23] Do not steal. Do not lie. Do not fight. If you meet a woman on the path, turn off toward the right, never toward the left. Do not address her as though you had the right to take liberties with her.[24]

Thus did they speak. Remember the words I have told you and take them to heart if you desire to be a good member of the Rite. Only so will you secure that full measure of life which I and all your relatives and fellow members, so earnestly desire for you.

Again, we greet you; ancestors, we greet you.

Far back, in the very distant past, our ancestors began the preparations for this Rite with a Tear-Pouring ceremony for the ghost of him who had just departed. This we shall now repeat and those of us here assembled will join in pouring out our tears in grief for him. Verily, this must become the lodge of tears, tears through which we make our appeal to the ghost of the departed, so that he may ask the spirits to distribute among us all that he left behind that was

88

still his due. For this we beseech him. Always, in the past, has the request of a ghost been successful and, doubtless, it will be successful this time, too. The life-residue you obtain for us, to good purpose will we put it and that is why we appeal to you so earnestly. It was no different at the beginning than today, we have been told.

But now we must sing you a song. A wail for the dead we shall chant, sincere and reverent. Our voices must not tremble as we intone this mourning song lest people doubt the integrity of our grief. Often this has been stated. Again we extend full greetings to you, our ancestors, and will begin at once, nephew, to tell you, of our life-entreating acts and prayers. First the song, the mourning song, we shall sing, one that has come down to us from the remote past of our ancestors. When that is done we shall again send our greetings to you, that you may take pity on us and that we may be benefited by the greetings with which you respond . . .

Long ago the Winnebago lived at Mogacutc.[25] The heads of the four divisions of the Medicine Rite were good and staunch friends. Then one of them died and one of the great plate-holders [26] brought the news to his wife. Her heart was sore and she began to weep. Her weeping was unabated. It became no better with time. Then her two grown-up sons had the following dream:

In the middle of the night the remaining three members of the Rite came after their mother and asked her to accompany them. They took her to a secluded place, away from the village and told her to sit down. When she had sat down, one of them arose and speaking, greeted her. 'When your husband died your heart indeed became sore, did it not?' 'Yes,' she replied. 'And do you wish to obtain your husband's knowledge of the Rite? If that is what you wish, lie down on the ground and put your body at my disposal.' In a similar strain did the second leader speak and, after him, the third one.

When they were finished the woman arose and answered, 'I care to know nothing of such a proposal.' Barely extending her greeting to them, she walked away.

Now, before the dream, the two sons had noticed that their

mother's weeping had stopped for a while and they were happy about it. But now it began again, just as intensely and continuously as at first. Her sons were perturbed and questioned her, asking: 'Why you were not that way a little while ago? Some man must have insulted you!' And then she answered and told them, 'The three friends of my husband, after he was dead, came to me one night, in the middle of the night, and asked me to accompany them to some secluded place, away from the village. There they spoke to me and told me that if I would stretch out my body for their disposal they would give me my husband's knowledge of the Rite. I refused to do it: I refused to listen to such a proposal. I did not desire that knowledge if it had to be acquired in such a manner. And so I got up and, barely greeting them, left. Again I began to weep just as I had done at first.'

'Mother,' exclaimed the sons, 'do not grieve anymore, for you will soon obtain ample knowledge and power. These three men are not the only ones who possess them!'

They took their mother to the edge of the water where there was a fairly large number of jack-oak. From the center of this jack-oak grove protruded a large rock, like a small hillock. Upon this rock they placed their mother. Then the two boys commenced running around the rock on which their mother had been placed. Again and again they circled it until, finally, a rumbling noise was heard within the hillock. Faster and faster they circled the jack-oak grove until suddenly it turned upside down and, around it, arose a lake. Without stopping they still kept on running although they were up to their ankles in water and the shells of their anklets could be heard jingling.

Throughout their running they kept shouting to their mother, 'Mother, dear, whatever is about to happen, be resolute, and do not run away!' The woman sat there in the midst of the commotion, singing to her children, so it is said. Suddenly various objects floated up from the depths of the water and, as each one appeared, she said to herself, 'Surely, this must be the one intended for me!' [27] And yet it was not so. Finally various kinds of animals floated up, the last one a very large snake.

90

When the turmoil subsided and the lake became quiet and calm, there, on the surface of the water, lay a waterspirit, a very white one, carrying under its red and extremely round armpits the material from which we compound the goods of life.[28] Immediately the two boys killed it and from its body they manufactured various articles. Then they began the songs we use today as well as the greetings. . . .

From this waterspirit's body they obtained the materials with which to make the shells for their anklets so these might rattle when they danced. From it [29] they made the bells that jingle when the Medicine Rite members swing their feet in dance; from it they made the iron decorations on their moccasins; from it, finally, they compounded the poisons to be used by those who are selfish, to kill those who had caused them heartache and pain. Not before this time had poisons been used in this Rite. (songs)

Ancestor-Host rises and speaks again:

A N C E S T O R - H O S T :   Our ancestors are waiting to show compassion upon us, on all of us, however great our numbers. They will send their life-begetting greetings to us and we shall return them. Indeed we intend to extend our greetings far back to those ancestors who had pity upon us in the distant past, so that we might some day see them face to face. With all these ancestors do we desire to celebrate our mourning ceremony. May they show compassion to us!

I beseech the ghost of the departed to think of us as he beholds us rising again and again at this Tear-Pouring ceremony in remembrance of him. May he not forget us as we tearfully ask for that residue of life he left behind him unfinished. And do you who are present make this demand sincerely, in response to true grief. Do not let your voices tremble and break. Not in such wise does one make a request of the ghost of the departed! But if your appeal is sincere, do not doubt it, the life-residue will be yours to use in the future.

Let us then begin the Tear-Pouring, let us begin the mourning songs, so that we may bring to a termination this portion of our ceremony. Remember it is life for which we are appealing and what-

91

ever extension of it is vouchsafed us. Thus do we repeat what has been passed down to us. Blessings through compassion, this we are requesting. For these we shall render thanks in the form of songs, negligible songs to be sure, but pity-compelling we hope.

Ancestors, we greet you! (song)

When the song is finished Ancestor-Host rises and speaks again:

ANCESTOR-HOST: I greet you, my relatives. My nephew, not only these present here, but all their ancestors, far back, will be your guides. Surely you will heed what I say and obey their injunctions. On their words and speeches we can and we must live. Ancestors, as many as you are, wherever you are, we greet you . . .

Keramanic'aka, they tell us, used to pay visits to the Iowa who were settled at a place named Mo'uitca on the Mississippi.[30] Every fall, for three years, he went to see an Iowa named Tcacex'inga. On his fourth trip he loaded his boat with presents for Tcacex'inga and his family. There was clothing, enough for a long time, for Tcacex'inga, his wife and his child. Ample food he brought, too, and a gun. Two hunting dogs tied together, he placed in front of the lodge as well as some twisted buffalo hair.

When Tcacex'inga saw these presents, he turned to Keramanic'aka and said, 'I accept them, younger brother. By your gifts and your behavior toward me you have earned the right to become a Medicine Rite man. That for which you have been exerting yourself so strenuously, you have achieved. However, I will not give you the object you have been coveting, now. You must return to your home first and, on the fourth night after your return, I shall bring it to you. On that fourth night, younger brother, you must not sleep. If you do, you will bring great misery upon yourself.'

Keramanic'aka, thereupon, went home. Early on the morning of the fourth day he lay awake listening. A bird suddenly cried out from nowhere. It was a black hawk. Almost immediately it alit on the roof of the lodge and settled down as an owl. The bird strained its neck looking into the lodge. 'Well, younger brother, I see you are

92

awake.' 'Yes, indeed, I am awake.' 'You have done well, you have succeeded.'

Then he, *Tcacex'inga*, entered the lodge and put before *Keramanic'aka* the two objects from which he had derived his powers and which had made him holy. 'Younger brother,' he said to him, 'you must select one of these two medicine pouches that I have placed in front of you.' *Keramanic'aka* looked at them and fell into deep thought. Then he said to himself, 'If I take this pouch, made of a child's skin, doubtless it will give me the power to obtain many scalps.' As he thus weighed the matter in his mind the Iowa said to him, 'If you do not take this pouch, it will become the possession of your younger brother!'

Keramanic'aka had now emptied the pouch of its contents and was still hesitant. Then he turned away resolutely and took the other pouch, the one made of a woman's scalp. Had he taken the first pouch, it would have meant the giving of offerings far beyond his power. This fact it was that induced him to refuse it. Then *Tcacex'inga* spoke to him, 'Younger brother, together with this pouch I present you the song belonging to it. Now this fact I wish to impress upon you. Never turn this pouch the wrong way up. Always place it vertically on your lap, if you wish to obtain added life for your child' . . .

But now, my nephew, it is about time for you to sing your songs and start dancing so that you may acquire and retain the goods of life for which you have yearned and worked. My entreaties to the spirits will not be of much avail but they are yours to be used immediately. Remember, at the same time, that this tale I have just told you, can only be acquired in the manner in which you have done it. (8 songs)

Ancestor-Host rises and speaks again:

A N C E S T O R - H O S T : To all of you assembled here I extend greetings as Earthmaker has ordained I should. As morning follows morning, we hasten forward to the day for the Rite itself. It will not be given to us to perform it as our ancestors were able.

We are indeed only imitators. But we will try our best, in a pitiable, humble, fashion.

Nephew, never abandon this Rite; never withdraw from it. Keep to its way and its precepts that you may attain to its goal. *He-whom-we-call-our-nephew*, Hare, obtained for us a full and complete life in this Rite. Only there is this present; only there can we become reincarnated.[31] Thus has it been said in the past and thus has it been handed down. If we observe its rules then, surely, we shall, some day, come to the abode of Earthmaker . . .

Nephew, once there lived a man named *Kerexūsaka*,[32] a Winnebago, who was in the habit of paying visits to a Sauk, named *Nimāxguawa*. It so happened that *Kerexūsaka's* little son died and that *Kerexūsaka*, in his grief, kept four nights vigil at the child's grave.

When *Nimāxguawa* heard of this, he took two sacred pouches and started out to visit him. When he reached the grave, there he found *Kerexūsaka* weeping disconsolately. He tried his best to console him. For this purpose he had brought the two pouches. So, speaking to him gently, he said, 'Listen to me, younger brother. I have come to you with these gifts, to persuade you to cease crying. No one is my equal. If one of the many spirits Earthmaker created came to console you, he, alone, might, conceivably, be comparable to me and my powers. If the four great spirits sitting at the corners of our island, came to you, even they would not be my equals. Indeed, if all the spirits Earthmaker created, every single one of them without exception, came and huddled around you and pressed themselves upon you, even they, all of them together, would not be my equal. Earthmaker himself, were he to speak to you and bless you with unequivocal gifts and powers, even he would not be my equal. Well, possibly, that is not so, possibly I am slightly his inferior. But if I am, it is to a slight degree only. Indeed, I should contend that this greater gift that Earthmaker might bestow upon you, would not endure very long.

'Younger Brother, as you extend your piteous cry for life and consolation to the furthest reaches of the spirits' domain, listen to

94

what I am offering you. Your lodge shall be filled, piled high with meat; your lodge shall be filled, on all sides, with pails of fat. As long as the earth will last so long will you have meat and fat. And if you desire the same for some other Indian, he, too, will obtain food and fat ever after.

'Thus, your vision.

'Younger Brother, six times I embarked on the road of war, and never, not even when I was unattended by my nephew,[33] did I fail to obtain and bring home the highest honor, the necklace of wampum. Finally, there came a critical day of war indeed, a really difficult time. With great care and circumspection I prepared myself. The bullets, when they fell upon me, lost their power to penetrate my body and fell to the ground, cold.

'Thus, your vision.

'Younger Brother, this I tell you. In my fast, I dreamt that a man of another tribe appeared to me and said, "My intentions are in no wise different from your own. I, too, shall be bereft of my most prized possessions because of my gifts to a member of another tribe. It is a Winnebago, in my case as in yours, who will have access to my war-bundle and the songs belonging thereto."

'Younger Brother, as long as you and yours endure, that long will you have the right and power to use my songs. All I demand is that you offer me a handful of tobacco at times. The songs will obtain for you whatever it is you have in your mind. And when you sing, when, in the ceremony, you are about to start the dance songs, there I shall be, dancing up and down behind you, encouraging you. If you concentrate your mind and heart upon attaining that which you ask for, I, too, will be present to hear your demands for the full life and help you. For the tobacco offering, I will do it. I will be there in person, if you so desire it and, if, for some reason, I should not happen to be present, sing these songs and they will constrain me' . . .

Thus did the pity-invoking ancestors speak to one another.
Oh, ancestors, we greet you! Now we shall intone our songs so

that we can ask of you, of all of you, as many as you are, wherever you are, to have pity on us, so that we may feel the touch of your hands when you approach. (songs)

2. THE SECOND NIGHT

Now the time has come for the practice-singing of the second night. After they have all entered and sat down Ancestor-Host arises and, greeting them, speaks:

A N C E S T O R - H O S T : You, sitting in the path there, my nephew, my son, my uncle, my grandfather, my grandmother, my daughter, my niece, my aunt, my younger sister, my niece, my grandfather, my nephew, He-for-whom-we-seek-life, my sister-in-law, all of you, to all of you, I send my greetings.

As you sit there expectant, we pass around our life-engendering greetings to you, ancestors and relatives, that you may have compassion upon us and send us your greetings in return. From its inception, those who knew this Rite have always waited until everyone was fully prepared. Then, as soon as one group began, the others followed. That has caused delay. Our guests, surely, will pardon us if we cause them to wait.

We have come together here to perform the Tear-Pouring ceremony for the ghost of our recently departed member, piteously to pray for the full life. Ancestors, we greet you!

Then they sing a mourning song and when that is finished Ancestor-Host again arises and speaks:

A N C E S T O R - H O S T : Our ancestors have sent you their life-engendering greetings. We are to make haste on this night in our appeal for life, in our attempts to obtain life by songs and words. It was this same full life they tried to obtain, those distant ancestors of ours whose bones long since have mingled with the dust, and it is to them that we now send forward our greetings. Thus we have been told to do; thus we do.

Ancestors, we greet you. We shall now let a song and the sound of the drum, welcome you. Dance songs, too, shall issue from our throats. We greet you, we greet you! (songs)

Those who are not singing, get up and dance. Some may not even do this if they have not bought the privilege of dancing. Those who are present for the first time, get up from their seats and stand there singing. Then they make the circuit of the lodge and, returning to their seats, send a greeting to all those present. Then they sit down. Ancestor-Host arises again, sends his greeting to each one present, in succession, and as soon as they have acknowledged it, speaks as follows:

A N C E S T O R - H O S T :   Ancestors, we greet you. Our song for you is about to appear. Assuredly the members of the Medicine Rite, those who are far ahead along the Road, as they turn their heads, will see us stumbling, weaklings, men without power. But even though we are such weaklings, they will extend their compassion to us and bless us. It is for them, these members of the Rite, that we are giving this performance; it is for them that we break out in song and word. It is for them and for ourselves. Today we are to fix our mind and heart upon the initiate, He-for-whom-we-seek-life. It is for him that the song will now be sung and the drum beaten. Thus has it been handed down. Ancestors, we greet you, we greet you! (song)

But now we must get ready for the dance song. All those present are to arise and attempt to beseech the spirits for life, through dance. Not all those who sing will have to arise and dance. Life can be obtained by song alone they say. This is a sacred Rite that we are performing and all our desires and yearnings are directed toward the attainment of our goal, a full life. We are now ready for the dance song, for the beat of the drum to be heard. Ancestors, we greet you. (dance song)

Now for the third time they sing the completion song, and, after that, the dance song. When they have finished this one, then Ancestor-Host rises and speaks again:

A N C E S T O R - H O S T :   Ancestors, generous it was of you to have been so willing to keep on your feet for me!

97

Then they all return to their respective seats where they stand and sing. Each one sends his greeting around the lodge, from one person to the other. When everyone is seated, Ancestor-Host arises and speaks again:

A N C E S T O R - H O S T :   We have finished the greetings for tonight and it is about time for us to go home to rest and sleep. For tonight, then, we are done. Ancestors, we greet you, we greet you!

3. THE THIRD NIGHT

Everyone has now assembled for the third night, to practice the songs and speeches they know and to try to learn others, as well as to invest themselves with more life. Then when all is in readiness Ancestor-Host arises and speaks:

A N C E S T O R - H O S T :   Ancestors, we greet you, we greet you! My grandfather cautioned my father about all the various types of actions in the Rite that were forbidden. He warned him, for instance, against grouping together his greetings when he sent them around. It is necessary to greet each person individually, repeatedly, and in his proper turn. However, I did not listen to my father. Had I listened to him I would indeed have gained a blessing! He told me that it would be entirely my fault if I did not listen to him. And yet I dare speak to you here tonight! If you listen to me you will have gained possession of the song I am about to sing, be able to retain it and keep it as your own.

Our ancestors are waiting for this performance of ours, for the song and the greeting. What our pity-inspiring ancestors were able to say and do, that, of course, we will not be able to accomplish. And yet, perhaps, our one song will not appear too trivial. No matter how poorly we sing it our ancestors will deign to accept it. Ancestors, we greet you!

To our ancestors, whose bones long since are mixed and mingled with the dust, to them we are about to send our greetings. This, that we are performing, is what they called the Tear-Pouring ceremony.

It is said that if one loses a beloved relative, a man is apt to say to himself, 'If I perform this ceremony in remembrance of him who has died, it will be a good deed.'

As my father lay dying, he told me that he had lived a full and proper life and that this life would be mine if I acted properly and allowed him to secure the offerings made.

This promise I am fulfilling tonight in the mourning ceremony in his honor, the ceremony at which we are to beseech him with tears to grant us the years he left unlived. 'Let me have a Tear-Pouring ceremony!' he used to plead. (mourning song)

And now, if we follow what our ancestors told us, we must hurry along in this plea for life. We greet you, we greet you!

It is now about time for the dance song to begin and for the participants to renew their plea for life. After the dance song has been begun those who are allowed to dance, do so but those who do not have that privilege, simply get up and stand in their respective places singing till the dance is over. Then all sit down. Then, for the second time, they prepare to sing and Ancestor-Host arises and speaks:

A N C E S T O R - H O S T : We send you all our greetings. We will soon sing the completion song and repeat our greetings to our ancestors, for, it is said, we must try to accumulate an ample supply of greetings. The drum is about to be beaten, so be ready to receive it. Ancestors, we greet you, we greet you! (completion song)

When Ancestor-Host is ready for the dance song he arises and greeting everyone, speaks again:

A N C E S T O R - H O S T : Ancestors, we are about to greet you, to greet you. The dance song is now to be sung. We greet you, we greet you! (dance song)

Everyone now arises to dance and as they are moving along on their feet, Ancestor-Host waits till they finish their song and then addresses them:

A N C E S T O R - H O S T : Ancestors, you who have been keeping yourselves so unceasingly on your feet for me, I thank you. All of us who have invited you here send you our greetings.

Then they return to their respective positions and, passing along the greetings, sit down.

Once again, for the third time, they are ready for their dance song and, once again, Ancestor-Host stands up and speaks to them:

A N C E S T O R - H O S T :   Ancestors, we greet you. Wherever you are, we ask and supplicate you to have pity on us and bless us. Deign to accept the greetings we are about to extend to you! We are thankful. We greet you, we greet you!

The song that we are about to sing, let it be a greeting to all of you. (completion song)

The dance songs are now about to be sung for the fourth time. Again Ancestor-Host arises and speaks:

A N C E S T O R - H O S T :   We have spent no time indulging in sleep during these nights. It is not by sleep that we can expect to obtain anything, least of all, a full life. To obtain that we must apply ourselves and work. That we shall do. Ancestors, we greet you, we greet you!

4. THE FOURTH NIGHT

The fourth night of the ceremony has now arrived, the night before the first part of the Rite proper. The Rite begins at daybreak. Then Ancestor-Host rises and speaks:

A N C E S T O R - H O S T :   Ancestors, we greet you, we greet you! As many as there are of you, we ask you all to have pity on us. If, tomorrow, anyone comes, do you think he will find us sleeping here? Ancestors, to hasten our coming together tomorrow at the Rite we will hurry along with our activities and only sing a few songs apiece so that we can have a good night's sleep. This is what I wish to tell you. Now let us start with our song, with our greetings. We greet you, we greet you! (mourning song)

When the mourning song is finished Ancestor-Host asks them to ask for life. Rising he speaks again:

100

ANCESTOR-HOST : Let us send our supplications to our ancestors and beg them to give us a full life. We greet you, we greet you! (completion song)

ANCESTOR-HOST : Now I shall get ready for the dance songs. I shall start each one in its turn. (dance song)

Now for the second time he is to sing. After he has greeted each person in turn and each one has responded, Ancestor-Host begins to speak again:

ANCESTOR-HOST : Relatives, be diligent in what you have to do and then our ancestors will take heed of your requests. If they find you asleep they will not consider that a good sign. So have we always been told. Ancestors, we greet you, we greet you. (completion song)

Now again Ancestor-Host sends forward his greetings:

ANCESTOR-HOST : Ancestors, we greet you, we greet you. The song we are going to sing will be our life-engendering greeting to you. That is what we have been told to do from time immemorial. But now the beat of the drum is to be heard and so we shall greet you, greet you, O ancestors!

After they finish the completion song they get ready for the dance song and when they have finished the dance song Ancestor-Host arises and speaks:

ANCESTOR-HOST : So we have acted. Tomorrow night our ancestors will arrive. We will be there to await their appearance. Now we have finished for the present. It is time to rest, to fan ourselves to sleep. We greet you, we greet you!

III. The Preparatory Four Nights of East's Band

1. THE FIRST NIGHT

The leader of the division who is to occupy the east position in the Rite invites all those who belong to his band to assemble for the first of the four preparatory nights. He also asks some people to attend who do not belong to his band. When they are all assembled, he arises and speaks:

E A S T : Ancestors, we greet you, we greet you! Remember that it is forbidden for anyone to greet people in groups; only singly must you do it. However, if you get old and your body is still strong and steady then, indeed, you may, if you so desire, greet people in groups. Our ancestors had compassion upon me and, for that, I am grateful.

Our songs and prayers we must offer up seriously and sincerely, never frivolously. Behold! our ancestors have prepared an excellent day for us. They have connected us with the true life. It is good. What our ancestors told the members of the Rite to do, that they are doing. They told them to have compassion upon our poor and pitiable Indians. They were not to appeal to the spirits, but to a pitiable member of the Rite. In this way were they to show compassion. To lead a good and full life, that is the surest manner of securing this compassion.

Here along the Road we have been stumbling, weaklings, dependent upon others. Yet it is a good thing. To bring the one to be initiated, He-for-whom-we-seek-life, into connection with the full life, for that, the members of the Rite have assembled here. To have compassion upon him and to bless him, for that they themselves ask compassion from the spirits.

I have but little to say, nothing of importance. Yet they, Ancestor-Host and his people, did not forget me and mine. They know very well that I have nothing to tell them, yet they have brought us into connection with the life they are about to distribute. That is all they thought of and it is because they had this purpose in view we shall soon intone our song for them.

They say that, once, when a member of the Rite had lost a beloved child, he kept on thinking to himself, 'How must I behave to compensate myself for this child?' So he tortured himself.[34] He wore his fingers sore from hard work. He let himself stand in the full heat of the sun; he let himself get thoroughly baked. Thus did he hope to keep his remaining children alive so that he might have them with him for many years. With such a deep and fervent desire was he inspired. Thus impelled, he went to the leader of the Rite and compelled him to listen to his plea. Willingly enough did the leader consent to his request. And so, in this manner, did a man start to walk in the Road.

With the knowledge of all this were we blessed. And now we shall begin the Tear-Pouring ceremony for the ghost of the departed, to beseech him to distribute among us the unused years of life he left behind him. They say that this can be obtained by word and song and that we will be strengthened by them. So we will let our messenger, the drum, be beaten. We greet you, we greet you! (mourning song)

E A S T :   Making haste, our ancestors pleaded for life and we shall do likewise, saying exactly what they said. We greet you, we greet you! (completion song)

E A S T :   Now that the completion song is over we will greet you again, ancestors, and get ready to begin the dance song. We extend our hands in greetings to all the members of the Rite here assembled, greetings that, we know, will be returned. May the return greeting be gentle! Thus, it is said, it should be done. All of us present here extend our greetings to our ancestors, those ancestors, whose bones, long since, lie mixed and mingled with the dust. As you proceed with the ceremony, relatives, remember that nothing can be obtained by sleeping and listlessness.

In the old days, they say, that only those were allowed to sit within the lodge who had the right to sing the songs, and that all the members present would get up and dance in the ghost ceremony. As the old people used to say, nothing is to be gained by just sitting and observing one another. So, therefore, whoever you are, members of our band or not, get up and dance and we will include you all in our plea for life.

They get up and dance. When it is over the singer, East, expresses his gratitude.

E A S T : You have done well, you who arose and danced! We greet you, we greet you!

The greeting is extended and returned. East now arises and speaks again:

E A S T : Ancestors, we greet you again. This Rite was given to us from above, by the creator. It is a Rite only for those who are real Indians. Truly, it is a refuge-place for us. For us alone is it a ceremony of great significance. Of such importance is it that even if a member is sick when the Rite is about to be given he must attend. No one is allowed to stop for such a reason. Let him continue, sick and delicate though he be. Indeed, attendance will make him get well. Participation in the Rite will cure him. All those ancestors of ours, now dead, who properly observed the customs and beliefs of the Rite, have become like spirits. There are so many of them that the ground before my door has been worn away by their ceaseless coming and going. As they pass one another their greetings are innumerable and frequent just as are ours.

It is said that no matter how long ago it is that a person has been dead, if he had performed this Rite of our ancestors well, when he was alive, he will remain happy.

But now we must get ready for the songs. We shall sing them as they were sung at the very beginning and attempt to obtain through them what they then obtained, even though we use but one song. We greet you, we greet you! (completion song)

The completion song has been sung and the greetings passed around. East now speaks:

E A S T : Ancestors, we greet you again. This is the place where we can plead for life. To greet one another is pleasant and good, it

104

has always been said. But now we must get ready for the minor dance song, thereby to sanctify ourselves. We greet you, we greet you! (dance song)

All get up to dance and when it is over East extends his greetings and waits for them to be returned before he sits down. Then he speaks again:

E A S T :   We greet you again. I, who have been blessed, greet you. Our ancestors have indeed had pity on me and taken cognizance of me. I feel truly proud.

We have been taught to accumulate as many greetings as we can. Tonight, particularly, we are to take meticulous care of our manner of greeting.

On the fourth night, however, we are permitted to hurry through it and still receive our blessings. It is for these blessings that we repeat the songs and speeches of those who have become spirits. Carefully, meticulously, will we do it tonight, our heart full of thankfulness. Toward the one to be initiated, He-for-whom-we-seek-life, toward him, too, must our thoughts be directed. In singing the songs our thoughts must indeed be specifically directed toward him. That he may attain a full life, we are pleading for that. As for myself, I know too well that I cannot attain any life by my pleading yet I can at least put my mind upon the matter and, perhaps, it may then be granted. Ancestors, we greet you, we greet you! (completion song)

E A S T :   You who sit around me here, my relatives, we greet you again. Soon the dance song will start up and we will try to dance and sing as did the Indians of old in the beginning.

This was always an Indian ceremony and, in the old days, everything was done with the greatest of care and circumspection. Every single seat in the lodge was occupied and all who were present had been blessed by the spirits. Every night the members gathered in the lodge to ask for life. They did everything well. When it was time to begin the dance song, all arose and danced, doing it with zest and vigor. To sing and dance in this fashion, to ask for life in this manner, we must encourage one another to do just that. This is my admonition to you. In a moment I shall begin the dance song. That is why I am addressing you thus. Ancestors, we greet you, we greet you! (dance song)

E A S T : Now I am going to sing the last completion song and then we will rest. Ancestors, we greet you again.

Even if a man knows only one song as a greeting, it will help him in the securing of life, we are told. Our fellow members long for a fuller measure of life and are glad to send some life-begetting greetings toward the members of the Rite. How can we not but be thankful for their permitting us to participate? They have had pity and compassion upon us and we are thankful and grateful. But this, likewise, you must remember. Whosoever the person is who is to be initiated, concentrate your mind and heart upon him as you make your pleas for more life. Ancestors, we greet you, we greet you! (completion songs)

E A S T : Ancestors, we greet you again. When the creator created the different spirits, he put them in charge of certain songs that were to be used when they bestowed their blessings upon people. With these songs it is always possible to obtain life. And just as it was in the beginning, so it is now. The songs of the Rite will always retain the power they had at their first inception and, if they are properly and zealously cultivated, life can always be procured through them. Thus did our elders teach us. And they taught us, likewise, never, under any circumstances, to doubt the truth of the Rite. Ancestors, we greet you, we greet you! (dance song)

All now rise and dance. When it is over the greetings are passed around and returned. As each greeting is reciprocated the person receiving it sits down. Finally, East rises and speaks:

E A S T : Ancestors, we greet you. The first night of òur ceremony is about over. Let us hope that the second night will be an excellent one so that we can all be blessed again and offer up our prayers of thankfulness. See to it that as many as possible come tomorrow, for that is the proper way to behave, our forefathers said. We thank you, we thank you!

2 . THE SECOND NIGHT

When it is time for the smoking of tobacco to begin, on the second night, all the various members of the band gather together again, as well as all those who have been invited. Then, he who is to be the leader of his group in the Rite, East, rises. First, he sends his greeting around to those who are present and then he speaks:

E A S T : Ancestors, you who are sitting here, we greet you, we greet you. Our ancestors had compassion upon us, repeatedly and, today, on this beautiful night, they will have compassion again. Here, in this ceremony that the creator instituted, one can be truly invested with love and the full life.

Only in this Rite that has come from above is this true. The life that we have asked and obtained from the creator, this we shall put to good use. It is ours. He has put us in control of it. Remember that Earthmaker put the means of obtaining the goods of life in control of every single spirit he created. Let us, therefore, concentrate our minds upon the creator above. Be assured that he will not take anything from us without giving something in return. That is what he himself said. So if we pour a handful of tobacco for him who is up above, he will indeed take it; he will not reject it.

Very great and various are the spirits Earthmaker created, great the powers and gifts which he put in control of them. Particularly is this true of the great Island-Anchorers. If, then, we pour out a handful of tobacco for them, we will put ourselves in the position of receiving thanks from them; we will be clothed with life.

Let us now puff life upon one another as we smoke. Those who are real Indians know that this Rite is the place where life can be acquired easily. It is as if they said to themselves, 'I have obtained life!' In a few moments, I shall begin with the smoking ceremony, the medium by which we can acquire that life for which we should all be so grateful and thankful. Ancestors, we greet you, we greet you!

He now fills his pipe, lights it, and puffs, first toward the east, then toward the north, then toward the west, and finally toward the south. Then he extends the pipe toward the one nearest to him who seizes it and, accepting it, thanks him with an 'Ancestors, we greet you.' This man then smokes the pipe, takes

107

four puffs and stops. He now extends the pipe to the next person and when this one is ready, he seizes it, passes the greeting along, takes four puffs, and in turn, extends the pipe to the next one. And thus it goes, from person to person, until all have received the pipe and taken four puffs. Some of the little girls do not smoke. They do not make them smoke because they do not like it. However, even small children, so it is believed, would obtain great benefits in life and live longer if they smoked on such an occasion. Then when the tobacco ceremony is over, East rises, and, calling upon each person present by name, he greets them and speaks:

E A S T :   Ancestors, who are sitting here, we greet you. The members of the Rite blessed us so that we might have something to be thankful for. To the spirits and to this Creation-Lodge [35] we wish to extend our greetings. To the feast-giver and to all the Rite members that are seated, to all these we send a life-begetting greeting. We greet them together with all those who possess the open-faced otterskin pouches.[36] We greet the messenger of those who sing together and we shall tell them of the ghost ceremony in which they are to participate. We are now ready to ask the ghost of the departed member to beseech the spirits to distribute among us, his relatives, that portion of his life which he left behind him unused, this being the purpose for which we have come together here in the Tear-Pouring ceremony. Ancestors, we greet you, we greet you! (mourning song)

E A S T :   We are now to make haste in our prayer to express our plea for life by a song. Put all your thoughts upon the one to be initiated since it is for him you are to offer up your pleas. Ancestors, we greet you, we greet you! (completion song)

Those who are to dance now pass along their greetings and then the East speaks again:

E A S T :   From times past, we have been told that, on this occasion, we must ask our ancestors to have pity on us and put us in the way of being amply thankful to them. We greet you, we greet you! (dance song)

When the dance is finished East rises for the second time, calls each one present by his name, and, greeting them, speaks:

108

E A S T : Ancestors, all those gathered here and who are sitting in their respective seats, I greet you, I greet you!

Sometimes, a man who has no qualifications for being blessed, is, nevertheless so blessed. He, then, of all people, should show his gratitude.

Relatives, be diligent in your actions. Do not fall asleep. You know that nothing has ever been obtained through sleep. If the Rite members bless you and you inflict suffering upon yourself, if you exhaust yourself through being on your feet all the time, this Rite will become a refuge-place for you and you will obtain life. Thus has it always been, our elders told us. For all those within this lodge, this is the greatest of stories.

My friend compelled me to hear about myself and as a result the world is being informed of my insignificant name. A performance of the Rite is to be given and, behold! I feel as if someone were pointing at me and saying, 'There he is!' There are numerous members of the Rite and yet the giver of this one invited me, an unimportant person like myself, and allowed me to be the one to offer him thanks and to be the recipient of the means-of-thankfulness.[37]

But, now, let me sing you a song. We greet you, we greet you! (completion song)

E A S T : Ancestors, we greet you again. We are about to start up a minor dance song, the kind with which the older people used to obtain their blessings. Let us now pass along the greeting and the means-of-thankfulness through which we have been blessed. Ancestors, we greet you! (dance song)

When the dance is finished all sit down and East rises again and greeting each person in turn, speaks:

E A S T : Ancestors, we greet you. We shall try to bring ourselves into connection with the life that is tied up in the invitations you sent us.

There we were, a handful of people that death had spared, a mere remnant, taking care of a home in the absence of its true owners.[38]

109

Yet the giver of the Rite and his people thought us worthy of being brought into the proximity of life. We were people to be pitied, of low degree, yet they enabled us to be connected with life. Our hosts have listened to the advice of their ancestors and have gone out of their way to show compassion upon us, pity-inspiring objects! These ancestors must have told our host, who is now about to lead the Rite, to pray to the spirits, to appeal to all the spirits to whom the creator had entrusted powers. They must have told him to offer tobacco to them so that, in return, the spirits would take cognizance of us human beings.

Now I, you know, am not a member of the Rite and, look! they have even thought of me; they have even brought poor me into connection with life. Even toward me was their concern directed! Let us then greet them now, these, your ancestors, with an old and pity-inspiring song. Not, of course, in the way in which they sang it. That we cannot do. Yet it will be a greeting of some sort. Ancestors, we greet you, we greet you! (completion song)

E A S T : The dance songs are about to be started. Those we sing correspond to the greetings used of yore. Remember not only the spirits are to be greeted but the host likewise and the members of his band seated here who have obtained life for us by their songs and their utterances. They come here bringing their open-faced otterskin pouches so that everyone here could be forced to look upon life. This it is they have done. We greet you, and, in a moment, ancestors, we shall have our grandfather, the announcer, make known his presence. We greet you, we greet you! (dance song)

When the dance is over all sit down and the leader, East, rises and speaks:

E A S T : We greet you, ancestors. After the greeting is over we will ask our friend to help carry the messenger, the drum, to the next person so that he might aid us. When he has finished it will be about time for us to rest.

Then they carry the drum to those who are present but who had not been specifically invited to the Rite proper. Their leader rises and speaks:

110

L E A D E R : I, the one on whom you have had compassion, greet you. I greet you all, each one separately. It is good. 'Grandfather,' someone said to me, 'they have had pity on you, at first on you as an individual. And now they have gone one step further and actually invited you to the ceremony! The life with which they have invested you is without equal.' And I answered, 'Grandfather, it is indeed good.

'With what you have blessed me, me alone, for that I am indeed thankful. We shall take hold of the messenger [39] of the spirits and of his utterances. It is good. Far back, in the distant past, they used a certain song that was to be a greeting to the spirits themselves. That very song we shall use tonight. We have been told that a young person is desirous of securing a full life. We shall beseech the spirits to grant him that life and we shall direct toward him the same life-begetting greeting that you directed toward an initiate in the days of yore.' Ancestors, we greet you! (completion song)

L E A D E R : Ancestors, we greet you. The dance song will soon be started. We shall greet our fellow members with these songs, this shall be our method of addressing them. Ancestors, we greet you, we greet you! (dance song)

I, the one you had pity upon, your friend, greet you. In succession I greet you all and call upon you by name. Ancestors, you who are present here, I greet you, too. I have attached my hand to our grandfather, the announcer, and thus brought myself into connection with that life which I shall from now on, always retain. But now, let us get up and carry the messenger back to our host and place it before him. Ancestors, we greet you, we greet you!

All now get up and carry the drum back to East and place it in front of him. Then he rises and speaks:

E A S T : We greet you, we greet you again! So we must act. Now, however, we can rest; now we can cover our faces for a while. [40] We greet you, we greet you!

3. THE THIRD NIGHT

All of those who have been invited to the Rite by the leader of the band have gathered together again in the lodge to sing the ritual songs, etc. When all are in their seats, East rises, calls upon each one by name, and extends the greeting to them:

E A S T : Ancestors, we greet you again. Our pity-invoking ancestors were told to have compassion even upon us, the most pitiable and helpless of beings. They have caused a lovely day, a lovely life, to descend upon us. It is good. They have done all this so that everyone in their band might feel that they have been brought into relation with life. We are indeed filled with gratitude toward them, and shall show it by presenting them with tobacco. It is said that if people are invited to this Rite instituted by the spirits, and do nothing but listen, even, under such condition, the good, the true life will have touched them. Thus has it been handed down.

Weaklings, we would be, stumbling about this earth helplessly, were it not for the life guaranteed by this Rite and so, from time immemorial, it has been our refuge. From He-whom-we-call-our-nephew, Hare, we obtained this Rite. He, alone, knew how to secure the power of shedding our skin for us. Difficult it was for him but he finally succeeded. Tobacco, he took along with him, to obtain success. Thus if we use tobacco, we, too, will be successful. So did the creator ordain it. If any member of the Rite holds this tobacco foremost in his life and concentrates his mind upon it, then, whatever blessings he is asking of the spirits, these they will give him and he will obtain life. It is said that tobacco is our means of calling upon them and that if we cause the spirits to smoke, they will speak. This means of supplication I myself, shall now attempt to offer up, my nephew. You have filled this pipe for me, all of you, and lit it so that we who are present could hold life in their mouths, puff life upon one another.

Ancestors, we greet you, we greet you!

Then the leader, East's nephew, taking the pipe in his hand, gets up, sends the greeting along, and lights the pipe. He puffs smoke from it four times, to the east, to the north, the west and the south. Then he points the pipe toward the one seated on the right side of the doorway saying, 'Ancestors, we greet you,' after which he puffs smoke at all the persons in the lodge. They, in turn, one at a time, smoke, and when they are finished East rises again and speaks:

E A S T :   Ancestors, once again we greet you all. We are thankful for the compassion you have bestowed upon us and shall try to model our manner of greeting upon that of the Rite members of the old time. Still, however inadequate our greeting may be, they say it will be acceptable. Wherever is the place from which these ancestors sent their thoughts to us, to that place we send our greetings. We shall dispatch our greetings to all those sitting here as representatives of the spirits, to all those with open-faced otterskin pouches, to all those sitting here who intend to participate in the feast. But now, the messenger is about to be heard, now, indeed, is the time. Ancestors, we greet you, we greet you!

E A S T :   We have come together to weep tears with him who has sustained a loss, one who was a member of our Rite. By inviting us here tonight we were informed of this loss. Tonight, let us all share our tears with him, let us place this Tear-Pouring ceremony at his disposal. Let us remember, too, that we are to beseech the ghost of the newly departed to put at our disposal the life he left unused— the years, the deeds, the food. For these we are to pray. Ancestors, we greet you! (mourning song)

E A S T :   Hurriedly, let us now proceed to pray for life. To do it in this fashion is the custom. Ancestors, we greet you, we greet you! (completion song)

E A S T :   Ancestors, we greet you again. The dance song is now about to start up, a life-engendering greeting it shall be from us. Let us perform the Rite properly and well. We have always been taught that if anyone dies as an observant member of the Rite then the creator will send him back to earth to live again, back to the kind land that lies below the sky in which he dwells. Such is the request we must make of the creator. And so when you sit in your positions during the performance of the Rite, see to it that you do not spend

113

your time simply watching one another, see to it that you are not backward and without initiative. Comport yourselves as people sanctified, as people filled with awe.

The messenger is now to be sounded, as is the custom. Ancestors, we greet you, we greet you. (dance song)

As soon as the dance is over East rises again and greeting those present speaks:

E A S T :   We greet you again ancestors and we thank you for the compassion you have shown us. It is said that one can never get enough of the various objects, of all the various utterances, by which we exhibit our gratitude, particularly of the songs that are used. As you know our purpose is to beseech the spirits and beg them to grant a real and full life to the one who is to be initiated, He-for-whom-we-seek-life. We ask this humbly, pity-inspiring individuals that we are. That is the significance of the words spoken here. The creator gave us both life and death. If we act properly it is life that we shall receive and thus, likewise, we shall obtain life for those we love. Sincerely we desire to become holy and we know that this can be obtained only by proper attention to this Rite founded by the spirits. Our grandfathers thought of all these facts and therefore it is that we try to repeat what they said. Ancestors, we greet you, we greet you! (completion song)

E A S T :   Now, once again, we are ready for the dance song, the means we use to plead for life, so that, as the old people used to say, we might become virtuous and good. As soon as the dance song is to be started, the voice of the messenger will be heard. The privilege of striking him is not really mine, but, some time ago, it was bought for me and I was compelled to strike our messenger. We greet you, ancestors, we greet you! (dance song)

All sit down as the dance is over. Then the one who has been blessed, the leader, East, again rises and speaks:

E A S T :   In former times, the old people thought very highly of this Rite. It is even claimed that our ancestors could become reincarnated eight times. For that reason they prized this Rite so greatly

114

and concentrated their minds and hearts upon it so intensely and uninterruptedly, and selected their members with so much care. If, in those days, a person wished to be initiated, he was tested for four years. If, after that time, they found that he had proven his worth and trustworthiness, then, and only then, would they initiate him. So, in the beginning, they were able to re-enact the initial performance of the Rite perfectly, exactly as it was originally given. At all times they encouraged one another to do just this, so that they might be given an opportunity to live again when they were finished here.

In the beginning they were able to do all this, but we, today, cannot so re-enact the Rite. We do it imperfectly for we possess little of the true life. We are of no significance. Yet we desire earnestly to proceed along the path of life as they did and so we are going to attempt to utter the cry for life in their manner. Let the song now be started, let the messenger be heard!

Ancestors, we greet you, we greet you! (completion song)

E A S T :   It is about time for the dance song to be started and so we greet you once again. We cannot, of course, sing and speak in the holy manner our ancestors did in the early days. Our utterances assuredly, will not be comparable to theirs. Yet by what excuse could we keep silent, we who are sitting here? Let us, therefore, begin the dance song. We greet you, we greet you!

When the dance is over all sit down and East speaks again:

E A S T :   Ancestors, we greet you once again. We must indeed be thankful to you for being so willing to have compassion upon us, for making us feel so happy, for bringing to us the means of showing our appreciation. You have caused a lovely and happy day to descend upon us. Those of our ancestors who dwell below the earth have left us behind here, to tend our homes, left us behind here, in an empty house to await our time. Day after day we sit here wrapped in our thoughts. You have helped us to attain the good life, you have made me truly feel that I have not lived in vain. It is good. The greetings we have been taught to use, these we will now extend. This is all I have to say. We greet you, we greet you! (completion song)

After the completion song East speaks again and greets all, each in his turn.
(dance song)

When the dance is over all sit down and East rises again to greet everyone.

E A S T :   We greet you, we greet you. For tonight the giving of thanks is over. Now we must take some rest and sleep. We greet you, we greet you!

4. THE FOURTH NIGHT

All are expected to come back for the fourth night. On the following morning the Vapor-Bath ceremony is to be given, and so, on this night, no one receives any special consideration. East is only to sing the songs, and everything must be hurried along. The songs must be sung fast and those who know them do not have to come. Finally East rises and speaks:

E A S T :   Ancestors we greet you again. Tonight we shall dispense with the usual greetings and instead hurry along as fast as we can. We shall therefore proceed immediately to the Tear-Pouring ceremony for the ghost of the deceased. Let us then start up the songs at once and sing only one. Ancestors, we greet you, we greet you! (mourning song)

E A S T :   Ancestors, we greet you once more. Custom dictates that we make haste with our prayers for life both for ourselves as well as for him who is to be initiated, He-for-whom-we-seek-life. Ancestors, we greet you, we greet you! (completion song)

E A S T :   Ancestors, we greet you again. The dance song is now to start up. Again, we shall sing only one song apiece. We greet you, ancestors, we greet you! (dance song)

When the dance is over East rises and speaks again:

E A S T :   Ancestors, we greet you once more. We are extending to you the greetings that, we hope, will induce you to have compassion upon us. We shall be thankful. Tomorrow we are to meet our

116

ancestors, face to face, and to greet them. Not by falling asleep, remember, can anything be obtained. For that, it is necessary to pass along the greeting and to express our thankfulness. Ancestors, we greet you, we greet you! (completion song)

E A S T : Ancestors, we greet you. In a moment we shall have the dance song appear before you as it has been handed down from the past and make our plea for the full life. Let us then start up the dance song at once and have the voice of our messenger be heard. We greet you, we greet you! (dance song)

When the dance is finished the leader rises once more and, after greeting those assembled, speaks:

E A S T : Ancestors, we greet you once more. It is by extending enough greetings, we have been told, that we shall be in a position to be thankful. Again we express our gratitude and send forth the greetings to you, ancestors! (completion song)

E A S T : Ancestors, we greet you once more. In a moment the dance songs are to appear before you and the plea and prayer for life is to be made. If we do it quickly then we will be able to go home and rest. So let us do it immediately and let us hear the announcer! [41] Ancestors, we greet you! (dance song)

When the dance is over East rises again and, after greeting those present, speaks:

E A S T : Our ancestors have taken pity on us. This Rite is a place of refuge, a road along which we travel, feeble and weak, and tired from ambling along in the hope of securing a gift of value. It is the goal and destination for our journey. If we encourage one another to dance it is always with that object in view. So let us start up the bird-tail songs in order to enliven and encourage the otterskin pouches. Thus will our leaders keep themselves in a holy state and direct us to that destination we all desire. Thus may our leaders also guide those who have deviated from the teachings of the Rite and escort them back into the proper path.

We are now ready for the songs again which are to bring the ceremony of the fourth night to an end. Again we shall greet you, O ancestors, and sing the shell song in honor of the medicine pouch. (shell song)

E A S T :   Ancestors, we greet you again and this will be our last salutation. Tomorrow, the morning toward which we look forward so eagerly, we shall see each other once more and repeat the same procedure. Ancestors, we greet you, we greet you!

IV. The Preparatory Four Nights of North's Band

1 . THE FIRST NIGHT

After the members of the Rite have assembled, the leader of the North Band arises and greets them as follows:

N O R T H :   You who sit there, the first one, my son, I greet you. You, my niece, my sister, my friend, to all of you I send forth my greetings.

You, too, O ancestors, we greet! Our ancestors performed this Rite for us, they had had compassion upon us. How then, can we show our gratitude otherwise than by performing this Rite in the prescribed manner?

When those four prominent leaders who began the Rite and thus gave prestige to the Winnebago name, invited a person in the village to join the Rite, his name became audible to all the tribe. 'Ah, they are speaking of me,' such a person would say to himself, 'and thus I, too, have gained the right to speak about myself.' All our ancestors felt themselves connected with life as they went through their performances and we are deeply grateful to them and to you.

It is told of one of our grandfathers that he kept his desire to join the Rite deep down within himself and only when he was fully prepared did he make his wish and his thoughts apparent and public.

118

He had projected his desires and thoughts [42] everywhere, but first up above to the creator. From there he had extended them far down below the earth. Finally he brought them up to this earth, to those living on it. He was thinking of us, his descendants; he was thinking of the life we were to obtain by his actions. Indeed, he and the others, even then had me in mind, were thinking even then of how they could use me.

Oh, it is good, the life that they were thinking of! For that reason it is incumbent upon us to spread this knowledge by the compelling force of our songs and speeches.

And yet, what value will what I have to say possess?

None. But still, you had better begin to light the sacred pipe, you who are assembled here. Ancestors, we greet you, we greet you!

Then he strikes a light and has the pipe passed around so that it can be filled. When all is ready he lights it and sends his greeting to those assembled in the lodge. Then each one smokes in turn and as the pipe is passed from one to the other so, likewise, goes the greeting. Finally, when the pipe has come back, the leader, North rises and speaks:

N O R T H : Ancestors, we greet you. What you have done is good. We should all be thankful for this Rite.

Once, long before our time, so it is told, there lived a man who in a vision, saw the four Island-Anchorers, our ancient grandfathers. Every day they brought him a song, a song destined for us. Each one of these spirits taught the dreamer a song. First the one from the east approached him with his song, then the one from north, then the one from the west and finally the one from the south, the Down-Stream one as we call him. Then, when they had all given him their songs he composed a song for himself, one in which he recounted all that had happened to him.

What his grandfathers, the Island-Anchorers, had taught him, these songs he now decided to try out. Each of his grandfathers had told him that if he wished to poison a person, he had but to sing his song and that, then, the man would die.[43] If he wished to compose another song about the one he had thus killed, that, too, he was told, he could do. The songs that have come down to us in this manner, these we shall now attempt to sing and to use. Ancestors, we greet you, we greet you!

We have come together to weep for him who has departed, for a member of the Rite lost to us. We beseech him to ask the spirits to distribute among us all that he left behind, unlived. Here at this Tear-Pouring ceremony we cry for life. The messenger, the drum, is now to become audible and tell you what we wish to say, ancestors. We greet you, we greet you! (mourning song)

NORTH : Ancestors, we shall extend our greetings to all of you. Then hurriedly we shall utter our cry for life. We greet you, we greet you! (completion song)

Ancestors, we extend our greetings to you. The dance song is about to appear but, before we sing it, we send out our life-engendering greetings to all the fellow members of the Rite. They have, indeed, concentrated their thoughts upon this Rite. All those who have performed the Rite properly and carefully, will, when they die, ascend to the place where Earthmaker dwells. There they will all go. We know that all those who performed this Rite properly and carefully in the long distant past, whose bones long since have mingled with the earth, are living there, happy and joyful.

When we perform this Rite we, too, shall feel happy. No feeling of discontent and uneasiness will then assail us. So let the dancing song sing out! This is my speech. Ancestors, I greet you, I greet you! (dance song)

When the dancing is over North rises and greets those present as follows:

NORTH : We send our greetings out to you. From the time the Creation-Lodge was erected, right down to the present day, it has always been said that you cannot have enough of such greetings. These greetings are requests for life, begetters of life. That is why we utter them so often. But now it is about time for us to send our greetings to the spirits, it is time that we have their messenger, the drum, become audible again. Ancestors, we greet you, we greet you! (completion song)

N O R T H :   Ancestors, we greet you. We shall now immediately have a minor dance song appear. This is a song that has come from another tribe, a spirit-song with which someone in that tribe had been blessed. A Winnebago had begged him to give it to him, if he could spare it. He consented and thus was it obtained. Ancestors, we greet you, we greet you! (dance song)

N O R T H :   Ancestors, we send forth our greetings to you. I do not even know the particular songs a man should know for this occasion but, let me, nevertheless, sing those I do know. For what is it that we have been told? 'Keep up the songs that have come down to you. Do try to do so. Then when a member dies those who survive will continue on with them. Listen to what they are singing so that when those who have the knowledge of these songs pass away, you can sing them without difficulty. Then, when you are dead, your spirit can console itself with the thought that what you left behind remains in good hands. Thus, you will indeed, have the right to feel happy, from then on. The greetings, too, you must keep up.' I beg of you, then, if you know the greetings, use them now. Indeed let us likewise use them immediately. Ancestors, we greet you, we greet you! (completion song)

N O R T H :   Ancestors, we send forth our greetings to you. As we told you, we have not much to say but, yet, is it not said, that any songs, whatsoever, may represent the material for obtaining happiness? One song, then, we shall have appear before you. Ancestors, we greet you, we greet you! (dance song)

N O R T H :   Ancestors, we send forth our greetings to you. We greet the spirits with the songs that we are about to use. We will use them to beg for life, piteously. My grandfather, wisely he spoke to me, told me that what the older people did was not done foolishly or without thought. He advised me that, if one does not buy the knowledge and the privileges of the Rite, not long will one be here upon our grandmother, Earth, who is in charge of our life. But if, on the contrary, one purchases this knowledge and acts properly and virtuously, then our grandmother will soon have knowledge of our actions.

Nothing of this kind, of course, have I been able to accomplish. I did, however, realize that if I lived virtuously, I might obtain some of the goods pertaining to the true life. So I obtained a song but I cannot even now sing it properly. Yet what else can I do for you but to attempt to sing it? Ancestors, we greet you, we greet you! (completion song)

N O R T H :   Ancestors, we send forth our greetings to you. The completion song has been sung and I wish I knew how to deliver the life-begetting speeches that accompany it. But I do not know how. The others present have, however, shown that they can. By their actions and their utterances they have attempted to obtain life for me. I am grateful. Ancestors, we greet you, we greet you! (dance song)

N O R T H :   The dance song which we have just finished we sang as best we could. I know that we have not done it as correctly as our ancestor did. Yet if anyone wishes to dance by it, assuredly it would suffice to bring him in some connection with the life we are trying to achieve. I am not one of those privileged to hold in my hands an otterskin pouch.[44] But, still even though I do not possess one, possibly if one tried to secure some portion of life, one might obtain life by participating in the dance. This is what was always told us and this is what I wish to tell you. Ancestors, we greet you, we greet you!

2 .   THE SECOND NIGHT

Now the members of the Rite are again to come together. There are Four Preparatory Nights, the leader, North, tells them and then they will be ready for the fifth night, for the ceremony proper where they can put into practice what they had learned. When North is certain that all the members of his band are assembled, he rises and, greeting them, speaks as follows:

Ancestors, we greet you. . . .

Once one of our ancestors thought to himself of how he might be of benefit to one of his friends. Deep and widely he let his thoughts and desires travel until he felt he had accomplished his purpose. Far below the earth he sent his thoughts and then he tied together his tobacco offerings. Then as Ancestor-Host, as leader, he directed his thoughts and desires toward the place where Earthmaker dwelt. There, in front of Earthmaker, a human being suddenly stood. Earthmaker heard him speaking and telling him what he so fervently desired. And these were the words that the man uttered as he stood there before Earthmaker.

'Earthmaker, our father, listen to me. On earth, most pitiable is the life we lead. Falling and dying, we stumble along the road. True it is that you told us what to do so that we might obtain the goods and benefits of life. That we are aware of. To achieve the good life as you ordained, this, too, we know and we shall attempt. We shall indeed attempt to secure light and life. But do you, nevertheless, cause real life to appear among us. This is what we ask of you in all humility.'

Earthmaker heard the request. Below him stretched the earth, the world that was in charge of the very first being Earthmaker had created, Trickster, the Foolish-One. There lived Trickster and to Earthmaker he dispatched his thoughts, reinforcing the thoughts and requests of the man who stood before Earthmaker. Then, in turn, the thoughts and requests were sent upward to that blue expanse which our eyes can see, by the second of the spirits Earthmaker had created, Turtle, the being we call The Warrior. Then the third spirit Earthmaker created he, too, sent his thoughts upward to the blue expanse. Finally, he who had been placed in charge of the earth we live on, Hare, the spirit men call nephew, he who obtained for us this Medicine Rite, spoke to the man who stood before Earthmaker, saying: 'My uncle, you are indeed speaking the truth.' And having said this, Hare sat there absorbed in his thoughts.

Then the man who had dispatched himself to Earthmaker, returned to the earth. With what he had obtained he proceeded to one of the great and quiet Island-Anchorers, one of those given his position by Earthmaker. He entered the lodge and addressed the Island-Anchorer and made his thoughts audible to all the various spirits assembled within. And, behold! light was seen to emerge, light and life. Gracious and life-begetting thoughts the spirits sent to those within this lodge, people just like us in body. To have compassion on man, the spirits had been told by Earthmaker and this they did . . .

So runs the account. This ancestor of mine who had been thus signally blessed, to whom life had been granted, he knew all this. But not I. I indeed can say nothing. Since, however, I had already received the invitation to the Rite and so little time remained at my disposal, I had to accept it, in spite of my ignorance.

And, now, let us fill the sacred pipe and light it so that we may puff life upon one another. This have we always been directed to do. Ancestors, we greet you, we greet you!

Then he fills his pipe, lights it and puffs first toward the east, then toward the north, then toward the west and, finally, toward the south. Then he extends the pipe toward the one nearest to him who, after accepting it, thanks him with an 'Ancestors, we greet you.' This man then smokes the pipe, takes four puffs and stops. He now in turn, extends the pipe to the next person and when this one is ready he seizes it, passes the greeting along, takes four puffs and extends it to the fourth one. And thus it goes, from person to person, until all have received the pipe and taken four puffs.

When the smoking ceremony is over then North rises and, extending his greeting to those present, addresses them as follows:

N O R T H : Ancestors, we extend our greetings to you. We are about to begin the ghost-ceremony, the Tear-Pouring ceremony, for the one who has just left us. When that is done then we shall again extend the life-begetting greetings to one another. So now, let us intone the mourning song just as it has always been commanded we do. Ancestors, we greet you, we greet you! (mourning song)

N O R T H : Ancestors, we extend our greetings to you. And now we shall immediately beg for life just as our ancestors did. With the thoughts and aspirations they possessed we ask to be greeted. We

124

ask the same of all the feaster-participants seated here, as well as of all the different spirits gathered within this lodge. This, too, we ask—that all those present who possess open-faced birdskin pouches, that they, too, extend to us their life-begetting greetings. Ancestors, we greet you, we greet you. (completion song)

N O R T H :   Ancestors, we send our greetings to you. The dance song is now to be started and it will be sung just as we have always been commanded to sing it. Ancestors, we greet you, we greet you. (dance song)

And now they get ready to repeat the compassion-engendering actions so that all those present can benefit from them. The leader, North, rises, passes along the greeting and speaks as follows:

N O R T H :   Ancestors, we greet you. The actions and the utterances of the old people who have performed this ceremony have come down to us unimpaired. You, who are present today, have followed their lead and thereby obtained renewed life. Always it has been said that if we emulate their example we would obtain such life and happiness. Until recently this Rite had remained unchanged just as it was when He-whom-we-call-our-nephew created it and if, today, men and women, when they die, are simply shoved into the ground without the prospect of being born again, that is their own fault.

Anyone who desires to obtain the life He-whom-we-call-our-nephew created for him, can still do so by adhering to the tenets of this Rite. In that way he will also enable the members of his household, his children, to travel safely and happily along the Road of Life. If the members of the Rite, on the contrary, do not perform the ceremony correctly or piously, then, be assured, the Road they and theirs will travel, will not be easy or good. In the bygone days, the members of this Rite ended their days as old men. To this old age we, too, can attain if we give proper attention to it. Then we, too, will travel along the same Road as did these old men of yore. Otherwise, as I have just pointed out, the Road will be difficult and our life will be hard. I admonish you then to call to mind the life-benefits

125

that came to those in the past from their adherence to the tenets of the Rite; I admonish you to emulate their behavior. This is something we have not been doing of late. Nowhere else can man obtain a place of refuge like this and that is why I am so insistent in my admonishments that we beseech the spirits to extend to us their greetings and that we ask the members, long since dead, to have compassion upon us.

Not as they did, can we act or sing. However, it has always been said that, even if we know only one song and we sing it with due humility, it would suffice. Ancestors, we greet you, we greet you! (completion song)

N O R T H : Ancestors, I send forth my greetings to you. The dance song is soon to be begun. Now even if you do not know how to sing it correctly and even if you feel yourselves quite unable to carry on the ceremony as it should be done, do what you can. Then, if you sing it in the proper spirit, it will be acceptable. So we have been told. A life-begetting greeting it will be to us, this song. Compassion and blessings it will bring us. All the various spirits who preside over the Rite, they all will salute and greet us. The birdskin pouches, the open-faced and covered-faced,[45] they will enable us to behold and, with it, light and life. All those present here tonight will act as councillors and teach us how to secure the true life.

But now, the announcer, the drum, is about to be sounded so I send forth my greetings to you, ancestors! (dance song)

N O R T H : Ancestors, we greet you, we greet you! The members of old were able and clever people. Well-versed in the Rite they were and blessed with life. When they died they left an empty house. Day after day it remained empty as if waiting for some occupant. It is for us that the empty house was waiting so that we might carry on the blessings these old Rite members had obtained. That is why we are so happy and joyful at being invited. The Rite members have made us feel connected with life. They have had compassion upon us, they have filled us with thankfulness. It is good and we are grateful.

126

When our grandfathers, the spirits, hear of how the Rite has been performed here they will assuredly say to one another, 'Now we know what life is! Indeed these people have brought us into connection with life just as they did for themselves. Indeed, for all eternity, they will be thankful to us. As long as the earth lasts they will bring us into further connection with life!' Thus spoke the spirits. It is for this, among other reasons, that we humbly pray that you have compassion upon us and give us life. It is with gratitude and sincerity that we say this. Ancestors, we greet you, we greet you! (completion song)

When they have finished the completion song then North rises again and, greeting everyone, speaks as follows:

N O R T H :   Ancestors, we send forth our greetings to you. In a moment we will get ready to prepare for the dancing. That is all I have to say to you. Ancestors, we greet you, we greet you! (dance song)

N O R T H :   Ancestors, I greet you. We have been told repeatedly that life can, in no wise, be obtained in this Rite by sleeping. I need not therefore admonish you that the creator expects us to be most attentive to everything connected with its performance. If we pay proper attention to what we are doing then, our grandmother, Earth, will keep careful watch over us. But if we are careless and evil, then she will see to it that her back will become visible to us. We will die. Take the advice of our ancestors therefore and obey the tenets of the Rite. Then will our grandmother hold us at her broad breast until we have grown old.

Such is the manner of obtaining life. All the good spirits that Earthmaker created, those living up above, those living on earth, and those living under the earth, never have they failed to attend a single performance of this Rite. As Earthmaker created it so have they followed it. Always have they added their own powers and thoughts. That is why the life we obtain here is so good and full.

Thus have the members of the Rite talked to one another, from the remote past down, one parent handing it down to the other. And

127

so, eventually, it reached even me. Soon I was told that if I performed the ceremony really well then my journey through life would be prosperous and propitious. That information I now pass on to you here assembled, you sitting here listening. Remember, if you perform the ceremony well, excellent will be that Road in which you travel. I am indeed grateful to all of you who have invited me and permitted me to speak. Ancestors, I greet you, I greet you! (completion song)

N O R T H :   Ancestors, we send forth our greetings to you. They say it is best to obtain as large a number of life-engendering greetings as possible. But if you are unable to do so, it would suffice if you obtained just one. So it has been with me. And now we must again start up the dance. Now it is time for our messenger, the drum, to be heard. Ancestors, we greet you, we greet you! (dance song)

N O R T H :   Ancestors, we send forth our greetings to you. This night we have offered up our thanks. Now we must rest, fan ourselves to sleep. Tomorrow, if some of you should deign to come, we shall again offer our thanks just as we did today. Ancestors, we greet you, we greet you!

3 .   THE THIRD NIGHT

The third night has come and again all are assembled. Then he who is to ask for blessings, the leader of the band, North, rises and speaks:

N O R T H :   Ancestors, we send forth our greetings to you. Indeed it is good. In the past our ancestors acted just as we have been doing. They tried to obtain life. Diligence and piety were required then as now.

At times, so we are told, the old men used to say that the work and perseverance necessary for the proper performance of the Rite would weigh down some member completely. He would act as though the Rite did not agree with him. The others, looking at him, would whisper, 'I wonder if he's going to live very long?' Then, perhaps, the older members would sing the Medicine Rite songs that they knew. But all to no avail. He would only get tired and fall asleep. He would move about incessantly, without purpose. That is what was meant when the older members said that the Rite did not agree with him. Such a person, the full members of the Rite insisted, would never have much life at his disposal. If a person of this type pays little attention to the speeches and utterances of the other members, you can be certain that the explanation lies in the evil life he is leading. Clearly this man has but a short time to live.

It is good, at all times, never to let yourselves get tired during the performance of the Rite. Above all, however, it is good to attend all the meetings. We came here to obtain life. All our efforts, yours and mine, are directed to that purpose. It is good and I thank you.

When a member of the Medicine Rite loses a relative on the warpath, a loss he dreads to think of, then he will let down his hair and cease combing it. In this fashion will he sit down to eat. Thus will he recline, mourning, weighted down as it were with heavy clouds. The fire of his hearth is stirred but no smoke filters through the roof of his lodge. The smoke stays within the lodge and permeates it. Muttering to himself he thinks of suicide. Ah! but there is a solace for one who has lived up to the precepts of the Rite when death has thus struck—the life that is there obtainable. But he can secure even more. He can beseech the departed to bestow upon the living all the years he left unused, the deeds he left undone, the food he left untasted. For that purpose the Tear-Pouring ceremony was created. And this I now call to your mind as I send forth my greetings to you. (mourning song)

NORTH :   Ancestors, we greet you, we greet you! In a moment we shall again make our cry for life, humbly beseeching you. In a moment we shall have the announcer, the drum, make his appearance, accompanied by our words of thanks and gratitude. Ancestors, we send forth our greetings, to you! (completion song)

NORTH :   Ancestors, we greet you again. The dance will at once begin. (dance song)

N O R T H :   We have been told to attempt to accumulate an abundance of life-engendering greetings, an abundance of songs, as did our grandfathers in the days gone by. That we are, however, incapable of doing but I feel confident that the possession of just one song will somehow suffice. That I now offer you in my piteous appeal. Thus have we been told to act. Ancestors, we greet you, we greet you! (dance song)

N O R T H :   Ancestors, we send forth our greetings to you. My father and my grandfather, when they were alive, spoke to me repeatedly about this sacred Rite. 'Son,' they said, 'if you do not hearken to what we say, if you do not put yourself in a pity-inspiring condition, something like this, for instance, may happen to you. Some day a member of the Rite may invite you to take a place that has become vacant and will call upon you to say a few words of thankfulness and gratitude. There you'll be, dreading the opportunity that has come to you, to be a source of happiness for them and for your own family. And all this because you did not listen to what your elders were telling you for your own good! As you stand there, embarrassed, attempting to speak, you will be like one scratching himself as if he were being bitten by lice! Nothing will emerge from your mouth. Even if you did try to say something, a spell of coughing would prevent it. You will cough without the slightest desire to do so, simply because there was really nothing else you could do but cough.

'If you listen to me it will be quite different. Then if a member of the Rite were to ask you to be an instrument-of-thankfulness, you would be more than anxious to comply and the manner in which you spoke would indicate your very profound gratitude. There would be no hesitation in complying with their request and your words would correspond fully to what they expected of you. Pleased and happy will you make those who invited you. You, yourself, will secure new life thereby. So why should you make your listeners nervous and uneasy through your indifference? The members of the Rite will dislike you and you will, assuredly, not add to your years by such behavior.'

130

Thus spoke my father and grandfather. I was, in consequence, more than anxious to have the opportunity of being invited to the Rite.

Now it has happened and I am overwhelmed with pride. All I can say, however, is that I am sorry that I did not listen more attentively to what my father and grandfather told me concerning the means-for-offering-thanks. More particularly, I am sorry that I did not listen to the sacred words they recounted to me. Had I done so I would not now be standing here unable to utter any of those life-begetting speeches for your benefit and mine nor would I be suffering from the hindsight now overwhelming me. Here I stand. I know nothing, I can do nothing. Ancestors, I greet you, I greet you! (completion song)

N O R T H : Ancestors, I send forth my greetings to you. The announcer, the drum, is now to make his appearance and with it will come a song. Those who listen to it will be brought into connection with life. For that purpose do we sing the song. Ancestors, we greet you, we greet you! (dance song)

N O R T H : Ancestors, we send forth our greetings to you. In bygone days our ancestors performed these rites slowly and calmly. Just as they were accustomed to act during the Four Nights' Preparation so should we do now. Carefully, reverently, let us pass on the life-begetting greetings and offer up our thanks and gratitude, during these four nights, in the traditional manner.

In the old days men did not join the Medicine Rite until they had passed middle age, nor were performances within the Creation-Lodge frequent. The lodge would be filled with white-haired men and women. With this in mind and, as if these ancestors were present, let us now pass along the greetings, let us now meditate in true Medicine Rite fashion, all of us, all of us, as we sit here passing along the greetings. Ancestors, we greet you, we greet you! (completion song)

N O R T H : Ancestors, we send forth our greetings to you. For that gift of life which the creator bestowed upon us, for that we are

131

now attempting to ask. That is why we shall now immediately start up the dance and see to it that the drum is struck. Thus shall we extend the life-begetting greetings. Ancestors, we greet you, we greet you! (dance song)

N o R T H : Ancestors, we send forth our greetings to you. I possess a snake song, one that has come down to me and one that I could use, so they told me, whenever I wished to give a life-engendering greeting. This song was obtained from a large yellow snake by a person who had been blessed under the fork of a tree where there was a crow's nest. With a large portion of life was he blessed, with herbs and grasses, beneficent grasses, those that would restore health to a man. Yet, nevertheless, some of them, it is said, could cause a person to become weak. All these plants were to bring prestige and honor to the possessor.

Now, in the beginning, people associated with these plants just as if they possessed life like ourselves. They were worshipped and honored. Not today do we do so. Yet these herbs and grasses are still being used and are still efficacious.

This snake song I shall now sing. Ancestors, we greet you, we greet you! (completion song, snake song)

N o R T H : Ancestors, we send forth our greetings to you. We shall immediately start the dance so that we may ask for life through it and, having asked for life, that we may send our greetings to you. (dance song)

4 . THE FOURTH NIGHT

The members of the different bands are gathered together again and when those of the North Band are all assembled, the leader rises and addresses them as follows:

N o R T H : Ancestors, we send forth our greetings to you. It is good. Through their compassion and pity, our ancestors placed me in possession of a good life. They have brought me into connection

132

with life and they have enabled me, with my words, to bring all those within this lodge into connection with life. Indeed it is good.

Let me now scatter life among all of us here present by the force and power of my words. Undoubtedly, all has already been said that should have been said. However we can still bring out the pipe, fill it and puff life upon ourselves. Ancestors, we greet you, we greet you!

Then he fills his pipe, lights it and puffs, first toward the east, then toward the north, then toward the west and, finally, toward the south. Then he extends the pipe toward the one nearest to him who, after accepting it, thanks him with an 'Ancestors, we greet you.' This man then smokes the pipe, takes four puffs and stops. He now, in turn, extends the pipe to the next person and when this one is ready he seizes it, passes the greeting along, takes four puffs and extends it to the fourth one. And thus it goes, from person to person, until all have received the pipe and taken four puffs.

When the smoking ceremony is over then the leader arises and extending his greeting to those present, addresses them as follows:

N O R T H :   Ancestors, we send forth our greetings to you. Whenever, in the old days, an old man suffered a loss, it was his custom to call together the members of the Medicine Rite and then, all together, they would make their plea for whatever residue of life was still coming to the deceased, asking that it be passed on to the living. Thus, so it was said, can the good life be secured. Ancestors, we greet you, we greet you! (mourning song)

N O R T H :   Ancestors, we send forth our greetings to you once again. We must make our plea for life immediately just as the older members used to make theirs. Ancestors, we greet you, we greet you! (completion song)

N O R T H :   Ancestors, we send forth our greetings to you. We shall now start up the dance songs; one apiece, we shall sing. Ancestors, we greet you, we greet you! (dance song)

N O R T H :   Ancestors, we send forth our greetings to you. We must immediately extend our life-engendering greetings, an ample amount it should be, so we have been told, and then, tomorrow, we

133

will be able to greet you all again as you enter the Creation-Lodge. Would that we could do that right this minute!

We shall now attempt to obtain life as best we can even though we are really incapable of saying anything and must rely upon the mere passing of the greetings. Yet that will suffice, we have been told. Ancestors, we greet you, we greet you! (completion song)

N O R T H : Ancestors, we send forth our greetings to you. The drum, the messenger, will now immediately make its appearance so that we may be blessed by its greeting. Needless to say, I have told you this before, I am incapable of making any utterance of value. Ancestors, we greet you, we greet you! (dance song)

N O R T H : Ancestors, we send forth our greetings to you. I know this is not a matter to be hurried but we are anxious to greet our ancestors tomorrow and we will have an abundance of life-engendering greetings there. For the present, then, let us start up a song immediately. Tomorrow, it is said, a new life will come for the one to be initiated into this Rite, the one we call He-for-whom-we-seek-life. Then everyone will have to concentrate his mind upon this ceremony. Ancestors, we greet you, we greet you! (completion song)

N O R T H : Ancestors, we send forth our greetings to you. In the beginning, the song we are now about to attempt, was sung perfectly and it was handed down accurately until it came to me. But I, of course, will not be able to sing it in that manner for, as you know, I am incapable of saying anything. Let me therefore call upon the announcer to come forth; let the drum be sounded at once. Ancestors, we greet you, we greet you! (dance song)

N O R T H : Ancestors, we send forth our greetings to you. The time for the real performance of the ceremony is now at hand. Tomorrow, at the Creation-Lodge, the birdskin, the otterskin pouches will guide us, Medicine Rite members, along the path of life until we reach our destination up above. Let us then chant a song so that we can start off to reach our destination. Let us intone a birdskin

134

pouch song. And this we ask: that even if we, by chance, fell asleep at times during the last four nights, no evil befall us as we enter upon our journey. May the birdskin pouches, the otterskin pouches, lead us successfully through the evil obstacles we will encounter or, if need be, lead us around them. That these obstacles exist, of that we can be certain. So let us then see that the song is made ready. Ancestors, we greet you, we greet you! (shell song)

N O R T H : Now this is all that we have to do. Ancestors, we greet you, we greet you!

V. The Preparatory Four Nights of West's Band

1 . THE FIRST NIGHT

W E S T : Ancestors, we send forth our greetings to you. When my ancestors pondered over the question of whom to hand down their knowledge to, most assuredly, they could not have had me in mind, for I am not a fit person for such knowledge. And yet, though unworthy, they did include me in their thoughts. It is good. They have brought new life to me. Certainly these ancestors of mine did not do it just for me. They had everyone in mind, all those gathered here in fact. It was their concern to find a seat for me here in the Rite so that I might extend to it the life-begetting greetings. This then let me do. I greet you, feast-participants, all of you sitting here. I greet you, spirits, all of you, wherever you are. I greet you, all those who have concentrated their minds on the birdskin pouches, open-faced and closed. May this be as a life-engendering blessing to you! What I have to tell you is this. Let us all scatter life among ourselves and the means of obtaining life. So now let us fill our pipe. Ancestors, I greet you, I greet you!

Then he fills his pipe, lights it and puffs, first toward the east, then toward the north, then toward the west and, finally, toward the south. Then he extends

135

the pipe toward the one nearest to him who, after accepting it, thanks him with an 'Ancestors, we greet you.' This man then smokes the pipe, takes four puffs and stops. He now, in turn extends the pipe to the next person and when this one is ready he seizes it, passes the greeting along, takes four puffs and extends it to the fourth one. And thus it goes, from person to person, until all have received the pipe and taken four puffs.

When the smoking ceremony is over then the leader arises and extending his greeting to those present, addresses them as follows:

W E S T :   Ancestors, we extend our greeting to you. The messenger of the spirits, the drum, is about to be heard in connection with the Tear-Pouring ritual they established. Sincerely will our tears flow during this ceremony as we try to obtain life, as we beseech the ghost of the departed to distribute among us what he has left unlived. Ancestors, we greet you, we greet you! (mourning song)

W E S T :   Ancestors, we send forth our greetings to you. But now we must again ask for life immediately just as it has always been done. Ancestors, we greet you, we greet you! (completion song)

W E S T :   Ancestors, we send forth our greetings to you. A dance song is about to be released. He who wishes to dance must however not hold a birdskin pouch in his hand while dancing. If a person should, however, try to obtain life in this fashion, let him see to it that no one watches him as he stands there in his defiance. Let him also remember that such a dereliction brings with it great physical weakness. So it has always been said.

But, now, let us proceed with the ceremony. Let the song appear at once. That is the gist of what I have to say. Ancestors, we greet you, we greet you! (dance song)

W E S T :   Ancestors, we send forth our greetings to you. Up above where stretches the blue sky visible to us, once dwelt an extremely white and sacred spirit. He pitied and blessed my ancestor. 'Human being,' he said to him, 'Earthmaker placed me in charge of very much life when he first created me. With the life he gave me, with that I now bless you. For a long time have you been standing

136

there weeping. You have now fasted for a long time. You have almost thirsted yourself to death. Of this life that I bestow upon you, you can give some portion to those who ask you for it. I put at your disposal my song, likewise, and you may use it for those who wish to obtain life through you! This, then, is what I have to say.

Let the song make its appearance now and do you use it together with the life-engendering greetings, from now on to eternity. Ancestors, we greet you, we greet you! (completion song)

W E S T :   Ancestors, we send forth our greetings to you. If there is any one present here who wishes to dance, let him do so and let him obtain whatever portion of life is obtainable in that manner. Ancestors, we greet you, we greet you! (dance song)

W E S T :   Ancestors, we send forth our greetings to you. . . .

I once had a grandfather named Manixede. It is said that once, as he looked through space, he saw ahead of him a piece of land called Wa'uni. At that place he was blessed by a very white and sacred waterspirit. He was blessed with everything he could possibly have hoped for. A song, likewise, the waterspirit had appear for him. 'Manixede,' said the spirit to him, 'you have drummed yourself into life, drummed yourself and the members of the Rite into life. You will become a source of dependence for help and goodness for them.' Thus did the very white waterspirit speak to him when he blessed him.

Now near the waterspirit was a very white martin who had been working for him. This spirit, in his turn, now spoke to Manixede and said, 'Human being, I also bless you. Behold! with this I bless you.' Then the man looked at the white martin as he lay there stretched out on the water and noticed that a plant protruded from the top of the martin's back, a most desirable plant. Erect it stood there. Once again did the white martin address Manixede. 'Human being,' he said to him, 'I, too, wish to bless you. Here it is, the object with which I wish to bless you, a medicine to cause vomiting. It will enable you to sweep away all the evil you encounter, to sweep it up and cast it outside. Similarly if some enemy has poisoned you, if you

137

have eaten the evil thing set out for you, then take this medicine. It will cause you to vomit four times and I, in my spirit home, will sweep your stomach clean. Indeed, your stomach will be swept clean and nothing evil will remain in it.' . . .

This is what was told me. Thus has it been handed down. A song, likewise, we were to use and that is the one I now offer. Ancestors, we greet you, we greet you! (completion song)

W E S T :   Ancestors, we send forth our greetings to you. The Medicine Rite drinking song I now put at your disposal and I will show you how to use it. I offer it as a life-engendering greeting to you. In such manner was it offered to me. Ancestors, we greet you. (dance song)

W E S T :   Ancestors, we send forth our greeting to you. . . .

There was once an Ojibwa, a seer, one who had been richly blessed. A clever man he was and as he traveled around at night, visiting people, it was always high up in the air and as a witch. This Ojibwa had made friends with three other witches and poisoners. All possessed this power of traveling in the air at night. Because of his cleverness and their powers people were afraid of them. One night one of the most powerful of these Ojibwa agreed to fly across the sky at night. They were to have a contest of power.

He whom they call Manixede, a Winnebago, heard of it. He was a seer himself, a richly blessed individual. So, when the time came, he proceeded to the appointed place, using his night-traveling power to get there. He knew exactly where they were starting from and he waited for them, for each one separately. Patiently he stood there waiting for them. One after another he saw to it that three of these night-travelers failed to return. The fourth Ojibwa dived deep down from above and landed on the strip of a piece of land. There this Ojibwa stood, deer-horns (?) on his head. Manixede seized and held him tightly.

Now the four other Ojibwa had come together again and, as a sign of defeat, they asked Manixede to come to them, to which he will-
138

ingly consented. When he arrived, the Ojibwa tried to persuade *Manixede* to let them bestow their powers upon him, but he refused for he did not want their powers, but the medicines and plants that gave them these powers. So he asked them first for their drinking potion, but they found excuses for not giving it to him. Then he asked them for the beneficial plants which they possessed, but they found excuses for not giving them to him. 'Indeed we have no knowledge of such matters,' they maintained. Finally he asked them for their life-engendering greeting and all the power it possessed. This they gave him and this it is with which we salute you. . . .

O spirits gathered here from all directions! Ancestors, we greet you, we greet you! (completion song)

W E S T :   Ancestors, we send forth our greetings to you. What these Ojibwa gave *Manixede* and which was passed on to me, was spoken in another language and I, of course, am ignorant of it. However, I shall try to do the best I can. Ancestors, we greet you, we greet you! (dance song)

W E S T :   Ancestors, we send forth our greeting to you. As soon as we have finished offering up our thanks and gratitude we shall rest for the night. Ancestors, we greet you, we greet you!

2 .   THE SECOND NIGHT

When they are assembled again, he who is to dispense blessings, the leader of the West Band, rises and greeting each person in turn speaks as follows:

W E S T :   Ancestors, we send forth our greetings to you. Abundance of blessings the different members of the Medicine Rite have bestowed upon us and we are properly grateful. Grateful, likewise, we are because they concentrated their minds upon our welfare. We extend, at the same time, our greetings to all the various spirits. Those that possess open-faced birdskin pouches have all been in-

139

vited and to these feast-dispensing members of the Rite, as many as are gathered around here reclining in their seats, to these, we extend our greeting . . .

Once a man, fasting, had a vision of an elk waterspirit. He felt himself in possession of very great power and thought to himself, 'This spirit is not my equal.' Now this man had a younger brother who was also a seer and a seeker of visions and to this younger brother there appeared a real waterspirit. Because of this, the one who had seen the spurious elk waterspirit, became jealous.

Then the older brother determined to tease and irritate his younger brother, the one who had seen the true waterspirit. He determined to tease him by words and actions. More than that. He even meditated upon how he could poison him. Finally the older one appeared before his brother and said to him, 'Younger brother, you are in no way my equal in power. But let us, nevertheless, have a diving contest to decide that point. I am ready to try.'

The two lived near the water at the time. The younger brother dived headlong into the water first and soon emerged, right there in the middle of the lake. 'You are not my equal,' he shouted to his brother, 'you will fall far short of accomplishing what I just did.' Then the older brother dived into the water and there, in the middle of the lake, he emerged as a waterspirit. Then he spoke to his younger brother, 'Younger brother, remember, I warned you about my superiority but you would not take cognizance of it.' Saying this, he stepped out of the lake.

The time for the fall moving had now arrived. The older brother went along, the younger one did not. When the older brother returned and he came in sight of his home, there a grave was visible, a truly white one. So he composed a song for the younger brother he had killed and this song, here it is . . .

I extend it to you as a greeting, a greeting of the same kind as the older people used in the past. Ancestors, we greet you, we greet you! . . .

When a member of this Medicine Rite, one who has lived up to its precepts, loses a child he has loved dearly and tenderly, then he always thinks of how he is to fill the place of the deceased at the Rite and how he is to plead with him to distribute among the living the years the dead one left unlived. All the others present here are making the same plea so, perhaps, it is not effrontery on my part to do the same.

Life, then, let us pray for. Let us try to obtain it through our utterances, by song, just as it has always been done at the Tear-Pouring ritual. Ancestors, we greet you, we greet you! (mourning song)

WEST : Ancestors, we send forth our greetings to you. Now we shall immediately offer up our prayer for life again. That is all I have to say to you. Ancestors, we greet you, we greet you! (completion song)

WEST : Ancestors, we send forth our greetings to you. The dance song is now to be started in the manner in which it has always been sung. I, of course, will doubtless make many mistakes but I will try to do my best. Ancestors, we greet you, we greet you! (dance song)

WEST : Ancestors, we send forth our greetings to you. People have given me the means for rendering thanks, but these life-compelling materials that they put at my disposal were lost to me through my incapacity. I know only too well that the actions we perform here come from the spirits and that what we do here is sacred. But I do not belong here; I can perform none of these things.

Once, it is true, I knew and held everything done here in the highest esteem. Now, however, when I attempt to say anything I always think to myself, 'you are probably going to embarrass the members of the Rite when you speak.' That is what my older relatives warned me against and from that fact flows my reprehensible shyness. 'You cannot learn the speeches of the members of the Medi-

141

cine Rite unless your intent is really serious. It is just impossible to acquire these speeches or make the proper use of them, if you take them lightly. They are sacred. Our grandmother, Earth, she will always know what you do. He-whom-we-call-our-nephew, Hare, he it was who obtained this Rite for us, and only by attending to its ritual reverently, can we show our respect for it. Remember, then, without the proper attitude, you can do nothing with it.' Thus did the old people speak to me.

I know well how life-begetting the greetings are and that is why I shall try my very best to extend them to you correctly. But now the song is about to be started. So it must be. Ancestors, we greet you, we greet you! (completion song)

W E S T : Ancestors, we send forth our greeting to you. In a moment we will prepare to start up the dance song. We will do it to the best of our ability. The messenger, the drum, is about to be struck. Ancestors, we greet you, we greet you! (dance song)

W E S T : Ancestors, we send forth our greeting to you.

In olden times there was once a prominent member of the Medicine Rite who spent four years trying to obtain additional power. Finally he was able to obtain a song with which he could extend a life-engendering greeting to those around him. In addition to the song, other members of the Rite gave him all they knew. Then they took the gifts through which he was to become holy and put them in front of him. Afterwards, they gathered other objects for him: good and useful plants, plants that are vibrant with life; good and useful blossoms such as those that cover the body of our grandmother, the earth; sweet-smelling plants and sweet-tasting plants. Then they brewed some sweet concoction that could be added to the medicines which give life. In short, all the good plants and herbs they knew, they put at his disposal.

Subsequently they composed a song called the sweetened-drink song and it was to be used in a life-engendering greeting. This is the song that is now about to be heard. Ancestors, we greet you, we greet you! (completion song)

142

W E S T :   Ancestors, we send forth our greetings to you. Although it is impossible ever to track down and obtain all of the actions, privileges and speeches that belong to an important member of the Medicine Rite, I tried, nevertheless, to do so. Not that I would ever be able to put them to the proper use, of course! So, whenever an important member of the Rite gave a feast for the other members I saw to it that the food was provided. I provided the apparel [46] he was to wear at the feast. Indeed I saw to it that his body was properly covered and enveloped with clothing. I saw to it that he received a cane. When the time came for erecting a Vapor-Bath lodge, I saw to it that it was covered and closed, that the matting blankets enclosed the structure properly. Then when he stepped out of the Vapor-Bath Lodge, I saw to it again that he was provided with the necessary clothing. When another feast had to be given I was there to provide him with the materials required for it. He had food to eat. Supper I provided for him.

My father and grandfather, seeing how well I was providing for this man, spoke to me, saying, 'Now if you make a request from such a member of the Rite, doubtless he will not just brush aside your question.' And to my grandfather I said, 'Grandfather, have compassion upon me. It is for this, your religion, that I am exerting myself.'

Then, once again, I went to this member of the Rite and entered the lodge where he was sitting. I came so that I might again provide the materials to enclose his body, every part of it completely. Tobacco, I likewise brought so that he could smoke. I placed it in front of him. Food, adequate food, I piled up for him in the rear of his lodge. Mattings for the floor, these too, I provided and spread out before him. A bearskin I brought to him so that he could spread it out over his seat in the Creation-Lodge. Two belts, tied up, so that he could have a leash for his dogs, these I brought and gave to him. 'Have compassion upon me,' I beseeched him. 'Nephew,' he answered me, 'of what importance do you consider me, that you exert yourself so much in my behalf, that you are doing all this for me? Tell me!' Thus he spoke. But I did not answer. Instead, when I came to him for the fourth time, I brought a horse for him to mount. Then he arose and placed in front of me the materials from which he himself had derived his powers and made himself holy. Then he spoke, 'Nephew, what I am placing before you is the material through which men attain honor and respect. With this in your possession, all the members of the Rite will honor and respect you. In addition, the medicines therein contained can be used to guard your lodge against encroachers and will act as a protection to you, if you place them in the rear of your lodge. No night-travelers [47] will then be able to roar over you. They will be forced to avoid you.' Thus did he speak to me.

Then, again, he placed before me good and useful plants, the kind that enable sick people to arise from their sickbeds. These plants whose virtues and powers he well knew, he placed in front of me. Finally he put before me as a gift the most important sacred things that had been placed in his possession for all eternity. On receiving them I assured him that I would give them the most careful attention at all times. Songs, likewise, he gave me so that I could use them as life-engendering greetings. These, I assured him, I would use as a greeting when the time came as it now has come. Ancestors, with these songs I now greet you, I greet you! (completion song)

W E S T :   Ancestors, we send forth our greetings to you. The dance song is now about to be started. I intend it as my life-engendering greeting to all of you assembled here. Ancestors, I greet you, I greet you! (dance song)
We have finished.

3. THE THIRD NIGHT

When all are assembled again and the leader, West, has extended his greetings to each person in turn, he rises and speaks as follows:

W E S T :   Ancestors, we send forth our greetings to you. The men of old blessed us amply and placed an abundance of thank-offerings at our disposal. This is what they told us to say and this we are repeating. Tonight, following the directions of our ancestors, we shall again beg for life. We shall beg life for ourselves and for the

144

one to be newly initiated whom we call He-for-whom-we-seek-life. May he and his people likewise have pity and compassion upon us. For all those present here we humbly ask life; we ask that they be blessed.

One of the pious members of the Medicine Rite has sustained a loss; his hold upon the birdskin pouch has been weakened.[48] And so we have come together to join him in his piteous appeal for that residue of life that the deceased has left behind. At all times, everywhere, the members have been able to obtain their request through speech and action. By their pleas they have always assured themselves of the possibility of reaching old age. Whenever a pious and observant member of the Rite dies before his time, it has always been the custom to beseech his ghost that he present to the living members the years he left behind him unlived. This we now do. Ancestors, we greet you, we greet you! (mourning song)

W E S T : Ancestors, we send forth our greetings to you. In a moment we shall again ask piteously for life, in a moment we shall extend our life-engendering greetings to you and express our thanks and gratitude. Ancestors, we greet you, we greet you! (completion song)

W E S T : Ancestors, we send forth our greetings to you. We are about to start up the dance song as a greeting to you. But first, the messenger, the drum, will make its announcement. Here it is. Ancestors, we greet you, we greet you! (dance song)

W E S T : Ancestors, we send forth our greetings to you. Our ancestors who preceded us always asked light and life for one newly to be initiated, for He-for-whom-we-seek-life. They must have already said all that could be said. Indeed they left behind for us, and passed on to us, before they died, the proper utterances, the proper songs and speeches. They left behind more than an ample number of songs and speeches for us to use and thus obtain light and life. They were indeed true Medicine Rite members. But we, unfortunately, are not. We know no speeches. All we can do is to extend the life-engendering greetings. However, the old people assured us that, in the absence of anything else, even that might suffice. We greet you then, spirits, wherever you are, and we greet you, possessors of open-faced birdskin pouches, we greet you, councillors and life-obtainers, leaders, as many as are sitting around here. Ancestors, we greet you, we greet you! (completion song)

w e s t :   Ancestors, we send forth our greetings to you. In this Rite love is the foremost objective. That and life, it is our desire to seek and find. That is our objective. Our ancestors who felt themselves connected with life, presented us with a new life. They gave us ample materials, the wherewithal for thankfulness and gratitude. Thus did they speak to and instruct us. We greet the sacred lodge, the Creation-Lodge. No spirit-weakling, no one whose mind is hesitant, can enter that lodge. Only with tobacco can we enter it to good purpose. This it is, tobacco, which we must thrust forward into the lodge, with greetings, with the most sincere and deepfelt, life-engendering, greetings. We shall make the attempt. This is no place for foolishness and indifference. Here we are concerned only with obtaining that life and light which permeates all things and penetrates all beings. This it is we have come here to obtain tonight. We extend you our thanks and gratitude. Ancestors, we greet you, we greet you! (dance song)

w e s t :   Ancestors, we send forth our greetings to you. If it should so happen that at a performance of the Rite, there be a superabundance of dishes from which one can partake, that is, seats one can occupy, see to it that you have enough knowledge to say something. My father once spoke to me as follows: 'If you utter no word, then people will say to one another, "what manner of man could this have been to whom no knowledge has been passed on?" Listen to me, accordingly, my son, so that if, some day, the members of the Rite have compassion upon you, you will not stand there hesitant and blundering. Instead, you will be able to start right out. Nor should you try to guess at the words of the song I shall now teach you. If you ask your ancestors to pity you then your utterances must

146

be clear and distinct and you must speak with full understanding of their significance. Do not mumble your words but enunciate them carefully and piously. If the host gives you an offering, accept it and extend a life-begetting greeting to him.' Thus spoke my father.

I, however, am afraid that I cannot sing or talk accurately or piously. Properly and thoroughly was I taught but I only became bewildered from what they told me, because of my unworthiness. I am not a man of knowledge. On the contrary, I am an ignorant and wayward individual. I should indeed have been in a position to teach you things, carefully and piously. I should have been a man of virtue and knowledge. But I am not. However, in spite of that, the time has now arrived.for the messenger, the drum, to be heard so, ancestors, I greet you, I greet you! (completion song)

W E S T : Ancestors, we send forth our greetings to you. The minor dance song is now to be started. This song is to serve as a life-engendering greeting to everyone. That is its purpose. So we greet all of you again as this song is uttered. Ancestors, we greet you, we greet you! (dance song)

W E S T : Ancestors, we send forth our greetings to you. The song which we shall now use is one concerned with medicinal herbs. Here it is. I send it out as a life-begetting greeting to you.

When Earthmaker created the spirits he put each one in charge of great powers. Let us, then, beseech these spirits to bestow upon us the means for obtaining life. The creator hoped that the spirits to whom he gave these powers would bless us with them . . .

It is said that one of my grandfathers in the past made his plea to one of the spirits for life. He rubbed ashes on his face, ashes taken from our grandfather who stands in the middle of the lodge.[49] Fasting, he uttered his pity-inspiring cry, with tobacco-offerings in his hands. Our grandmother, Earth, heard it and spoke to him:

'Grandson, I bless you. With the good and useful plants that the creator, living up above, bestowed upon me, the plants that raise the sick man to his feet, with these I bless you. These plants will be

147

good no matter for what purpose they are used. Whatever request is made of them, they will fulfill. Grandson, not only you as you pass through life, but all the roots you send out, your descendants, will possess and enjoy them as long as this earth lasts. If you and your descendants offer up feasts for these plants, never will they fail you in any way. But this I must tell you. Never attempt to pull out these plants with your bare hands, that is, without proper ceremony. When you are ready to pull out these life-sustainers, first pour an offering of tobacco for them. Then you may dig them up from the earth and they will remain unimpaired. If, at the same time, you sing a song for me as you dig them up, I will appreciate it and be grateful and grant you what you have asked.' Thus did our grandmother speak . . .

A song therefore we shall now sing, a plant song. Here it is. We send it forth to you, as a life-engendering greeting. Ancestors, we greet you, we greet you! (completion song)

W E S T : Ancestors, we send forth our greetings to you. We must now finish immediately. The dance song is about to be started. It is to serve as a life-begetting song today just as it served in the past. We greet you, we greet you! (dance song)

4 . THE FOURTH NIGHT

W E S T : Ancestors, we send forth our greetings to you. This is the last night at which we are going to offer up our thanks and we shall go through our parts as rapidly as possible. We shall sing only one song apiece and we will have that serve both as our expression of thanks and gratitude, and as our greeting. Tomorrow we will gather in the Creation-Lodge, to be there with the birdskin pouches of those who are in search of light and life. There we shall pass on to them the life-engendering greetings. There we will be sitting with all the materials for securing true life and there we will extend the life-engendering greetings to one another. Through the few songs we sing will these greetings be extended.

148

Tomorrow the great day will come, the day I have already mentioned, a day, fair and propitious for us, where we can greet the members of the Rite and see them face to face. The messenger is already here, the drum is about to be sounded. Ancestors, we greet you, we greet you! (completion song)

W E S T :   Ancestors, we send forth our greetings to you. But now, without saying many words, let us see that the messenger, the drum, makes its appearance. Ancestors, we greet you, we greet you! (dance song)

W E S T :   Ancestors, we send forth our greetings to you. Here is a small number of songs that we present to you as a life-engendering greeting for tonight. We are indeed grateful to you and thank you. The first song is one with which an otter blessed a man and with which he bestowed life on him. The next is an earth song, also sung by the otter. These we put at your disposal as we extend our greeting to you. Ancestors, we greet you, we greet you! (completion song)

W E S T :   Ancestors, we send forth our greetings to you. Again we must, immediately and without fail, have the dance song appear, for a group of songs are still to be sung and many things to be done tonight. Let us go to work immediately for, tomorrow morning, we shall meet them, the members of the Rite, face to face. We send our life-engendering greetings to you. Ancestors, we greet you, we greet you! (dance song)

W E S T :   Ancestors, we send forth our greetings to you. We must sing the next song very fast and let it serve as our life-engendering greeting. Those present made us feel connected with life and we are deeply grateful. When I finish the song I am about to start up, then I shall extend a greeting to all. Ancestors, we greet you, we greet you! (completion song)

W E S T :   Ancestors, we send our greetings out to you. Our messenger, the drum, will immediately be sounded and, with it, we extend our greeting to you. Ancestors, we greet you, we greet you! (dance song)

W E S T :   Ancestors, we send forth our greetings to you. I know that when I am in a hurry, it is difficult for me to make my words audible. However, it has been said that even a dance song given in this fashion is acceptable and can serve as an expression of thanks and gratitude. I greet you with words and dance, as it has always been our custom to do. Ancestors, we greet you, we greet you! (dance song)

W E S T :   The time has now come for us to rest. Let us all do so now. Ancestors, we greet you, we greet you. I am finished.

VI. The Preparatory Four Nights of Ghost's Band

1 . T H E   F I R S T   N I G H T

G H O S T :   Ancestors, we send forth our greetings to you. The members of the Medicine Rite do all things well. Indeed, they do things superbly well. And that is why people who wish to be blessed, direct their thoughts toward them. Dispensers of life they are to those who ask them for compassion and pity. They have blessed me with a new life and I am thankful and grateful for it. They are really great, these Medicine Rite members. But we others, who are here, are clearly of no importance, consumed as we are with fear and indecision. Yet these great men would like us to be blessed, would like to see us participate in the cry for life and thus, properly humble, obtain knowledge! All this they desire. In spite of their kindness, however, we are unable to say a word because of our deep ignorance. Now the leader who invited us here did not do so unintentionally or without purpose. He did not make any mistake. He knew what to expect. He was just thinking of us and of bringing us into connection with life.

150

I am now going to do the untying of the invitation sticks [50] in the lodge. Reverently I shall do it. There, within the lodge, I shall puff on myself that life with which I feel connected. It is a very pure and true life that is being directed toward me. The atmosphere of this Island-Lodge, as far as it stretches, is murky with tobacco smoke.[51]

The creator ordained that all the spirits throughout the world should sit in their lodges and be obsessed with a longing for the wonderful odor of tobacco, for the taste of it. As it penetrated their dwellings, spreading itself everywhere, they sat in their homes wondering who would be put in control of it. 'Where else,' so they thought to themselves as they sat in their homes expectant, 'where else could they take care of this life-invoking possession but here among ourselves.' So each spirit sat there convinced that he and he, only, was to be the one selected to take charge of the tobacco.

Then He-whom-we-call-our-nephew, Hare, arose and spoke, 'Thus it shall be. My uncles and my aunts, the human beings, to them is tobacco to belong. As long as mankind exists never will you, O spirits reclining in your lodges, be permitted to take it from them without some recompense! Thus did he who is above, the creator, ordain it. Even the creator, he above, would have to accept it and grant human beings what they asked if they offered him a pipeful of tobacco. In such manner did he arrange things for the human beings. If, therefore, all you spirits, whoever you are, wherever you are, if, as you recline in your lodges, human beings pour out a pipeful of tobacco, seize it, take firm hold of it, smoke it eagerly and grant them their request! In no other way will you be able to obtain the means of smoking. This is how the creator, up above, ordained it.'

In this manner did the creator present to the two-legged walkers a beneficial gift. All the spirits, in their various homes, were aware of it. They realized that when he had created them, Earthmaker had given the two-legged walkers only a short span of life. With this life-compelling gift, with this tobacco, the span of years could now be increased. For all eternity were they to employ it.

All the various members of the Medicine Rite are about to send the life-invoking tobacco to the spirits who sit at the edge of the island, the East, the North, the West, the South. A blessing they have caused to come in our direction. It is good. But, now, let us proceed to puff life upon one another. Ancestors, we greet you, we greet you!

Then he fills his pipe, lights it and puffs, first toward the east, then toward the north, then toward the west and, finally, toward the south. Then he extends the pipe toward the one nearest to him who, after accepting it, thanks him with an 'Ancestors, we greet you.' This man then smokes the pipe, takes four puffs and stops. He now, in turn, extends the pipe to the next person and when this one is ready he seizes it, passes the greeting along, takes four puffs and extends it to the fourth one. And thus it goes, from person to person, until all have received the pipe and taken four puffs.

When the smoking ceremony is over then the leader rises and extending his greeting to those present addresses them as follows:

G H O S T : Ancestors, we send forth our greetings to you. We have been scattering new life among ourselves. Thus did the spirits, every one of them, direct us to behave when these ceremonies were performed at the first Creation-Lodge. And now we are to sing a song. What kind of song is explained in the following story: . . .

Once a man went out to fast and obtain a vision. A waterspirit blessed him with his body. The man cut it open and, from the various parts of the body, prepared a liquid medicine, the kind called to-tap-the-head-with. This he took home with him and it was to be used for distribution among his children. Then this man prepared many evil medicines from what remained of the waterspirit's body. After this he went home and, subsequently, looked about for some hiding-place where he could secrete his medicines. In the corner of a perpendicular cliff he placed his medicine-container with his evil medicines enclosed within it.

In preparing these medicines he had as his object the purpose of making himself a prominent and distinguished man, one that people would fear because of the great powers he had acquired from his fasting visions. He wanted people to flatter him and truckle before him and that is why he became a night-traveler.

However, it so happened, that, before him, there had been another seer and seeker of visions. This seer knew where the first one had deposited his medicine-container. So he proceeded to this place and took all the medicine bundles he found there. Then he continued until he reached a grove of thick timber near his village. To one of the many large trees he found there he brought the bundles. He poked his hand into the core of this tree's trunk and, into the opening he made, he inserted one of the first seer's bundles. Then he covered and sealed the hole. From this sealed hole in the core of the tree no one could possibly extract the bundle. Then he proceeded to another tree with another of these bundles and inserted it likewise right into the center of its trunk. He continued to do this for each one of the first seer's bundles. Thus did he empty the contents of the medicine-container. The container was a black one, they say. When he was finished with the disposing of these bundles, he returned home.

About this time the first seer decided to pay a visit to his medicine-container. When he got to his hiding-place he found that the container was gone. 'How can this have happened?' he said to himself in consternation, 'the waterspirit, when he blessed me, assured me that I was going to become holy and powerful.' He looked around and finally found where his bundles had been deposited, but he could not extract them from the tree.

The older seer was indeed holy. He had the power of poking his hand right into the center of any kind of a tree. He could put anything he wanted to inside and keep it there permanently. The other seer only thought himself holy and strutted around a good deal as though he were. He was deservedly defeated and humiliated . . .

Such is the story of the song we are about to sing. It is still in our possession and we shall use it as a life-engendering greeting for you. This is what I thought I would do tonight as an offering to that old member of the Rite who has just sustained a loss and who has asked us to join in mourning with him. In order to weep with him and his and to show our sympathy, for that we have come to this ceremony.

Together with the mourners, we shall, here at the Tear-Pouring

153

ceremony, pray and beseech the ghost of the deceased that he bestow on us the residue of life still due him. Ancestors, we greet you, we greet you! (mourning song)

G H O S T :   Ancestors, we send forth our greetings to you. To ask for life we have been told and that we shall do immediately. We greet you all, you Medicine Rite members who have concentrated your thoughts upon our welfare; we greet you, spirits, wherever you are, wherever you are; we greet you possessors of birdskin pouches, open-faced and closed, and lastly we greet you, all you councillors and warners who are sitting around this lodge. We greet you all, we greet you all! (completion song)

G H O S T :   Ancestors, we send forth our greetings to you. We are now about to start up for you some dance songs, O ancestors, to serve as a life-engendering greeting. It has been said that the larger the number of such greetings, the more thankful the recipients will feel and, thus, through their gratitude, receive additional blessings. Thus did the older people speak. We now pass these greetings along to you. But here is our messenger, the drum. Ancestors, we greet you, we greet you. (dance song)

G H O S T :   Ancestors, we send forth our greetings to you. He-whom-we-call-our-nephew, Hare, secured this Rite for us. It was not a ceremony acquired through a vision.[52] This Rite was taught to two human beings in the first Creation-Lodge. He-whom-we-call-our-nephew became a human being in order to succour us. In order to obtain a larger span of life for us, he looked for and obtained the promise of reincarnation, the shedding of our skin, at this Rite. If any member adheres to its teachings meticulously and sincerely, then will he obtain this new life, this shedding of skin. Here, at this ceremony, I tell you again, we can be put in the way of acquiring the materials that lead to the shedding of skin, to reincarnation. For this reason the members of the Rite have always been encouraged to live up to all their responsibilities when they perform this ceremony, and to lead virtuous lives. Then will Earthmaker, sitting up above,

154

send human beings down to the earth to live their lives once more, there to attain a good old age. Ancestors, we greet you, we greet you! (completion song)

G H O S T :   Ancestors, we send forth our greetings to you. Now it is time for our messenger, the drum, to make its appearance so that we may extend the life-engendering greeting to you. We shall all dance again and make our pleas for life. Ancestors, we greet you, we greet you! (dance song)

G H O S T :   Ancestors, we send forth our greetings to you. Four spirits attempted to succour our forefathers. Three of them failed. The last one, however, succeeded and he trampled under his feet all the evil spirits who were molesting the human beings. But he was not able to obtain for us an immortal life like his own. In fact it was through him that death was made possible for us. After this, however, he brought down from above, for our forefathers, this Rite and allowed them to make their choice of the kind of life they desired to live again, whether as human beings or as animals.

If any human being performs this ceremony correctly and sincerely, if his thoughts are honest and loyal, then, so those who have gone before us have said, he will obtain this new kind of life. If, however, anyone questions or doubts its truth, then, between the layers of the earth, our grandmother, will be placed when he dies, to lie there permanently. Quite otherwise will be the fate of that one where doubt of the truth of the Rite does not enter his mind. He will never know death, never experience that sensation, and forever and forever, will our grandmother, Earth, hold him pressed to her broad breast. Thus will it be they said; thus did they act themselves. Ancestors, we greet you, we greet you! (completion song)

G H O S T :   Ancestors, we send forth our greetings to you. Again we greet you, all you members of the Rite, all you councillors and exhorters sitting around this lodge with your birdskin pouches, open-faced and covered. May our greetings serve as a request for life! So, too, may the dance songs we shall now attempt to sing, serve the

155

same purpose. Thus were we told to act; thus shall we act. Ancestors, we greet you, we greet you! (dance song)

G H O S T :   Ancestors, we send forth our greetings to you . . .

They say that once there lived an old man, a member of the Rite, who had obtained great powers. All the other Rite members feared him greatly. If, at a performance of the ceremony, he was not given the first place of honor then he would forcibly take it away from whoever happened to possess it. If anyone tried to resist him then this old man would threaten him and say, 'On this particular day, at such a particular time, you will die!' At different times attempts were made to kill him, premeditated attempts, plain for all to see. But when these men approached to kill him, he would thwart them all by shooting claws in their direction and they would fail in their purpose. Or, if he did not shoot claws, he would use feathers, stripped to the quill. Then before they reached their home, they would be dead. Even individuals who had no children, even individuals who had no wives, even such he killed.[53]

At last, in desperation, the people approached a very holy Winnebago, a young man, and made him a tobacco offering. This man took his arrows and the peculiar sound that he had obtained from the spirit called *Heroka*, He-Without-Horns, and then he made his way to the old man's lodge. The old man received him by shooting claws at him. But they did not kill this Winnebago. He caught the claws and pressed on. In fact, after he had collected a handful of these claws, he took them to the old man and said, 'Here take these claws back. Apparently you are in the habit of using them.' He gave them back to the old man. Then the young man sent out his breath toward the fireplace. Then he directed the special *heroka-shout* straight into the center of the fireplace and dispatched an arrow at the old man. The old man bounced forward violently and fell headlong into the center of the fireplace, dead . . .

So did they kill this old man. Nevertheless we still possess the powers he had and we shall include them in our greetings. Members

156

of the Rite, all of you, we greet you. Ancestors, we greet you, we greet you! (completion song)

G H O S T : Ancestors, we send forth our greetings to you. We must immediately proceed with the dance song as well as with our life-engendering greetings. One can never extend enough of them to Rite members, we have always been told. Ancestors, we greet you, we greet you! (dance song)

2 . THE SECOND NIGHT

G H O S T : Ancestors, we send forth our greetings to you. In the beginning the members of the Rite were extremely attentive to the ceremony. They left absolutely nothing undone. All the members, far and wide, would be asked to attend and, when they sang their songs, it was to a full lodge. When they danced, their gourds did not rattle. When they arose to extend the life-engendering greetings, throughout the lodge they resounded. When they had finished the dance songs and the dance, then they would again extend the greetings. Then they would sit down and again the greetings would go around. After they had sat down for the last time, when everyone had gone through his part, then and only then would they stop. Not before that moment, would anyone ever go home.

In the beginning, the person to be newly initiated, He-for-whom-we-seek-life, was not given four sacred shells. He was not allowed to do anything. After he had once entered the ceremonial lodge, he was not allowed to leave it until the ceremony was completely over. Nor was he allowed to stretch out his arms when he shot the sacred missile.[54] Not any of these actions was he permitted to indulge in.

In the beginning thus they acted and so has it been handed down to us. In this Rite the privilege of doing certain things is acquired slowly. Not right off can a person expect to participate fully in everything. Thus did the old people speak. Ancestors, we greet you, we greet you! (completion song)

G H O S T : Ancestors, we send forth our greetings to you. And now we shall immediately have our messenger, the drum, make its appearance and then we shall extend to all the Rite-members gathered here the life-engendering greetings. Ancestors, we greet you, we greet you! (dance song)

G H O S T : Ancestors, we send forth our greetings to you. In the old days if a person had acquired the new light and life, it was a real thing and meant something. Then all those who were admitted to membership really obtained this new life. Now they do not. In those days if a newly initiated member had been permitted to see the sacred shell, he would surely have died. In those days there were really seers, people really saw visions and were blessed. They would live to attain a good old age. Later on these seers became poisoners and these poisoners would attempt to destroy those members of the Rite who possessed true knowledge and who were virtuous. Again and again it happened that a virtuous and prominent member of the Rite would be killed. How, under such circumstances, could one expect to attain long life? Ancestors, we greet you, we greet you! (completion song)

G H O S T : Ancestors, we send forth our greetings to you. A song, one dealing with fear-inspiring matters, these old people knew. With that song, that evil one, am I now supposed to greet you. Such is the tradition. Ancestors, we greet you, we greet you! (completion song)

G H O S T : Ancestors, we send forth our greetings to you. We extend our life-engendering greeting to the ceremonial lodge and to all the members of the Rite, everyone specifically, assembled there. Ancestors, we greet you, we greet you! (dance song)

G H O S T : Ancestors, we send our greetings to you. My elders told me that the Rite members possess many privileged actions and that we should try to emulate their actions if we desire to go to the spirit-home. That is what we intend to do and that is why we have

158

come here, to extend the life-engendering greetings to those present. May evil never come upon us and may all those who have been the object of compassion, secure the life that is scattered about this lodge as the members speed around it! May we reach the destination that has been promised us! Ancestors, we greet you, we greet you! (completion song)

G H O S T : Ancestors, we send forth our greetings to you. The dance song is now to be started immediately and so we extend the life-engendering greeting to all the old people assembled in this lodge, those with whom we shall soon play,[55] those whom we shall join in the Spirit-Lodge where we make our plea for light and life. Ancestors, we greet you, we greet you! (dance song)

G H O S T : Ancestors, we send forth our greetings to you. It was He-whom-we-call-our-nephew, Hare, who sought some way for us to live happily and securely. We had not been living well or securely before that and, only after He-whom-we-call-our-nephew, Hare, secured this new life for us did we know peace and well-being. This he obtained not only for us but for our children and our posterity.

My elders are not responsible for my acts of omission. They were assiduous enough in teaching me the ways of this ceremony. They only taught me what was good. It is through this Rite that I am still hale and hearty, that my skin is still wrapped around my bones, that I still can eat. Ancestors, we greet you, we greet you! (completion song)

G H O S T : Ancestors, we send forth our greeting to you. The dance song will now be sung and then we will once more extend the life-engendering greeting to you before we rest. Ancestors, we greet you, we greet you! (dance song)

G H O S T :   Ancestors, we send forth our greetings to you. Great has been the blessing you have brought us. You have brought us into connection with life. But we are not Rite members nor are we capable of doing anything. Yet, despite this, you desired us to receive this new life, to obtain ever additional life. It is good. How could it not be good? You have acted as if we were prominent and distinguished people.

We are proud to have had true living come to us. It was He-whom-we-call-our-nephew, Hare, who sought for and found, this refuge-place for us. That is how we procured the knowledge of this Rite, from him. He it was gave us this good counsel. It is indeed good.

Our elders told us about it. 'See to it that you are blessed and that you are properly thankful and grateful.' But how is it possible not to be thankful for the blessings our elders enabled us to obtain? The song they told us to sing, however, that we cannot do for, unfortunately, we are not like them. Nevertheless we shall try.

Once, many years ago, one of our ancestors sustained a loss. 'How am I to face it, how can I restore my peace of mind and be happy again?' he thought to himself. And then suddenly he thought, 'Thus will I do.' Up as far as the creator, he sent his thoughts. He tried to penetrate to the Creation-Lodge. Then far down below, to our grandmother, Earth, he made his thoughts travel. Thus far shall they go, he thought. Thus far did he make his own feelings known. In this fashion did he obtain solace.

From this the moral follows that when one suffers a loss through death, do not walk around excited, tearing things up in your violence. Such grief serves only to make your mind troubled. If you must cry, let your tears drop gently on the best of all grandmothers, Earth. So will your mind really attain peace when you weep, and it is this peace of mind, this happy weeping which will bring you solace and the only true life.

Our grandmother, Earth, has opened up a new day for us and our elders, through their utterances, have provided us with ample means

160

for securing a new life. Their words have led us to life, to the light and life we see spread all about us. It is good.

He-whom-we-call-our-nephew, Hare, was able to obtain this ceremony for our benefit and he assured us, so it is said, that we would never fail to secure this life.

But now we are to utter our cry for the ghost of the recently departed, to beg him to leave behind, for us, the residue of years still his due. The Tear-Pouring will now begin. Ancestors, we greet you, we greet you! (mourning song)

G H O S T : Ancestors, we send forth our greetings to you. In a moment we shall begin to make our plea for life. He-whom-we-call-our-nephew, Hare, trampled under foot all the evil spirits as he forced his way eastward on that memorable journey that was to bring us a new life. For this purpose only did he undertake that journey. So runs the story. Ancestors, we greet you, we greet you! (completion song)

G H O S T : Ancestors, we send forth our greetings to you. Now the dance song is to appear as an evidence of our gratitude. We have been told from time immemorial to express our gratitude in this manner just as we have always been told to extend the life-begetting greetings to all the various spirits, to all the possessors of open-faced birdskin pouches, in fact, to all the feaster-participants gathered around the lodge. Ancestors, we greet you, we greet you! (dance song)

G H O S T : Ancestors, we send forth our greetings to you. The original men, those to whom the term Medicine Rite men was first applied, were not initiated into the ceremony by human words and human utterances. Let me tell you about one of them.

'My various grandfathers,' so this man said, 'founded this Rite and, from then on, they began to initiate new members and instruct them. It was far in the distant past that this took place. Since then new members have always been initiated by others. But this is not true of me,' so the man continued. 'I was initiated directly, in the way in which my distant grandfathers had been, by the spirits who presided over the first Creation-Lodge. They told me to shoot the sacred missile at them immediately upon my entering the Creation-Lodge. Nor did they place me in the center of the lodge. They regarded me as holy and particularly blessed with supernatural power.'

The song that this man composed, this I was ordered to sing for you here. May it serve as a life-engendering greeting to all of you! Ancestors, we greet you, we greet you! (completion song)

G H O S T :   Ancestors, we send forth our greetings to you. With a number of dance songs, I shall now try to greet you, with those very ones that were used when our distant forefathers first entered the Creation-Lodge. Ancestors, we greet you, we greet you! (dance song)

G H O S T :   Ancestors, we send forth our greetings to you. Our forefathers had many customs and practices connected with this Rite. They always insisted that the Rite members should be of mutual insistence to one another in order thus to discover the means of obtaining possessions. In such manner have I been told did true members behave in the past and should they behave in the present. Always to be good and virtuous, always to beseech our ancestors to have compassion upon us. Thus must we, too, act if we do not wish to be forever limited by lack of knowledge to the right to have certain privileges. If we behave otherwise and just stay put, do not improve ourselves, we are bound to cause our fellow members to become uneasy and nervous.

Not anything do I amount to, that I know, yet I pine for some raiment for my body, some knowledge and privileges. I long for some food though I am not entitled to participate in the ceremonial feasts because I have failed so signally. Let me however start my song now, the song that is to serve as a life-engendering greeting for all of you. Ancestors, we greet you, we greet you! (completion song)

G H O S T :   Ancestors, we send forth our greetings to you. We must at once, without delay, begin the dance song. Ancestors, we greet you, we greet you! (dance song)

162

G H O S T :   Ancestors, we send forth our greetings to you. We have always tried to have all the members of the Rite have compassion upon us and enable us to be blessed. We are but naked men, originally without possessions, except for what the creator bestowed upon us after he had finished his work and had distributed to the various spirits the powers they were to have. The amount of life we then had was so small that it seemed no greater in size than are the tiniest insects that cover the earth. Almost invisible it was. Indeed not even as long as these insects was our life. To the beings the creator had fashioned before he made us, he had given such life-bestowing powers that what remained for us was really but half a life. We did not even have the power of looking into the future. And so we were inferior to every other being that existed. Then did the creator bestow a gift upon us, tobacco, the prayer-compelling means of life, the object through which we might obtain life.

Thus did our forefathers obtain from the creator, tobacco, the prayer-compelling means of life. So have we been told and so do we pass it on. Ancestors, we greet you, we greet you! (completion song)

G H O S T :   Ancestors, we send forth our greetings to you. In a moment, our announcer, the drum, will be sounded. Let that serve as an expression of the thanks and gratitude we all feel for being invited to this Rite. Let it be our life-engendering greeting to those present today. We greet you, we greet you! (dance song)

4. THE FOURTH NIGHT

G H O S T :   Ancestors, we send forth our greetings to you. Tonight we shall have to proceed fast for tomorrow we are going to see our elders face to face and extend our life-engendering greetings to them in person. But now we have time for but one song apiece. Tonight we shall have a chance to sleep well again and so we shall, at once, send along our greetings to you, ancestors, and proceed with the Tear-Pouring ceremony. Here is our dance song. Ancestors, we greet you, we greet you! (mourning song)

G H O S T :   Ancestors, we send forth our greetings to you. It is time for us now to continue with our prayers for life and so we send you, as a life-engendering greeting, a completion song. Ancestors, we greet you, we greet you! (completion song)

G H O S T :   Ancestors, we send forth our greetings to you. In a moment we shall have to call upon our messenger, the drum, to make his appearance and then we shall send a song to you as our life-engendering greeting. Ancestors, we greet you, we greet you! (dance song)

G H O S T :   Ancestors, we send forth our greetings to you. We must speak rapidly and then, when we finish the greetings, have the dance song ready. Ancestors, we greet you, we greet you! (completion song)

G H O S T :   Ancestors, we send forth our greetings to you. But we cannot pause. Here is the dance song, sent to you as a life-engendering greeting. Ancestors, we greet you, we greet you! (dance song)

G H O S T :   Ancestors, we send forth our greetings to you. Again we cannot pause. Here is a life-engendering greeting for you to serve as an evidence of our gratitude and thankfulness. Tonight, as we sing for you and greet you, we hope to receive your greetings in return. We pray that evil fortune never befall us. Ancestors, we greet you, we greet you! (completion song)

G H O S T :   Ancestors, we send forth our greetings to you. In a moment we shall attempt to bring you a song. This dance song originated in the following manner . . .

Once an old man, a member of the Medicine Rite, blessed with great powers, said, 'If I should die and you should have pity on me and dance in my honor, then I will always be there behind each dancer. When you pour out a handful of tobacco in my honor, I shall arise and dance behind you although not visible to any one' . . .

164

And now the song of that old man we shall intone. Ancestors, we greet you, we greet you! (dance song)

G H O S T :   Ancestors, we send forth our greetings to you. When we are on the way to our destination and approach the Creation-Lodge, see to it that your mind is completely at peace. Cheerfully, happily, must you step into that Road. This, too, remember. As you walk along that Road toward the Creation-Lodge, should you stumble and fall to the ground, do not get angry. Instead, have recourse to the various ceremonial utterings which the Rite members possess and rise from the ground in the very best of spirits. Let the birdskin pouches lead us on and be our example. But now, a song is about to appear.

It is of no consequence if we fall asleep from fatigue tonight, for we are headed where the kindly birdskin pouches lead. We cannot lag or stay behind for, then, evil would befall us. Ancestors, we greet you, we greet you. (tobacco pipe song)

G H O S T :   Ancestors, we send forth our greetings to you. We are finished but, tomorrow, we are to start on the journey which will lead to our destination.

VII. The Preparatory Four Nights of South's Band

1 .   THE FIRST NIGHT

S O U T H :   Ancestors, we send forth our greeting to you. This is the story that has come down to us, the story of a Medicine Rite member who had sustained a great loss. 'How am I going to bear it?' So he thought to himself. And this is what he did. Down into the very depths of the earth did he send the thoughts that he was carrying within himself. Above to where the creator sits he sent them. To every one of our forefathers, to each one in turn, he made these thoughts travel. Finally, he sent them out so that they penetrated below the earth itself. His thoughts of how he could regain peace of mind had now reached one of the great waterspirits. There he was helped. And now he was rewarded—his desires and thoughts caused light and life to burst forth from the Creation-Lodge. To his descendants, down to the present time, has he dispatched his thoughts and his desires. And so it can be said, even in that far-off time, he was thinking of me. It is good.

Not only to me did he bring this new light and life. He obtained it for all of us. He brought all his relatives, sitting assembled here, into connection with life. We are all enveloped in life in consequence. He has made me, in particular, try to live and enter into life. It is good . . .

To my great forebear there once came a certain spirit, an exceedingly white wolf (?), to exchange puffs with him. He stretched himself and was soon there bringing with him the material for smoking, the-means-of-asking-for-life which He-whom-we-call-our-nephew, Hare, had secured. Opening his tobacco-pouch, he walked toward the center of the lodge. He seized hold of this tobacco, this means-of-obtaining-life and, holding it in his hands, he crunched it and mixed it with the chief of all trees, the oak.[56] Then he filled the pipe and lit it. Four times he puffed at the pipe he had lit, and with every draught he imbibed, he scattered around the lodge, the whitest, the most sacred, type of light and life. Four times he drew in the tobacco smoke and, suddenly, he became very old. Like a person wearing moccasins, so worn out that only the tops remained, such was his appearance. The hairs on his back were gone save a few that stuck out here and there.

The lodge had now become entirely filled with smoke. In fact the whole earth, throughout its breadth and length, was filled with the haze of this smoke. And now the odor of tobacco permeated the whole world till it reached the lodge of the spirits, every lodge of every spirit. There they lay, expectant, and filled with longing for it. Life they had, but they desired more, as He-whom-we-call-our-nephew, Hare, had said . . .

166

Ancestors, we greet you, we greet you!

Then he fills his pipe, lights it and puffs, first toward the east, then toward the north, then toward the west and, finally, toward the south. Then he extends the pipe toward the one nearest to him who, after accepting it, thanks him with an 'Ancestors, we greet you.' This man then smokes the pipe, takes four puffs and stops. He now, in turn, extends the pipe to the next person and when this one is ready he seizes it, passes the greeting along, takes four puffs and extends it to the fourth one. And thus it goes, from person to person, until all have received the pipe and taken four puffs.

When the smoking ceremony is over then the leader rises and extending his greeting to those present addresses them as follows:

S O U T H : Ancestors, we send forth our greetings to you. The lodge of our distant grandfathers lay there completely filled with smoke and, in the middle, stood my forebear. Not steady on his legs did he stand but trembling as if afraid to walk.

The hairs and dandruff drop into the plates of the bereaved when they are eating and so they cease eating.[57] The sinews that bind together the poles of the sacred-lodge have worked themselves loose and we must tighten them by speech and song and prayer, tighten them so that the bereaved can make themselves whole again. The plate is overturned [58] from which one of our members had eaten. It must be turned up again and filled with food so that some child, some well-beloved one, can eat thereof. Bowed and lowered is the head of the birdskin pouch tonight.

But soon, very soon, indeed three days from now, light and life will be brought to us and upright, erect, the head of the birdskin pouch will become again. Any observant and virtuous member of the Rite can see to it that his child, his well-beloved one can arise [59] and be blessed with life at this Rite. Let us then proceed and offer up our prayers for light and life; let us raise our voices that this dearly beloved child receive it. More than this. It behooves every observant and virtuous Rite member who has sustained a loss to make a humble plea to the ghost of the departed that he leave behind for us all that which was still his due. So should he make his piteous cry.

But now we must start the Tear-Pouring ritual. Ancestors, we greet you, we greet you! (mourning song)

167

s o u t h : Ancestors, we send forth our greetings to you. In a moment we shall renew our pleas for life just as, in the past, people made these self-same pleas, uttered these self-same words and had the life-engendering greetings come and go from one person to the other. Ancestors, we greet you, we greet you! (completion song)

s o u t h : Ancestors, we send forth our greetings to you. In the beginning, when they gave a performance of the Rite and a plate was to be turned upright, all who were to fill it, crowded to attend the Rite. Everyone would dance. Nor would they shake their gourd rattles when they stood up. Only this ceremony could give them a peaceful life. Never would it be unquiet. In those days, if a person was not able to take part in certain ceremonies, then he would just get up and extend a life-engendering greeting as a gesture of respect. Ancestors, we greet you, we greet you! (dance song)

s o u t h : Ancestors, we send forth our greetings to you. Just as morning follows morning, so, day by day, does the number of the members of the Rite increase. Never has a renegade been heard of. Never must anyone drop out of the Rite after he has once joined it. At all times must we try to perform this ceremony correctly and with sincerity. Particularly must we be careful to perform the main cere- mony properly and sincerely. Remember, too, that you cannot obtain anything for nothing or in a trifling spirit. When you send your greet- ings to one of our fellow members, do not steal the speeches and songs. If you like some particular utterances, buy them in the proper manner. The members of the Rite are always willing to be ap- proached on such matters. Whatever you ask of them they will grant you.

When the old Rite members look back behind them, they will realize that we are quite in the rear of the line. The Road that stretches in front of us is strewn with those who have fallen down in death. That we, too, should be blessed and die in our time like them, for that do we pray.

So did our ancestors, the founders, speak and so should we speak and act, that we might be blessed and have compassion shown us.

168

Then will we return it in gratitude and thankfulness. And so we send our life-engendering greetings to you gathered around here. Ancestors, we greet you, we greet you! (completion song)

S O U T H : Ancestors, we greet you, we greet you. In a moment we shall start up the dance song as a life-engendering greeting to you. We have been told that one can never have enough of such greetings. Ancestors, we greet you, we greet you! (dance song)

S O U T H : Ancestors, we send forth our greetings to you. He-whom-we-call-our-nephew, Hare, tried to obtain for us a span of life equal to his, but he failed. Then the creator gave us this Medicine Rite, that we might learn it and gain its reward, reincarnation. He told us that if anyone performed it properly, and lived up to its teachings and stayed with it to the end, then, from above, where Earth-maker sits, the ghost might look down upon the earth. From above, he could see how those who lived according to the tenets of the Rite had become reincarnated. If he wished to enter a human body again, he too could do so. Many have been able to do this in the past, all those, indeed, who performed the ceremonies of the Rite properly and sincerely and who remained firm and loyal to the end. Today, unfortunately, we cannot do it any more. Ancestors, we greet you, we greet you! (completion song)

S O U T H : Ancestors, we send forth our greetings to you. In a moment, we shall extend a dance song to serve as a life-engendering greeting to you in accordance with the custom of our forefathers. Ancestors, we greet you, we greet you! (dance song)

S O U T H : Ancestors, we send forth our greetings to you. In the old days, whenever they were ready to give an enjoining-rite,[60] they always set plates for the four Rite leaders. They never omitted any one of these four from their invitations. Now we, too, have plates for four leaders and we, like our forefathers, will ask that those assembled here take pity on us and grant us the possibilities for living

169

well and contented, in other words, for living on earth as they did. We ask this of you. It is good. It is not within our power to extend to you greetings of the truly life-giving qualities of our forefathers. But since it would not be respectful for us to sit here without saying anything so we shall say what we have to say. Ancestors, we greet you, we greet you! (completion song)

s o u t h :   Ancestors, we send forth our greetings to you. In a moment, the dance song will appear and that is all I have to offer you. Ancestors, we greet you, we greet you! (dance song)

2 . THE SECOND NIGHT

s o u t h :   Ancestors, we send forth our greetings to you. When a man first joins this Rite he can participate in it only to a small extent. If such a person has been initiated he cannot, without the proper right to do so, indulge in any ceremonial activities. These he must purchase from an older member. Unfortunately I was not able to purchase anything. The leaders of the Rite, it is true, told me it is good to buy something from all four of them, but I have been unable to buy from any one of them. The best I could do was to buy a few privileges, few indeed. That is how important I am! Yet that much, the purchase of a few privileges, I did do. My elders forced me to do this when I joined this Rite.

In the old days and today, too, whenever a person wishes to show his affection for a child, he has him become a member of this sacred ceremony. It was for his happiness and welfare they did it. Now, if my elders had not done that for me, I would have died of hunger long ago. That would have happened to my father likewise. When my father spoke to me about it, I, in my ignorance, thought the matter of less consequence and easier to obtain than he stated it to be. Yet my elders assured me that there would be a day when I, myself, would realize that I was without food. For that reason they kept on encouraging me and said to me:

170

'Grandson, try your best. If you work diligently in this Rite, the members will see to it that you have ample food to eat and ample clothes to wear. Perhaps you never thought of that. They will bring this apparel and place it in front of you. So, grandson, you will be actually helping yourself materially by paying proper attention to this Rite. Not only we, but all those ancestors of yours who have preceded you in the Medicine Rite, will step into your footsteps, the footsteps that lie still before you. You will be securing yourself for the future. Then as you get older, so will your security increase. The members in the Rite will show more and more solicitude for you, give you increased blessings. After a while, as you begin to approach the end of your life, they will take complete care of you. This it is that your ancestors planned for you and this is why they and I have so persistently begged you to work zealously and hard in this ceremony. They wished you to have many people following you and helping you.

'Then, finally, when you die of old age,' so they used to say, 'when your body falls to pieces, you will be at the end of this Road. But the Medicine Road will still stretch before you. Take your staff and proceed until you can get a firm hold on the tree, the frog-leg, to your left. That tree is a red cedar tree, a chief tree, with a smooth bark, smooth and blackened from frequent usage. Hold it tight, for that frog-leg is imprinted with light and life. The staff with which you supported yourself that also belonged to one of your ancestors.[61] They helped to imprint the tree with light and life as they seized it and they hoped that you, too, would come to do the same. All your ancestors who lived up to the tenets and instructions of the Rite, finally came to the place where Earthmaker sits, up above. From there you will see, down below, men and women performing the ceremonies of the Rite, performing them well. Then you will realize that your elders must have had confidence in you and that what they did for you was only for your good. Then, indeed, you will say to yourself that they probably would have been satisfied had you done a little less.' Thus they spoke to me.

As a result I actually exceeded them in performance. How then could I be so disrespectful as to reject their invitation and yours?

It was because I know only too well how inconsequential I am that I always try to do my best.

I greet you, I greet you, O ancestors, and in a moment I will have the announcer, the drum, appear, to bring to you a life-engendering greeting. Ancestors, we greet you, we greet you! (completion song)

S O U T H :   Ancestors, we greet you, we greet you. We shall start up the dance song immediately for those whose body and whose resolve to continue has become weakened in their efforts to secure a position and prestige in life at this Rite. It is for the attainment of such a position in life that I am exerting all my efforts to be holy and that I shall try to live up to all my duties and obligations in this ceremony. In such fashion did my forefathers live and so they enjoined me to act. With all this in view I shall now start up the dance song and make our pleas for life. Ancestors, we greet you, we greet you! (dance song)

S O U T H :   Ancestors, we send forth our greetings to you. The major ceremony is soon to be given and, at this ceremony, all those who perform it well, will make those members who have died, happy. So we have been told. All those who have preceded us in this Rite and who knew it well, all of them, down to the present, will feel happy. Indeed all those who lived up to its precepts in the distant past and who now lie mixed and mingled with the soil, they will regain consciousness and be alive and conscious just as we are again. They will come crowding to the cleared space before our lodge. No sleep will be possible for us, these Indians of long ago assured us.

They who knew this Rite so well and obtained life therein will be walking to and fro before our lodge. Not to make us nervous and uneasy of course, but, on the contrary, to make us happy. Whenever they meet one another in this walking to and fro, they extend the life-greeting and they join that band to which they belonged at the end of their life. So likewise they invite their own Medicine Rite members to take part in the singing. There they are outside, jostling

172

one another, crowding about one another, longing and yearning for us and to be of use to us.

Only in the spirit, as ghosts, can our ancestors crowd around the entrance to our lodge, yet we hope they will be there. Ancestors, we greet you, we greet you! (completion song)

SOUTH : Ancestors, we send forth our greetings to you. The dance song is about to appear again and, perhaps, some of the members of long ago who stand outside will have compassion upon us and show this compassion by joining in my song. Perhaps they will pour a handful of tobacco for me as I dance and I shall pour one for them in return. These ancestors of mine will not know I am doing it but I will be doing it nevertheless. Ancestors, we greet you, we greet you! (dance song)

SOUTH : Ancestors, we send forth our greetings to you. In a moment the messenger, the drum, will be heard. All the spirits whom the creator formed will be gathering around to listen to their messenger and announcer. Even the creator himself, up above, will not disdain to do so. What we so ardently desire, Earthmaker, up above in the highest heavens, will hearken to. As he listens to his messenger drumming aloud our desires and requests he will tell all the spirits gathered within the Creation-Lodge to pay heed to them. This is what, sitting up above there in the clouds, Earthmaker will tell those whom he formed with his own hands. For all these who belong to the Medicine Rite, the drum, when it is sounded, will announce their desires and requests. Cry out the pity-inspiring plaints for life and well-being, will this messenger do. And he will beg us in his drum-voice to live properly and piously.

They say that when a person has some dearly-beloved child for whom he desires to seek light and life, whom he wishes to have initiated, he makes his plea to those in the Rite that they pray for new life for his child. He asks the Rite members to raise their voices to secure for him a long, a good life, on earth. Would that the helping light and life our grandfather gave us does not remain invisible and unseen by those many spirits toward whom we are speeding! They will recognize us, so the messenger of the spirits told us.

As we are about to start on that journey, we pray that we will not have to tread into anything evil. Such is our hope and plea. To the messenger who is now to make his appearance, of him we ask that he inform all those in the Creation-Lodge, of our desires so that they will become cognizant of our existence. Ancestors, we greet you, we greet you! (completion song)

s o u t h :   Ancestors, we send forth our greetings to you. In a moment, the dance song will appear and, with it, a pious, life-begetting greeting. That is how we should greet one another, our forefathers always insisted. And this we shall do as far as it lies within our powers to do so. But we are not able to give you any true spirit utterances. Would that we could! Instead we extend to you our life-engendering greetings, in a single song. Ancestors, we greet you, we greet you! (dance song)

s o u t h :   Ancestors, we send forth our greetings to you. I obtained little indeed from my grandfathers. They did try to teach me many of the things that I see you performing, but all to no avail. They enjoined me not to attempt to make an impression on you by talking too much or by being supercilious. 'If you do,' they said, 'some Medicine Rite members may think that you are depreciating them. Particularly be careful not to brag about your greatness before you are entitled to because of age and merit. If you do, some of the more prominent members may get to dislike you. You will not live long this way. No time will elapse before they will dip you into the earth, to lie there with our grandmother. So, above all be considerate and modest.

'Be advised. When you first enter the Medicine Rite lodge and take your place, you will not be in possession of any ceremonial privileges. Do not then carry yourself as if you were. Whatever action the others order you to perform, do it. If an older member of the Rite asks you to do some work for him, be proud to oblige him and be

174

happy at being asked to do so. You will be really using something that belongs to me. But above all, do not spy upon people.[62]

'In this way, all those in the lodge will like you and you will be able to reach a good old age. You will have obtained this life not because of anything about you, personally, but because you have acted with propriety and consideration.

'You must buy the right to perform certain actions and then, if you have bought enough of them, when you reach old age, you will be in a position to do anything you wish. You can cut across the lodge directly,[63] instead of having to make the regular circuit around it. Yet about one thing let me warn you. Do not try to buy privileges from all the four leaders. Buy less.[64] If you were to buy from all the four leaders and you did not live up to the obligations they entailed, you would injure yourself. In fact you might kill yourself.

'Never let yourself have doubts about this Rite, and do as I tell you.'

I, myself, am not able to do many of these things, but listen to me anyhow and do you try to do them. Ancestors, we greet you, we greet you! (completion song)

S O U T H : Ancestors, we send forth our greetings to you. In a moment the dance song will appear and we will send our life-engendering greetings to all the Medicine Rite members assembled here, to the Creation-Lodge and to the feasters sitting about us. We greet you all. It is said that one can never do enough of these greetings. Ancestors, we greet you, we greet you! (dance song)

3. THE THIRD NIGHT

S O U T H : Ancestors, we send forth our greetings to you. Anyone who ponders over the matter for a moment will realize that what our ancestors said and the actions they performed in this ceremony were good and valuable. It is because Hare flashed his eyes in concentration upon them in order to create this Rite, that you are alive.

175

The thoughts of our distant grandfathers, their interest in us, was never secret. He who created this Rite knows you.

He-whom-we-call-our-nephew, Hare, who is up above in the blue sky, he will know everything you think, will even know when you just raise your eyebrows. If anyone were to doubt what our ancestors attained in this ceremony—but, of course, such doubt is impossible—he will do injury to his own body. But he, on the contrary, who never doubts, his existence will ever be happy and peaceful.

That is why my ancestors wished me to act properly and circumspectly. But I was incapable of learning how to speak as they did. I knew that what they were saying was good yet I remained inattentive. Had I been attentive and pious, I know that I would be able to do what they told me to do, correctly. They wished me to be attentive and willing so that the spirits could show their compassion toward me. They were trying to teach me something that was good in itself and also useful to me. This they were doing, but all to no avail. Ancestors, we greet you, we greet you! (completion song)

S O U T H :   Ancestors, we send forth our greetings to you. The dance song is now about to be heard. If I could say anything, I would be greatly delighted to do so. It is good to be the means of asking for life. But it is quite beyond my powers. Let me simply greet you with a dance song. Ancestors, we greet you, we greet you! (dance song)

S O U T H :   Ancestors, we send forth our greetings to you. My grandfathers have known the sacred spirit songs and utterances from the very beginning of this Rite. They did not have to wait to receive them as gifts.[65] Anyone who was attentive could learn them, anyone who was attentive could understand them. They were willing to instruct anyone who was interested. They tried to make my grandfather interested and they did. He learned them and that is why he was able to live such a prosperous and happy life. 'If, then, any person is attentive to the ways and teachings of his ancestors,' so they spoke to me, 'and becomes versed in the knowledge of the Rite, to

176

such a one I will pass on what I know. Then, in peace of mind, I can depart and I will know I have not lived in vain. The song I wish you to know, here it is. That is what I wished to say to you.'

So my grandfathers and my father. Ancestors, we greet you, we greet you! (completion song)

s o u t h :   Ancestors, we send forth our greetings to you. The dance song will appear in a moment. In the meantime let me greet you, ancestors. Here is the messenger, the drum. Ancestors, we greet you, we greet you! (dance song)

s o u t h :   Ancestors, we send forth our greetings to you. Even though I am unable to offer you any adequate kind of thanks, I will ask you to have compassion upon me and bless me. That much, possibly, I may ask. With songs, at any rate, I can greet all of you assembled here. But I was told that if one is too weak and inconspicuous to be able to extend enough life-engendering greetings, there is always some Rite member to whom one can appeal, some one with ample knowledge. If one appeals to him, gladly and graciously will he comply with your request. By doing this, not only will you be helping yourself now, but you will be providing for yourself in the future. Indeed there will be more ahead of you than you have at the present.

An old man once had a son and he spoke to him as follows . . .

'My son, in the old days, our ancestors did not bestow the knowledge of the Rite upon a child just because they happened to love him. To have done so they would have been regarded as iniquitous and evil. Such knowledge is not taught to anyone, no matter how much he is loved, without recompense. No one would be able to obtain a secure existence in that fashion. You must learn to help yourself.

'To obtain this knowledge it is necessary, first, to be respectful to, and considerate of, one's parent, and to make him realize that you are prepared to endure hardships for the knowledge you desire to obtain from him. Remember, he had in his time to do the same. So, my son, try hard! Help yourself and then you will acquire the knowledge that will enable you to live in peace. It is proper to seek a blessing for a child dear to you, but only in this way. Try hard, my son! There is no other way of obtaining a happy existence here.

'A father always hopes and wishes his son to acquire his knowledge and his powers. He does not wish him to go to someone else and pay all this attention to a stranger. So, I repeat, even if a man loved his son deeply he should never make a present to him of the knowledge he possessed. That would be like borrowing something without returning it. Such knowledge would only spell death for the recipient. Try, then, to obtain knowledge properly and only from your own people!' . . .

They tell another story of how a man spoke to his son and said, 'O, my son, you have raised my spirits by your conduct. Indeed you will reach the bottom of the tree.'[66] This man, at the time, was in the act of using his powers for transforming himself into a night-walker. This power he placed before his son. Then a food-mixer he placed before him and a bundle. Again he brought him another bundle and told him that it contained medicines with which to cause blindness. Then he brought forward all the other important medicines which he had possessed but had always kept hidden and secreted, all the numerous grasses and herbs, the hair of our grandmother, Earth, as well as all the plants he knew. These he placed before his beloved son, gave them to him as a gift, so that he could help and improve himself. The songs he possessed, these too, he gave him, as well as the sacred speeches of our leaders that were delivered in the far distant past and that have come down to us, down to our very last Rite leader. The ancestors of the father blew these sacred speeches, as it were, into his very mouth. 'And this they did to me,' the man said to his son. 'Not one did they omit as I sat there, mouth wide open' . . .

Now all these utterances, these speeches and songs, that were blown into the mouths of our ancestors, all these, we, too, have

178

learned and we will present them to you as a gift and have them sung for you as a life-engendering greeting. Ancestors, we greet you, we greet you! (completion song)

S O U T H :   Ancestors, we send forth our greetings to you. In a moment we will have the dance song appear. Soon, O nephew, you who are to be initiated, will receive from us a blanket and you will be granted your wish of participating in the Rite. So that you might practice our dance song, we will now make it appear. Ancestors, we greet you, we greet you! (dance song)

S O U T H :   Ancestors, we send forth our greetings to you. The following tale will illustrate how, at the beginning, they were able to accomplish so much when they were zealous in their attention to this Rite . . .

Once there lived a very powerful Medicine Rite man,[67] honored and respected by the whole community. He had an only son and, because he was his only son, he had no knowledge of things. Never had he been told anything. But one day the father began giving him the various things he possessed. Then he put on a kettle for him and spoke to him. 'Dearest son of mine, be brave, become a real warrior!' 'What can he be meaning?' the son thought to himself. 'He must have something in mind when he makes me these gifts and speaks of my being brave.'

The father continued with his presents. He gave him his precious horse, the only one he possessed and, again, addressed him. 'Dearest of sons, in order to know how to become a warrior, one must obtain certain knowledge.' Finally, the son began to understand what his father meant and he acquired this knowledge.

After a while the boy married. His wife belonged to another tribe. She was a very handsome woman. She had very red hair and the young man's father cast longing eyes at her. The son understood and gave his father the woman. 'O, my son, how can I possibly thank you? You have made my spirits rise within me!' Then all that he, the

Medicine Rite man knew he scooped up for his son and gave them to him . . .

The daughter-in-law became sick and died and he made a receptacle from her skull. At the same time he composed a song, the one that I am about to start up for you and that is to serve you as a life-engendering greeting. We greet you, we greet you! (completion song)

s o u t h : Ancestors, we send forth our greeting to you. The dance song is to appear in a moment and we hope, grandfather, that it will be of benefit to you. So the old people used to hope. Ancestors, we greet you, we greet you! (dance song)

4. THE FOURTH NIGHT

s o u t h : Ancestors, we send forth our greetings to you. Tonight there will be some speeches and, then, we will speed up everything. All we shall ask is that the various Rite members concentrate their minds upon our welfare. And so we salute them with a life-engendering greeting. We send our greeting to the possessors of the open-faced birdskin pouches, to our elders attempting to secure light and life, in fact to all who are sitting around this lodge.

We have come together for the sake of a Rite member who has sustained a loss and who is about to make his piteous appeal for help and to mourn for the one he has lost. We wish to add our own appeal to his and, with his relatives, gathered here, to seek light for him, cry out for life. Like him we humbly beseech the ghost of the departed to leave behind, for us, the years he left unlived, the food uneaten, the deeds undone. Such is our request. Ancestors, we greet you, we greet you! (mourning song)

s o u t h : Ancestors, we send forth our greetings to you. The life we have been directed to ask for, for that, we shall now make our appeal at once. Here is a greeting for everyone. The messenger,

180

the drum, is now to make his appearance. Ancestors, we greet you, we greet you! (completion song)

s o u t h : Ancestors, we send forth our greetings to you. Let the dance song be begun immediately, for we have little time for speaking tonight. This dance song is one composed long ago, one that has come to us from the distant past. We offer it to you as a greeting. Ancestors, we greet you, we greet you! (dance song)

s o u t h : Ancestors, we send forth our greetings to you. As I have said before, as soon as we have finished one greeting, we will begin on another. That is the custom. Tomorrow we shall be together with our ancestors, we shall be able to extend to them all, a life-engendering greeting. We ask humbly that no evil befall us till then. That is our one request. Ancestors, we greet you, we greet you! (completion song)

s o u t h : Ancestors, we send forth our greetings to you. Here is a dance song. It must suffice as a greeting. Ancestor, we greet you, we greet you! (dance song)

s o u t h : Ancestors, we send forth our greetings to you. I was told that whenever I was in a hurry, I could use a small number of songs. Here they are and I send them with a greeting. In spite of their inadequacy, may they serve to call forth your pity and compassion and a return greeting from you! That is what we hope; that is what we have been told. But here is the messenger, the drum, to make his announcement. Ancestors, we greet you, we greet you! (completion song)

s o u t h : Ancestors, we send forth our greetings to you. In a moment the dance song will start up and the messenger make his announcement. We send our greetings to all the Rite members here. We greet you, we greet you! (dance song)

s o u t h : Ancestors, we send forth our greetings to you. This will be the last of the Preparatory Nights. Let us then show our birdskin pouches and start up our songs so that we can have our smoke and then go home to sleep. Not long will we be able to sleep, for the preparations for the ceremony are already in progress.

Let us sing our song at once and pray that no evil lies before us. Gently, with peace of mind, we will return. This is enough of words. Ancestors, we greet you, we greet you! (pipe song)

s o u t h :   Ancestors, again we extend our life-engendering greetings to you.

PART TWO

THE RITUAL OF PURIFICATION

On the morning of the Fourth Preparatory Night of his band, which is always the one giving the Medicine Rite, the initiate is sent to get the stone to be used in the Vapor-Bath ritual. He always selects one that is not too heavy for him to carry on his back. Before picking it up he offers it tobacco. As soon as it is brought home it is heated. The initiate, next, is sent out to obtain four oak twigs that should not be more than 2½ feet long. These he must trim, leaving the tops however. Sufficient grass is also obtained for the seats.

When all these things have been secured, the four poles are stuck in the ground at the back of the eastern end of the Medicine Rite lodge and bent so as to form a small Vapor-Bath structure. These poles are the representatives of the four cardinal points. The stone that is to serve as the heating stone is placed in the center.

The people who have been invited have now begun to gather outside. They cannot, however, enter the enclosure until they have been properly greeted by the leader of the Ancestor-Host's Band and the initiate. These two go in turn to the leaders of each of the other four bands and touch their heads with their hands. The order is East Band, North Band, West Band, South Band. When there is a Ghost Band this comes between the West and the South. As soon as a leader has had his head touched, he rises and follows the Host and the initiate into the enclosure, always keeping to the right of them. As they pass any people within the enclosure they give the ceremonial greeting, those greeted responding with a long drawn-out 'ha-a-a!'

As soon as the Ancestor-Host has been informed that everyone has been seated, he rises and speaks:

ANCESTOR-HOST : You who are sitting there, my grandson, I greet. I greet you, too, my friend, and you who impersonate the End-of-the-Road, South. All of you, elders and ancestors, all of you sitting in this lodge, do I greet. I have asked you to come here so that I can give and place firmly in your hands, these tokens of our grandfathers, the means-through-which-we-petition-for-life.[1]

183

Then the Ancestor-Host takes an invitation-stick to which tobacco has been tied and walks to the seat of East. He stops in front of him and speaks:

A N C E S T O R - H O S T :   I greet you, grandfather. I am bringing you the tokens of our grandfathers, the means-through-which-we-petition-for-life and ask you to take hold of them firmly. With them I also bring you the invitation-stick and the tobacco, those possessions of ours through which we can secure a happy existence. When you seize hold of them you must have a pure heart. Indeed contact with them will give you a pure heart.

When he is finished, he approaches the North leader and, standing in front of him, speaks:

A N C E S T O R - H O S T :   I greet you, my grandson. I touch your head in greeting. I have seen with my own eyes the blessing you have given me. It is good. I am thankful. When people speak to you of a life that has been blessed they are not thinking of material existence.

You have come here to bless me, to have compassion upon me. I am happy. In gratitude and thankfulness I return to you what is yours anyhow, the tokens of our grandfathers,[2] tied to tobacco, as well as the invitation-sticks tied to tobacco. It is through you that my existence has been made so complete.

Ancestor-Host now greets East and walks around the lodge until he stands in front of the band that impersonates the West. There he stops, extends the ceremonial greeting, and speaks:

A N C E S T O R - H O S T :   I greet you, my friend, and I offer you the small amount of life-imploring materials I possess. I give back to you what is yours. Here, too, is the invitation-stick with tobacco tied to it. I am thankful and grateful. Through you I have lived.

Then Ancestor-Host walks on until he comes to the Ghost Band. There he stops, extends the ceremonial greeting, touches the head of the leader and speaks:

184

A N C E S T O R - H O S T :   I give you my greeting. I am going to give you now what you deserve. Here is an invitation-stick. You, O leader of the Ghost Band, have given me the only life I know.

Ancestor-Host now gives the leader of the band a number of red invitation-sticks, tied together, as well as a tobacco bundle. He then thanks the members of the Ghost Band and extends his greeting to them saying, 'Ancestors, we greet you, we greet you.'

Ancestor-Host now approaches South, the one impersonating the spirit who stands at the End-of-the-Road. He stops in front of the leader, greets her, touches her head and speaks:

A N C E S T O R - H O S T :   I greet you, grandmother.

S O U T H :   He-e-e.

A N C E S T O R - H O S T :   The little I have, I return to you, to whom it belongs, I give it back to you. Here take this invitation-stick and the tobacco. I am very deeply grateful to you for having enabled me to live so completely.

Then he greets the leader and she greets him in return saying, 'Grandfather, it is good.' Ancestor-Host, in his turn, greets all those present, again saying, 'Ancestors, we send you our greetings.' After this, he returns to his own seat but, before he sits down, he speaks as follows:

A N C E S T O R - H O S T :   We will be listening to you, ancestors. We greet you, we greet you, you who sit in the First-Position, my nephew; you who sit there impersonating North; you who sit there impersonating West; you who sit there impersonating Ghost and you who sit there impersonating One-at-the-end-of-the-Road, South.

All now get up, holding the invitation-sticks in their hands, and extend their greetings to Ancestor-Host. Then the second one, the leader of the East Band, after the ceremonial greeting, speaks:

E A S T :   Just as the privilege of standing in front of a leader and his people was used by Ancestor-Host, so will I use it. I thank you. You who sit over there impersonating the Rite-Giver, the Host, I greet you; you who sit over there impersonating North, I greet you; you who sit over there impersonating West, I greet you; you who sit over there impersonating Ghost, I greet you; you who sit over there impersonating the End-of-the-Road, I greet you. I greet you all, ancestors.

Then the leader of the third, the North Band, extends his greeting and speaks:

N O R T H : You who sit over there impersonating the Rite-Giver, the Host, I greet you; you who sit over there impersonating the One-who-was-First, I greet you; you who sit over there impersonating West, I greet you; you who sit over there impersonating Ghost, I greet you; you who sit over there impersonating the End-of-the-Road, I greet you. I greet you all, ancestors. Without waiting, you have honored me with the privilege of standing in front of a leader and his people. I thank you.

Then the leader of the fourth band, West, extends his greeting and speaks:

W E S T : You who sit over there impersonating the Rite-Giver, the Host, I greet you; you who sit over there impersonating the One-who-was-First, I greet you; you who sit over there impersonating North, I greet you; you who sit over there impersonating Ghost, I greet you; you who sit over there impersonating the End-of-the-Road, I greet you. I greet you all, ancestors. Without waiting you have honored me with the privilege of standing in front of a leader and his people. I thank you.

Then the leader of the Ghost Band extends his greeting and speaks:

G H O S T : You who sit over there impersonating the Rite-Giver, the Host, I greet you; you who sit over there impersonating the One-who-was-First, I greet you; you who sit over there impersonating North, I greet you; you who sit over there impersonating West, I greet you; you who sit over there impersonating the End-of-the-Road, I greet you. I greet you all, ancestors. Without waiting, you have honored me with the privilege of standing in front of a leader and his people. I thank you.

Then the old woman, she who impersonates South, the End-of-the-Road, extends her greeting and speaks:

S O U T H :   You who sit over there impersonating the Rite-Giver, the Host, I greet you; you who sit over there impersonating the One-who-was-First, I greet you; you who sit over there impersonating North, I greet you; you who sit over there impersonating West, I greet you; you who sit over there impersonating Ghost, I greet you. I greet you all, ancestors. Without waiting you have honored me with the privilege of standing in front of a leader and his people. I thank you.

All the participants now make the circuit of the lodge four times. The reciprocal greetings are also passed along four times. Then, as each one in his proper turn sits down, he greets all the others again. The one occupying the first seat, Ancestor-Host, with the invitation-stick and the tobacco in his hand, now gets ready to speak.

A N C E S T O R - H O S T :   You who sit over there impersonating the One-who-was-First, I greet you; you who sit over there impersonating North, I greet you; you who sit over there impersonating West, I greet you; you who sit over there impersonating Ghost, I greet you; you who sit over there impersonating the End-of-the-Road, I greet you. I greet you all, ancestors. Ancestors, here is our chief, our means-for-obtaining-life, the invitation-sticks and tobacco. Through them we are to secure the right to be thankful. I, myself, have nothing to tell you. As far as supplying you with the means-for-obtaining-life or bringing you into connection with life, I am like one who cannot speak.

Then he offers them all a handful of tobacco. Ancestor-Host now steps forward to get the fire ready. He takes some tobacco, goes to the east side of the fire and throws some into it, in honor of those who occupy the East position.

A L L   P A R T I C I P A N T S :   E-ho-ho-ho!

Then he goes to the North side of the fire and does the same for the North position.

A L L   P A R T I C I P A N T S :   E-ho-ho-ho!

Then he goes to the West side of the fire and does the same for the West position.

ALL PARTICIPANTS : E-ho-ho-ho!

Then he goes to the South side of the fire and does the same for the South position.

ALL PARTICIPANTS : E-ho-ho-ho!

Ancestor-Host now lights the pipe and then greets the participants with 'I greet you, ancestors, I greet you all.' Then he puffs tobacco toward the East position and makes the leader of the East draw on the pipe. This he repeats for the North, the West, the Ghost and the South positions. Then the East leader takes the pipe and repeats what Ancestor-Host has done. The others— the North, West, Ghost and South follow. The South leader returns the pipe to Ancestor-Host. The latter then rises and speaks:

ANCESTOR - HOST : Ancestors, I greet you. Our forefathers told us that you would have compassion upon us, that you would bring salvation and life to those who appealed to you. Through the words of your mouth, you would do it. I greet you.

Then he makes all the others smoke and they thank him for having brought them the possibility of life and happiness. With this, the smoking ceremony is finished.

Now the leader of the East stands up and greets those present.

EAST : You who sit over there impersonating the Rite-Giver, the Host, I greet you; you who sit over there impersonating North, I greet you; you who sit over there impersonating West, I greet you; you who sit over there impersonating Ghost, I greet you; you who sit over there impersonating the End-of-the-Road, I greet you. I greet you all, ancestors. Through the invitation-sticks, these means we have for designation, you have given us the means-for-invoking-life. I am thankful. You have brought me into connection with life.

From the chief of trees, Earthmaker's tree, you have brought me a branch. You have come here bringing with you the life and light you possessed so that I too might seize hold of the means-for-securing-life. You are about to bring life to my relatives through the utterances of your mouth. Life we are to make use of and that is why I wish you to recognize my greeting. That is the only reason for my saying anything at all.

Ancestors, as many of you as there are seated here, I greet you! Soon, we shall see the birdskin pouches with open faces, all of them. But now I must greet you all, each one in turn. (song)

E A S T :   I shall now return our designators, the invitation-sticks, the means-through-which-we-ask-for-life, to the Ancestor-Host. What we are doing here is for the benefit of myself and my relatives. Unimportant though we are, weak and dependent upon others though we are in our performance, we hope they will be a source of strength to us. And so I now return the invitation-sticks, our means-for-imploring-life, to Ancestor-Host.

Hãhã, ancestors, I have completed my thanks and I now pass it on, the means-for-expressing-thanks, to the one ahead of me, he who sits there impersonating North. We greet you, we greet you!

N O R T H :   Ancestors, I greet you. You who sit over there impersonating the Rite-Giver, the Host, I greet you; you who sit over there impersonating the One-who-was-First, I greet you; you who sit there impersonating West, I greet you; you who sit over there impersonating Ghost, I greet you; you who sit over there impersonating the End-of-the-Road, I greet you. I greet you all, ancestors. I have been allowed to seize hold of the means-for-imploring-life, tobacco. Through these invitation-sticks, I have been brought into connection with a new type of existence. Those here have made me take care of my own welfare. Now I really know what it means to live.

At Earthmaker's home, up above, there exists the chief of trees. Its roots have never dried up, its leaves have never wilted. A branch of this tree was brought down.[3] It sped down through the light of day. Tied firmly to our means-of-imploring-for-life, tobacco, we, through it, have been brought into connection with life. Now I really know what life means. They have made me take care of my own welfare. My relatives have come here with me to seek life and, in a

189

moment, I shall try to make my voice audible to you in song. But first, so I was told, I must secure enough life-engendering greetings.

I send forth my greeting to you. I greet our means-of-imploring-for-life, tobacco; I greet all my relatives attempting to be brought into connection with life. If I succeed in obtaining possession of the life-imploring tobacco, then I know that I and mine will be connected with life and with a happy existence and that we will prosper as we travel along in life. (song)

I cannot speak like the rest of you and, yet, I beseech you, ancestors, to have compassion upon me. Little indeed can I say or do, yet I have held on firmly to the invitation-sticks, our means-of-imploring-for-life, and I know they will be a source of strength to us in our performance. I now pass them back to Ancestor-Host.

I greet you, ancestors, and I pass on to the one ahead of me the means-for-expressing-thanks. I shall now molest the one who, with his thanks, impersonates the Ghost.

G H O S T : You who sit over there impersonating the Rite-Giver, the Host, I greet you; you who sit over there impersonating the One-who-was-First, I greet you; you who sit over there impersonating North, I greet you; you who sit over there impersonating West, I greet you; you who sit over there impersonating the End-of-the-Road, I greet you. I greet you all, ancestors.

They have given me the life-imploring invitation-sticks, tied with tobacco. I have been brought into connection with life. I can say little; I can accomplish little. I have been told, however, that mere greetings, if there are enough of them, suffice.

I greet you, spirit-tobacco; I greet you, invitation-sticks; I greet you, all of you, who are sitting here in the lodge. As I sit here, be assured, I shall say exactly what my own people instructed me to say. I greet the means-of-imploring-for-life. And now let us intone the mourning songs. (songs)

G H O S T : I greet you, ancestors, and I pass on to the one ahead of me, the means-for-expressing-thanks. I shall now molest the one who impersonates the End-of-the-Road, South, with this thanks.

190

S O U T H : You who sit over there impersonating the Rite-Giver, the Host, I greet you; you who sit over there impersonating the One-who-was-First, I greet you; you who sit over there impersonating North, I greet you; you who sit over there impersonating West, I greet you; you who sit over there impersonating Ghost, I greet you. I greet you all, ancestors.

I thank you for the invitation-sticks, the means-of-imploring-for-life. I greet these means, I greet all my relatives who have gathered here to humbly petition you for compassion, for life. Through this tobacco we shall express our gratitude and thankfulness. Life we intend to scatter among ourselves by speech and song. In this way do I desire to greet you. I shall now attempt a song. (song)

When the song is finished South speaks again:

S O U T H : I shall now return the invitation-sticks to Ancestor-Host. I know they will be a source of strength to me and mine in our performance.

Now East rises and speaks again.

E A S T : You who sit over there impersonating the Rite-Giver, the Host, I greet you; you who sit over there impersonating North, I greet you; you who sit over there impersonating West, I greet you; you who sit over there impersonating Ghost, I greet you; you who sit over there impersonating the End-of-the-Road, I greet you. I greet you all, ancestors.

When this Rite was first established this seat and he who sat in it were strong. For me to occupy it now is not becoming or fit. I know nothing and I can do nothing. I have no knowledge of this, your Rite, ancestors. All that I can do is to ask you to have compassion upon me, to bless me. I ask you to excuse me for my incompetence and have compassion upon me. We are to paint ourselves, envelop ourselves with our grandfather, the sacred woman.[4] I direct all of you to do the same.

I, too, will paint and envelop myself with my grandfather. To you, sitting over there who impersonate North, let this be a haven and a

191

destination.[5] To you, too, sitting further along, who impersonate West, let our grandfather, the sacred woman, be as a final destination. This is what I have been told to do by my elders. I send forth my greetings to you.

He who instituted this Vapor-Bath rite liked it and offered up thanks accordingly.

Thus does East speak and thus does he greet:

E A S T :   You sitting still further along, you who impersonate Ghost and you, at the very end, South, you, too, I greet. For you, likewise, let there be this destination. I greet you. But now we have reached the point of undressing, the point of unbinding.

N O R T H :   I, too, greet you and will tell you about the undressing, the unbinding.

W E S T :   I, too, greet you and will tell you about the undressing, the unbinding.

G H O S T :   I, too, greet you and will tell you about the undressing, the unbinding.

S O U T H :   I, too, greet you and will tell you about the undressing, the unbinding.

East now speaks again.

E A S T :   You who sit over there impersonating the Rite-Giver, the Host, I greet you; you who sit over there impersonating North, I greet you; you who sit over there impersonating West, I greet you; you who sit over there impersonating Ghost, I greet you; you who sit over there impersonating the End-of-the-Road, I greet you. I greet you all, ancestors.

I was told that you cannot too often greet our grandfather, the sacred woman, she who is to be our destination and our haven. I greet you. (song)

Then East sends the greetings around again and speaks:

E A S T :   Here in this space, cut off from the rest of the lodge, will be the Vapor-Bath, our haven and destination.

Then East gets up and walks forward greeting North. The latter gets up and follows him. Then East greets West who gets up and falls behind North. Then East greets Ghost who gets up and falls behind West. Finally East greets South who gets up and follows Ghost. All five now walk to the eastern end of the enclosure and stop there facing the audience. East speaks:

E A S T :   Here is our destination and our refuge. Here we are to receive strength and power from our grandfather, the sacred woman. Toward her, the sacred woman, toward him our grandfather, I shall now undertake to walk.

Then as East puts his right leg forward he ejaculates 'wa-hi-hi-hi, wa-hi-hi, o-ho-ho-ho' and he makes the circuit of the enclosure until he returns to his starting-point. Then he starts around for the second time ejaculating 'wa-hi-hi-hi, wa-hi-hi, o-ho-ho-ho.' Now for the third time he makes the circuit of the enclosure ejaculating 'wa-hi-hi-hi, wa-hi-hi, o-ho-ho-ho.' When he has returned to his starting place he stops and speaks.

E A S T :   Ancestors, we have been told that it is impossible to cross right in front of our grandfather, the sacred woman.[6] Nevertheless, I tell you now that I am going to cross in front of him; that is just what I shall do! May it give me power and strength; may it bring me into connection with life!

For the fourth time now he starts. With each step he takes, he utters an ejaculation. He has come to the side of the Vapor-Bath lodge. Through this side he now bursts and crosses the path of the stone. Then he returns to where he started and once again starts for the Vapor-Bath lodge. With each step that he makes he ejaculates 'wa-hi-hi-hi-hi.' He is trying to make himself holy as he approaches the Vapor-Bath sanctuary. Finally, standing in the center of the Vapor-Bath lodge, he seizes the lodge-poles on both sides and shakes them violently, at the same time ejaculating 'e-ho-ho-ho.' Having done this he makes his way to where his own people are sitting and sits down near them. Rising, he goes in succession, to North, West, Ghost and South and sits next to them for a while. Finally he returns to his own seat in the east.
East speaks again:

E A S T :   There he sits rapt in his thoughts saying to himself 'We will obtain life if we do this, if we have complete faith and act

193

in sincerity. If our thoughts, on the other hand, are not sincere as we sit here, if they are not entirely concentrated on the Vapor-Bath then we will obtain nothing or something of no consequence. This is what would happen, in such cases, the members of the Medicine Rite used to tell one another.'

Five sticks are now daubed with life, with blue clay. Ancestor-Host gives all five to the first man, East. He seizes them firmly with both hands and speaks.

E A S T :   I greet you. It is good. What I have seized will strengthen me greatly, will give me life within life. I have indeed got hold, through these sticks, of that which will give me the expectation of life. That this life is to be only for me, I would not for a moment pretend to say.

But now I must turn them over to the one sitting there, he who impersonates North, so that he can do his part. Ancestors, we greet you!

N O R T H :   I greet you. It is good. What I have seized will strengthen me greatly, will give me life within life. I have indeed got hold, through these sticks, of that which will give me the expectation of life. That this life is to be only for me, that I would not for a moment pretend to say. But this is not for me. I am only in the middle.[7]

Now I shall pass the sticks on to the one sitting there, he who impersonates West, so that he can do his part.

W E S T :   I greet you. It is good. What I have seized, will strengthen me greatly, will give me life within life. I have indeed got hold through these sticks, of that which will give me the expectation of life. That this life is to be only for me, that I would not for a moment pretend to say. But this is not for me. I am only in the middle.

Now I shall pass the sticks on to the one sitting there, he who impersonates Ghost.

G H O S T :   I greet you. It is good. What I have seized will strengthen me greatly, will give me life within life. I have indeed got

194

hold through these sticks, of that which will give me the expectation of life. That this life is to be only for me, that I would not for a moment pretend to say.

But now I must pass on these sticks to the one over there, he who impersonates the End-of-the-Road.

s o u t h : I greet you. It is good. What I have seized will strengthen me greatly, will give me life within life. I have indeed got hold, through these sticks, of that which will give me the expectation of life. That this life is to be only for me, that I would not for a moment pretend to say. Life has been scattered about by you in profusion. It is good. But I have nothing to say and I will pass these sticks back to the First One, East, and place them before him.

When the sticks are returned to East he arises and speaks:

e a s t : Ancestors, I greet you. I shall now give one of the sticks to North that he can render thanks; to the one impersonating West, to him, too, I shall now give one of these sticks so that he can render thanks; to the one impersonating the Ghost I shall likewise give a stick so that he can render thanks; to the one at the End-of-the-Road I shall also give a stick so that he can render thanks.

As each person receives his stick he thanks East profusely. All four are now in possession of the sticks. East now rises again and speaks:

e a s t : I greet you, ancestors. Our grandfather, the pole,[8] I shall now pass to Ancestor-Host. I and mine are weaklings and dependent upon others but I know it will strengthen me. Ancestors, I greet you.

Then North, the second one, arises and speaks:

n o r t h : Ancestors, I greet you. I know it is forbidden to include more than one person in a greeting but I shall do so anyhow. Have compassion upon me and bless me, ancestors. I know I am not your equal yet I shall presume to take hold of the pole, our grandfather, and thus obtain connection with life. Then I shall pass our

195

grandmother, the pole, along to the next one. I am only a weakling, dependent upon others, but I know this will strengthen me and mine and give us life. Ancestors, I greet you.

Then the third one, West, rises and speaks:

W E S T :   Ancestors, I send forth my greetings to you. I shall now pass on our grandfather, the yellow pole, to Ancestor-Host. Weaklings we are and dependent upon others, but this will give us strength and give us life.

Then South, the End-of-the-Road, rises, sends forth his greeting and speaks:

S O U T H :   You who sit over there impersonating the Rite-Giver, the Host, I greet you; you who sit over there impersonating the One-who-was-First, I greet you; you who sit over there impersonating North, I greet you; you who sit over there impersonating West, I greet you; you who sit over there impersonating Ghost, I greet you. I greet you all, ancestors.

For the members of my band I have taken hold of our grandfather, the pole, and thus I have seized life for them. I am grateful and thankful. Yet I know I am a nuisance, bashful and without value here. In a moment I shall pass to Ancestor-Host our grandfather, the yellow pole. Weaklings we are and dependent upon others yet, ancestors, I feel myself connected with life through your efforts. I greet you, ancestors!

The four leaders—East, North, West and South—now enter the Vapor-Bath lodge, followed by Ancestor-Host and the initiate, He-for-whom-we-seek-life. There are six in all. As soon as they have taken their places Ancestor-Host rises and speaks, addressing East specifically.

A N C E S T O R - H O S T :   You who sit over there impersonating the One-who-was-First, I greet you; you who sit over there impersonating North, I greet you; you who sit over there impersonating West, I greet you; you who sit over there impersonating Ghost, I greet you; you who sit over there impersonating the End-of-the-Road, I greet you. I greet you all, ancestors.

196

All those present here are asking you to have pity on them and each one individually extends his life-engendering greeting to you. What they desire I ask you to give them.

O you who sit in the first position, I greet you. Our ancestors, whose bones long since lie mixed and mingled with the earth, they too bless and pity you. As they left, they must have bequeathed to you abundant sacred speeches to use in asking for life and happiness. Do not be selfish or petty with them. O grandfather, for the initiate, He-for-whom-we-seek-life, I covet something of yours, something you value highly, the shells, the arrows you possess.[9] I beg life for my own kinsman. Do you throw them at him and we will do the same.[10] Instruct him in life, in pious life! I ask you for this.

And this, too, I beg of you, who are here, that you always show respect and always value properly your birdskin pouches. Enough!

You who impersonate North, to you, likewise, I wish to speak, for from you I also desire something. Remember that Earthmaker placed a high value on your birdskin pouches. I send a life-engendering greeting to you and recall to you the many sacred speeches left by those ancestors of yours whose bones long since lie mixed and mingled with the earth. I ask for them, the speeches enabling us to live happily. Do not be selfish or petty with them.

I send a life-begetting greeting to you, my friend, sitting over there. To all your ancestors, dead this long time, to all of them whose bones lie mixed and mingled with the earth, I send a greeting. I ask you to use for my kinsman, He-for-whom-we-seek-life, all those various speeches that were bequeathed to you, the speeches that bring happiness and make us live well. Do not be selfish or stingy with them so that we may all obtain life.

To you, grandmother, sitting there, you who impersonate West, I send my greeting. I send those life-begetting greetings to your ancestors, dead this long time, whose bones lie mixed and mingled with the earth. I beg you to make ample use of the speeches and utterances they left behind for you. Tell my kinsman, He-for-whom-we-seek-life, about these utterances which will enable him and us to live happily here. It is to secure such a happy life that I plead with you. Do not be selfish, do not be miserly with these speeches. Have compassion upon us, bless us I ask of you. I send a life-engendering greeting to you, to each one in turn. Such my request.

Of you, my relatives, all of you who have sympathy with me and love me, of you, too, I ask a blessing. You have complied with my request; you have made me proud and happy. All the more is this true, for I was about to do a most humiliating thing for you and for me, to do it despite everything to the contrary. I thought you might be pleased by it. Do, therefore, have compassion upon me. You did help me, despite everything, and I am pleased and happy. It is good.

Hāhā, ancestors, I greet you. As far back as you will listen, that far back, you will be able to hear me, that far back I will annoy you and yours.

Then East, the one in the first seat, speaks in his turn.

E A S T :   You who sit over there impersonating the Rite-Giver, the Host, I greet you; you who sit over there impersonating North, I greet you; you who sit over there impersonating West, I greet you; you who sit over there impersonating Ghost, I greet you; you who sit over there impersonating the End-of-the-Road, I greet you. I greet you all, ancestors.

Although I have always tried to be accurate and truthful, I know only too well how fallible I am and how easy it is for me to make a mistake. Yet, keenly aware of this as I am, it is impossible for me not to think of helping you here and I shall, therefore, use my voice as best I can. Ancestors have compassion upon me. I cannot do much, I cannot say anything of importance, but do have compassion upon me! . . .

He-whom-we-call-our-nephew, Hare, secured the Creation-Lodge, the lodge of life, for us. From all the different corners of the universe, from above, from the earth, from below our grandmother, Earth, all, everyone of the spirits, the most select of them, all, crowded into this lodge. As they sat there, all concentrated their hearts and minds upon the center of the lodge. The day was nice and warm as the light flickered and sparkled. From up above, where stands the place where everything is created, from there it came, this Rite. From Earthmaker it came as all things do.

Earthmaker looked at this Rite of his and was pleased. Earthmaker looked at this Rite of his and looked at the Creation-Lodge as it lay there quietly and peacefully. He was, indeed, pleased. 'Only to human beings will this Rite belong,' he thought to himself. Then it occurred to him that the human beings he had formed would want companions. So he took a rib from the right side of his own body and out of it he created our grandfather, the sacred woman.[11] It was a well-shaped body he gave him. A fine voice he gave him too.

When he finished him he sent him hurtling to the earth. He landed in the east, there where a bluff protrudes out of the water. There he landed, there he set up his lodge, there he acquired knowledge and there he obtained visions.

One day he told the old woman, his wife, that Earthmaker was preparing Hare, He-whom-we-call-our-nephew, for the mission of bringing his uncles and aunts, the human beings, a new life. 'Earthmaker has already told Hare what it is he is to show his uncles and his aunts, what it is he is to instruct them in.' So spoke our grandfather. Continuing he said, 'Earthmaker, when I left, gave me a feather-case containing paints which I shall now use.'

Then he put on his apparel. The top of his head, the parting of his hair, this he painted blue. Two eagle feathers were attached to his head, and four more, one apiece, to each of his limbs. With the various things that grow and cover our grandmother, Earth,[12] he rubbed (?) his body, all four limbs. He stood there, finally, a completely and immaculately well-dressed man. No detail in his apparel was forgotten.

He took four steps toward the Creation-Lodge. At the end of the fourth step he stopped, tapped his mouth and ejaculated 'ehoho-o-o-o weha weha' and inhaled deeply—'hhu.' Then, for the second time, he started out to walk. At the end of the fourth step, he again tapped his mouth and ejaculated 'ehoho-o-o-o weha weha' and again he inhaled deeply—'hhu.' Now, for the third time, he started out to walk. At the end of the fourth step, again he tapped his mouth and ejaculated 'ehoho-o-o-o weha weha' and again he inhaled deeply—'hhu.' Now, for the last time, he started to walk again. At the end of the fourth step he tapped his mouth and ejaculated 'ehoho-o-o-o weha weha' and, again, breathed deeply—'hhu.'

As he strode along, the earth shook, shook as if someone were treading upon her heavily. She gave way as does an elastic object. He walked along with a mighty tread. The trees bent forward and he pulled their branches down to him.[13]

Within the Creation-Lodge the spirits sat huddled together, frightened.[14] 'We can do nothing,' they said to one another, frightened. 'Earthmaker has willed it so. How terribly is this earth shaking and rolling! Even our grandmother, Earth, itself, she upon whom we dwell, has no remedy. Let us, however, just in case it is necessary, leave a place free for this person who is approaching.'

Along he came. He was on his fourth start and he had just taken his fourth step. Indeed, he had just tapped his mouth and was ejaculating his 'ehoho-o-o-o weha weha.' By the time he had uttered his fourth cry, he was at the very entrance to the lodge. His last cry, in fact, was sent right into the lodge. As it spread into it, all those present felt themselves hot.[15] Now he entered the lodge. The occupants were trembling with fear. His appearance was prodigious. Completely and immaculately was he dressed. No detail had been forgotten.

As he entered he was addressed, 'There, over there, a place has been purposely left for you to sit in.' And he responded, 'Yes, indeed, but not, for a moment, should you have forgotten me, as you actually did. If that place you designate had really been meant for me, you should have come after me, not waited for me to come. Now I am going to do exactly what it has been ordained I should do, something no one else has the power to do because only to me did Earthmaker give this power. Now I am going toward that objective, to attain which I have come.'

Thereupon he walked toward our grandfather who stands in the middle of the lodge,[16] he whom it is not good to oppose. There, right in the middle of the lodge, he sat down. Not very long did his body remain the same [17] as he sat there near the standing-onè, near the one who stands in the middle of the lodge. Yet there he sat, in spite of this, with all of a man's apparel, the complete headdress, the head ornament. The light flashed blue from the headdress.[18]

Then four boys entered.[19] They walked straight to the center of the lodge and, right in front of East, in front of He-who-is-First. Then they walked over to stand in front of North. Again they started and walked to stand in front of West. Finally they walked over to stand in front of South. Thus they had stood in front of each one of the four directions.

Now, suddenly, there appeared a dark-furred, grizzled and awe-inspiring bear.[20] He seemed almost as large as the lodge when he entered. He did the same thing the boys had been doing. Then he turned to the four boys. First he jerked [21] the first limb of all four and pulled it toward him. Then he jerked the second limb and pulled it toward him. Then the third limb he jerked and pulled it toward him and, finally, he jerked and pulled the fourth limb toward him.

Now another group of four boys entered the lodge, and behaved just as the first four had done. Finally they walked over to where He-whom-we-call-our-nephew, Hare, sits and stopped in front of him. They carried stones on sticks and they placed them near the fireplace. [They really represent the sticks or stone-heaps surrounding the fireplace to prevent sleepers from falling into the fire.] [22]

Then Hare and his friends, Trickster, Turtle and our grandmother, Earth, all four of them, picked up the boys.[23] Turtle, thereupon, made himself invisible at the place where he was sitting.[24] After a short time he returned and what was impossible to others, he accomplished. He seized the sacred woman and threw himself upon her breast.[25]

When he had left before, he had gone to one of the waterspirits, the chief of the Island-Anchorers that Earthmaker had placed in the center of our island-earth to keep it motionless. From him Turtle had obtained holy water. He had to beg for it but, finally, it was given to him. This water he brought back with him and placed on the sacred woman's breast. As he threw the water upon her there burst forth from Turtle's navel, daylight and life. When the flashing of light had stopped there, upon his own breast, was impressed a mark, the mark of light and life. Through four rainbows the light streamed in.

Before all these things had happened, the chief, the bear, that had been converted into the covering of the lodge, had made everything within the lodge dark. It had been impossible to see anything. But now the inside of the lodge became extremely white, as light as day.[26]

Then Hare turned to our grandmother and said, 'Grandmother, have you no knowledge of anything, nothing you can do?' 'Ah, my grandson, you are quite right,' she answered. She took four pieces of her hair, of a very blue color,[27] doubled them, to make them strong and then, tied them together. Having finished this, she turned toward Hare and said, 'Grandson, for this that I have done I shall forever be remembered by your uncles and your aunts. In gratitude I beg them to pour a handful of tobacco in my honor. In the future, whenever they tie my hair as I have done and do it properly, then they will be collecting life in a knot.

Then East took the tied-hair of our grandmother,[28] threw Turtle upon the sacred woman, and touched his navel.[29] As East did so, Turtle breathed heavily and cried out 'eho-o-o-o, eho-o-o-o, weha, weha!' The sacred woman he now placed on his breast and, breathing heavily again, cried out 'eho-o-o-o, eho-ho-ho weha weha!' A second time he breathed 'e-ho-o-o eho-o-o weha weha!' Putting the sacred woman to his breast again he breathed 'eho-o-o eho-o-o weha weha!' All those within the lodge, all of them did the same. Then, a third time, he placed the sacred woman on his breast and breathed deeply 'eho-o-o-o eho-o-o-o weha weha!' Now, for the fourth time, he placed the sacred woman on his breast and breathed deeply 'eho-o-o-o, eho-o-o-o weha weha!' . . .

This, then, is what I have been trying to say. But, really, I have probably not told it correctly. Our ancestors, mine and yours, have asked me for a life-compelling prayer, for words and actions that will mean salvation to us. I have tried to tell it to you but I know that I have been unable to do so, that my account is inaccurate. May I receive your blessings, nevertheless! Have compassion upon me! Here are four songs we shall try to intone! (songs)

As soon as the songs are finished I shall start up some dance songs.

When he has finished the dance songs, then East speaks again:

E A S T :   Two men, one behind the other, have made me follow them. One of them came to my right side and whispered in my ear saying that he was going to give me an important, a chief missile, a shell, to place in the center of my heart. 'No one will ever see it,' he said. The other man whispered in my other ear that he would place a missile inside of my stomach. If I tried very hard I would be able to force it out of myself he assured me. Well, that I shall try to do now, so put your minds together and help me, ancestors.

Yes, my ancestors, I think I can succeed indeed, I think that I am about to cough it up right now. Here it comes—'khang, khang, khang ang ang!'

East succeeds in forcing up the shell within him. Then he lets his thoughts wander all around the Creation-Lodge, holding the shell straight before him. Now he is ready to swallow and then displace the shell again. Straight before him he holds the shell. Suddenly he swallows it and throws himself upon the ground. When he gets up he spits on his left hand and stretches his arm to make it ready for shooting.[30] Now he shoots and a man falls to the ground. Immediately East starts up a shooting song. All go around the lodge with the shell, singing four songs and each one shooting in his turn. (?) After they have shot the shell at the last person they cease their singing.

East then walks toward the second leader, North, ejaculating 'wahihihi, wahihihi, wahihihi, wahihihi' and places the ceremonial materials before him.

The second leader rises, sends his greetings around and speaks:

N O R T H :   You who sit over there impersonating the Rite-Giver, the Host, I greet you; you who sit over there impersonating the One-who-was-First, I greet you; you who sit over there impersonating West, I greet you; you who sit over there impersonating Ghost, I greet you; you who sit over there impersonating the End-of-the-Road, I greet you. I greet you all, ancestors.

East has passed on to me the materials-for-thankfulness and thereby enabled me to feel that I had been brought into connection with life. You, O East, have truly been blessed, and you have had the blessings actually placed here for me, for one in the middle. The blessings so amply bestowed upon you by your ancestors, let me partake of some of them, I beg you. Then would I indeed be full of thankfulness, replete with thankfulness. But, even if I had the capacity for learning just a few words, all I doubtless would do would be to repeat them indefinitely. The best I can do, then, is to show my gratitude and thankfulness by offering you some songs which my ancestors taught us, three completion songs, three regular dance songs and three minor dance songs.

North now sings the songs, three apiece. Then he speaks again:

N O R T H : Two men came and spoke to me. The first one said he was going to give me a shell, that he was going to place it under my heart. 'Never,' so he said to me, 'will you be able to see it, so deeply will it be buried.' The second man spoke to me likewise and said he would place a shell within my stomach.

'I shall try out my powers in the lodge as soon as I can.' I said to myself. Ancestors, I beseech you, put your minds together for me so that I may succeed! Such is my prayer.

North tries to cough up the shell. 'K-hang, k-hang, k-hang, k-hang, -ang, -ang.' There it is. He has succeeded. He is well pleased and sings to himself 'eho-eho-ho.' Then he sends his thoughts around the Creation-Lodge, stretches his hand straight out and, having done this, swallows the shell, and falls to the ground instantaneously. He gets up and, for the third time, he places the shell there. Again he falls to the ground instantaneously. Soon he snaps back into life and starts his three shooting songs. When the third shell has come back, the singer shoots the last one and the songs cease. He is now ready to pass on the ceremonial materials to the next leader, West. He approaches him ejaculating 'wahihihi wahihihi wahihihi wahihihi' and places the materials for thankfulness before him.

The third leader now rises and speaks as he accepts the materials-for-thankfulness.

W E S T : You who sit over there impersonating the Rite-Giver, the Host, I greet you; you who sit over there impersonating the One-who-was-First, I greet you; you who sit over there impersonating North, I greet you; you who sit over there impersonating Ghost, I

204

greet you; you who sit over there impersonating the End-of-the-Road, I greet you. I greet you all, ancestors.

As far back as we can go, that far back has come the blessing you have brought me and which my ancestors have forced me to live by. Of all this you have made me cognizant.

I greeted my ancestors in the Preparatory Four Nights' ceremony. There I spoke to them and saw them face to face. I told them that I was going to send a life-engendering greeting to them for having passed on to me the means-of-thankfulness. Yet I hesitated even then to attempt to say anything for fear of making a mistake and embarrassing them. Now you have passed on to me the means-of-thankfulness. Even if I do not succeed in making proper use of it, still I am grateful to you, and send you a life-engendering greeting. I have been told that this might be acceptable. Songs, likewise, I shall start up for you, two completion and two dance songs. The dance songs will be archaic ones.

Two men came and spoke to me. The first one he was going to put the shell firmly under my heart. 'Never will you be able to see it,' he told me, 'so deeply is it buried.' The second one said he would speak to me inside the Creation-Lodge. 'If they give me a person to initiate, if I were you, I would try to get the shell out of my body,' he said to me. 'I will get it out,' I answered. 'If you wish to see it, I will get it for you,' the man said. 'No, I will try to do it myself.' 'Well and good, then, concentrate your mind upon it! In that way you will succeed.' So he spoke.

Then West tries and coughs 'k-hang, k-hang, k-hang, k-hang, ang, ang.' He succeeds in throwing up the shell. Straight ahead he stretches his hand, saying to himself 'Now I shall try and see whether I am really in connection with life!' Again he stretches his hand out and then swallows the shell. Instantaneously he falls to the ground. Soon he is up and pounds along the road of the lodge, shooting the shell. One shell is returned to him. He goes on shooting and singing. He is now about finished with his songs. He has snapped back into life and is ready to place the means-of-thankfulness before the next leader, South. He approaches him breathing heavily 'wahihihi, wahihihi, wahihihi, wahihihi.' The means-of-thankfulness is now placed in front of the last leader and the life-engendering greeting is extended to him.

South accepts and speaks:

s o u t h : You who sit over there impersonating the Rite-Giver, the Host, I greet you; you who sit over there impersonating the One-who-was-First, I greet you; you who sit over there impersonating North, I greet you; you who sit over there impersonating West, I greet you; you who sit over there impersonating Ghost, I greet you. I greet you all, ancestors.

You have passed on to me the means-of-thankfulness; you have passed on to me life; you have made me realize that I had been brought into connection with life. Assuredly, those before me have already said everything that could be said. Yet I was always told that those in the South position had more life to dispose of than the others. I am very thankful and grateful. You have made me realize what life really it. As far back as one can go, from that distant time, my relatives have made new life come to me. From that distance past, on up to the present, they have concentrated their minds upon me and blessed me. I now have, at last, been given the chance to greet them.

Earthmaker established four stations of rest for us. Visible to all in this lodge is the means-of-thankfulness. To me they have passed on the privilege of greeting and the means-of-thankfulness. Here I sit a weakling, dependent upon others, occupying a place not meant for unimportant and fragile men. I am no Medicine Rite man. If I am here at all it is not so much because of my merit but because of my kinship to the giver of the present Rite.

Here I am, an ignorant and unworthy man, occupying the place of one who is supposed to be able to dispense more life than any of the others! How can I be anything but overwhelmingly grateful and thankful? Yet if I tried to speak I would succeed only in repeating, over and over again, the few words I happen to know. However, one unimportant song I do possess and that I will now sing. Apart from that I am simply a person sitting here and indulging in talk.

Then South passes on the means-of-thankfulness to the next one, East. He rises and speaks:

206

E A S T :   We are now finished with our grandfather, the sacred woman. Our grandfather's body had become that of an old man. The four small boys were bent, their backs were meeting. They were now, all, very old people. Their heads were white like men wearing swans as headdresses. The handle of the stone-sprinkler whose hair had been originally very black when they first tied it, that, too, was now very white, overcome by old age. The leader in the east who had, at the beginning, wrapped around him an exceedingly dark-haired skin [31] he, too, had become a very old man. He sat there in the east, his red gums showing, his teeth protruding, a fearful and awe-inspiring object.

The one at the End-of-the-Road now stepped out and produced, from his right side, a very young black bear [32] which he placed in front of himself. He carried himself as one frail from holiness.[33] He had clothed himself with that life with which Earthmaker had blessed him.[34] Then he pushed the top of the bear's head up and out.[35] Immediately light appeared above them. Then the top of the head of the second one was pushed up and out and more light appeared above them. Then the top of the head of the third one was pushed up and out and still more light appeared above them. Those inside now took heart as they saw the light appear above them. Now the top of the head of the fourth bear was pushed up and out and the full light of day appeared. All inside breathed a deep sigh of relief and were extremely grateful. 'E-ho-ho-ho-,' they ejaculated.

E A S T :   It is now time for me to begin redressing, and as soon as you start it, I, too, will do so. Songs, likewise, I shall sing, one at a time.

Then he sings a minor dance song, and when it is finished, he sings a regular dance song.

E A S T :   I shall now attempt to move the shell and if I can move it, the shell (?), again I shall start up a song.

Two men appeared before me and one of them said, 'I shall insert the shell tightly below your heart so that it cannot ever be seen. By

207

means of this you will obtain life.' The second one also spoke to me and said, 'I shall insert this shell below your heart. Then some day, in the future, you will be able to initiate a man if you wish to and you concentrate your mind upon it.'

I shall now try it. Ancestors, put your minds together for me for I am going to try the shell and I wish to succeed.

He forces the shell, 'k-hang, k-hang, k-hang, k-hang, ang-ang-ang.' Life he wishes to reconquer.[36]

E A S T :   Straight ahead, in front of the feast-giver, there I shall stop.

Now he sends his thoughts around the lodge, and then, arms stretched forward, he swallows the shell. Instantaneously, he falls to the ground. As soon as he snaps back into consciousness, he shoots one of the people in front of him and starts the songs around their circuit.

When the songs have been sung he starts over again. He swallows the shell and falls to the ground instantaneously. When he snaps back into consciousness, he rises and breathing heavily, ejaculates 'wahi-hi-hi-hi, wahi-hi-hi-hi, wahi-hi-hi-hi, wahi-hi-hi-hi.'

This completes the actual vapor-bath. They all leave the enclosure now and go out into the open, to cool off. When they have cooled off, they reenter the enclosure, stand for a moment in front of their seats and, sending around a greeting, each one sits down. East now rises and sends his greetings:

E A S T :   You who sit over there impersonating the Rite-Giver, the Host, I greet you; you who sit over there impersonating North, I greet you; you who sit over there impersonating West, I greet you; you who sit over there impersonating Ghost, I greet you; you who sit over there impersonating the End-of-the-Road, I greet you. I greet you all, ancestors. All you who have been blessed, to each one in turn, I send my greeting.

Then North rises and sends his greeting:

N O R T H :   You who sit over there impersonating the Rite-Giver, the Host, I greet you; you who sit over there impersonating the One-who-was-First, I greet you; you who sit over there impersonating West, I greet you; you who sit over there impersonating Ghost, I

208

greet you; you who sit over there impersonating the End-of-the-Road, I greet you. I greet you all, ancestors. All you who have been blessed, to each one in turn, I send my greeting.

W E S T : You who sit over there impersonating the Rite-Giver, the Host, I greet you; you who sit over there impersonating the One-who-was-First, I greet you; you who sit over there impersonating North, I greet you; you who sit over there impersonating Ghost, I greet you; you who sit over there impersonating the End-of-the-Road, I greet you. I greet you all, ancestors. All you who have been blessed, to each one in turn, I send my greeting.

S O U T H : You who sit over there impersonating the Rite-Giver, the Host, I greet you; you who sit over there impersonating the One-who-was-First, I greet you; you who sit over there impersonating North, I greet you; you who sit over there impersonating West, I greet you; you who sit over there impersonating Ghost, I greet you. I greet you all, ancestors. All you who have been blessed, to each one in turn, I send my greeting.

Although the seat I occupy is really of little importance it has been said that you will consider it as equal to your own.

Now all sit down and food is brought in. East rises and speaks:

E A S T : You who sit over there impersonating the Rite-Giver, the Host, I greet you; you who sit over there impersonating North, I greet you; you who sit over there impersonating West, I greet you; you who sit over there impersonating Ghost, I greet you; you who sit over there impersonating the End-of-the-Road, I greet you. I greet you all, ancestors. All you who have been blessed, to each one of you in turn, I send my greeting.

Using our grandfather, the sacred woman, they have prepared the boiled water. But now we shall pass on the means-of-thankfulness to the one who impersonates North so that he, too, may be able to benefit by it. Ancestors, we send forth our greetings to you.

North now rises and speaks:

N O R T H :   You who sit over there impersonating the Rite-Giver, the Host, I greet you; you who sit over there impersonating the One-who-was-First, I greet you; you who sit over there impersonating West, I greet you; you who sit over there impersonating Ghost, I greet you; you who sit over there impersonating the End-of-the-Road, I greet you. I greet you all, ancestors. All you who have been blessed, to each one of you in turn, I send my greeting.

It is good. You have passed on to me life, have made me feel connected with life. But I, who sit in the middle, I should hardly be expected to possess any knowledge. I cannot tell you anything.[37] Perhaps the one in front of me, perhaps he might be able to say something. What he says that will be correct. Let me therefore pass on the means-of-thankfulness to him.

West now rises and speaks:

W E S T :   You who sit over there impersonating the Rite-Giver, the Host, I greet you; you who sit over there impersonating the One-who-was-First, I greet you; you who sit over there impersonating North, I greet you; you who sit over there impersonating Ghost, I greet you; you who sit over there impersonating the End-of-the-Road, I greet you. I greet you all, ancestors.

Like the one before me I, too, am in the middle. I, too, am of little significance. The one in front of me, he who impersonates South, he will undoubtedly know what to do. I therefore pass on to him the means-of-thankfulness.

The last one, South, now rises and speaks:

S O U T H :   You who sit over there impersonating the Rite-Giver, the Host, I greet you; you who sit over there impersonating the One-who-was-First, I greet you; you who sit over there impersonating North, I greet you; you who sit over there impersonating West, I greet you; you who sit over there impersonating Ghost, I greet you. I greet you all, ancestors.

To the one in the first seat we shall now pass on the means-of-thankfulness and whatever he tells us to do we shall do.

East now speaks:

210

E A S T :   Take the food outside. We will divide it there, this life. But now I shall stand up and talk. I will not talk when I am sitting down.

N O R T H :   I, too, when my term comes, will stand up to speak.

W E S T :   We have been specifically warned against presuming to greet more than one person at a time. Nevertheless, I shall do so, well aware of the fact that I am not your equal and should not attempt it. I, too, when my time comes, will stand up to speak. I send my greetings to you, ancestors.

All now rise. East speaks:

E A S T :   I extend my greetings to our grandfather, the sacred woman, and to the water heated for us. To our kinsmen present here what we say will bring them life, will bring them the added life and prosperity we so ardently desire for them. Such is the greeting I extend to them. When we come to the food, that-with-which-we-ask-for-life, let us all, O kinsmen, think and feel as one, so that we can thus obtain double strength. Thus let us all behave as we sit together here, one next to the other, partaking of the feast.

I greet and salute all the birdskin pouches, the open-faced ones. As you see I am trying to extend the greetings in the proper fashion. I know I shall not succeed but do not think any the worse of me for my failure. Let me however start up a song before I greet you. (song)

He then finishes with a minor thanks-offering and passes the means-for-thankfulness to the second one.

N O R T H :   The minor means-of-thankfulness has been passed on to me. Let us all, O kinsmen, try to think and feel as one, as we sit down to the feast, to the heated water from our grandfather,[38] the heated water with which we ask for life. We must regard ourselves doubly strengthened from participation in this food through which we ask for life. Let me presume to extend one greeting and have it suffice for all. I greet you all. I greet you with a minor song. (song)

211

N O R T H :   I will now pass on the means-of-thankfulness to the third one.

The third one, West, accepts the thanks-offering and thanks North, speaking as follows:

W E S T :   Those before me have already said all that there is to be said so that the best thing I can do is to proceed at once with a greeting song. That is what I shall attempt to do immediately. Thus it should be. I greet both the food and the boiled water as one and the same and I beg all my kinsmen present to see that they strengthen themselves from what they partake of here. (song)

W E S T :   I shall now pass on the means-of-thankfulness to the last person. I greet you, I greet you!

S O U T H :   You who sit over there impersonating the Rite-Giver, the Host, I greet you; you who sit over there impersonating the One-who-was-First, I greet you; you who sit over there impersonating North, I greet you; you who sit over there impersonating West, I greet you; you who sit over there impersonating Ghost, I greet you. I greet you all, ancestors. I greet you too, visitors, sitting around this enclosure.

They have passed on to me life, they have brought me into connection with life. I now realize what life really means. Since I know that, what I have to say will only annoy you. I will cut things short and start up a greeting song immediately. I greet all those who have come here; I send a life-engendering greeting to the tobacco, to the invitation-sticks, to the tobacco pouches, to the lodge, to the feast-givers. All of them I greet. (song)

PART THREE

THE RITUAL OF EXPECTATIONS

Ancestor-Host and the members of his band enter the lodge. When they are seated, Ancestor-Host rises and speaks:

ANCESTOR-HOST: Ancestors, we greet you. When this Rite was first instituted everything that was done was perfect. Remembering this, we ask that our ancestors have compassion upon us, that they bless us. Indeed, it would be good if they had compassion upon us, upon every one of us. But you have already conferred the real blessing upon us when you honored us by your invitation to participate in this Rite. However, I must not waste time speaking, for the others are waiting. So let us begin immediately and send around the greetings. Soon we shall see the spirits face to face. As they enter, they will take charge of us and we shall greet them. But now, let me start up a song for you. (songs)

East and his band enter. They make the circuit of the lodge and, after extending a greeting, stop at the left end of the lodge in front of Ancestor-Host. East speaks:

EAST: I greet you, you who sit in the seat of the host. I greet you all, ancestors, all of you who are standing here.

A member of the Medicine Rite has sustained a great loss. 'How can I become reconciled to my grief?' he thinks to himself. In spite, however, of his intense grief and his tears, he did not permit this sorrow to interfere with his obligations to the Medicine Rite.

And now the thoughts which he had been thinking, made themselves felt. The spirits, came to the lodge that was theirs, from all directions. Smoke lay everywhere, circling up from the fire, circling up from he-who-stands-in-the-middle-of-the-lodge, but unable to get

213

out.[1] The spirits, every one of them, brought with them a blessing, that which we tie up in bundles, and when they got near enough they placed the obstacle-conqueror [2] close to him.

All this time the head of the birdskin pouch had been drooping, had been unable to look at the light. The dish from which it had been accustomed to eat was turned upside down.[3]

Tomorrow, however, a new day, even if small, is to come to us. It will come with life for him, who has lost some loved one, and for us. The time will then have arrived for the bad hairs to be thrown away.[4]

Tonight we must tie up this lodge tightly with blessings. Then the flames from the fire, from he-who-stands-in-the-middle-of-the-lodge, will go straight up and the smoke that lies in the lodge will disappear. Tomorrow will be pleasant and calm. The birdskin pouch will look up again toward the light. The plate will be full again, the plate will be rightside up again and the dear and beloved one will eat from it again.[5]

The time for the obtaining of that life which the creator appointed for us, has arrived. I greet you.

My grandson, He-who-sits-here-as-Host, Ancestor-Host, has had compassion upon me although I am not fit to be blessed in that manner. Repeatedly he and his have done this. But I would bless and greet you even if this had not been done. From the bottom of their hearts this life-engendering greeting has come.

In entering the Creation-Lodge I am in the presence of something utterly real and true. I greet its blessing. I feel as though the one sitting in the east, is that very Island-Anchorer placed there, at the beginning, to keep our island-world quiet. Now, I know what it is to be endowed with life! I, myself, have nothing of importance to say.

My grandson, He-who-sits-there-as-Host, is aware of that but he also knows that He-whom-we-call-our-nephew, Hare, founded this Rite for everyone, in spite of the insignificance of any particular participant. How to obtain true life for us was his objective and he has accomplished just that. I have no life-engendering greeting to extend to you nor am I compelled [6] to intone a song. But I will do so nevertheless, and beseech the ghost to leave behind for us all that

214

was still his due and which he left behind unused. To him I make this plea before I intone the mourning song. Ancestors, I greet you, I greet you! (mourning song)

E A S T : They say that when the leader of those who were to occupy the East position in the original Creation-Lodge, walked toward it, he took four steps and then stopped right there at the entrance. There was no way of closing this entrance, yet open though it was, no person of unstable mind, no weakling, would have succeeded in passing through it. Even an unimportant spirit would not have been able to force his thoughts into that Creation-Lodge. However, this first man entered without difficulty for Earthmaker had put him in control of light and life, had made him in appearance like himself.

As he entered, the light in the lodge shone with increased lustre. Around the lodge he walked until he came to the fire. The light spread as he shuffled along. It could be seen flickering within the lodge. There, at the entrance to the road, he stopped, sent his life-begetting greeting and intoned his song of greeting, even as I, myself, do now. (song)

E A S T : Ancestors, I greet you. The seat, too, I greet, the seat they have designated for me. To you, likewise, I extend my greeting, you feast-givers sitting yonder.

There where you sit down in the east lies the bear.[7] I will greet him. He cannot be missed with the missile [8] you throw. And yet, I am only an unimportant kinsman, mixed with other unimportant kinsmen. You cannot but hit him under his very armpits [9] as you limp and stumble along with your light. To miss would be impossible. I greet you with hand extended, straight out.

I am now finished with my speech and we are about ready to take our seats. Before that, however, let me start up a song, a real song. I greet you, I greet you! (song)

East and the members of his band now walk around the lodge until they come to the west end of it. There they pause and East speaks again:

215

E A S T : I greet our relative sitting over there; a life-engendering greeting I send to him and then I shall sit down to join him. We greet you all!

All now sit down, each one before sitting down, extending a greeting. Immediately after all have sat down, East rises again and walks around the lodge until he reaches the seat of Ancestor-Host. There he stops, gives the latter some tobacco and speaks:

E A S T : Hāhā, my grandson, you have made me obtain a hold on a new day, you have made me realize what life really means. The offering the creator gave us with which to ask for life and which we are to use for that purpose, I have presented to you. The creator let us have a handful of tobacco to present to you so that, in exchange, there would come back to me and mine the means for gaining new strength. Thus Earthmaker intended it; thus have I done. I ask you to have compassion upon me. But what am I saying? You have already taken compassion upon me. I greet you.

East and the members of his band now sit down. Now North and the members of his band enter the lodge. They go around it once and when they come to the east end, the place from which they had started, they stop and North speaks:

N O R T H : You who sit in the place of the Host, I greet you. You who sit in the east I greet you. I greet all of you, ancestors, who are standing here with me.

I have been given to understand that perhaps there is a seat designated for me in the north where they were to have compassion upon me, I was told. Unworthy as I was I was to receive life. They paid no attention to my unworthiness. I have been blessed by them. It is good.

Now, just as my elders said, I know what it is to live. All about me in this lodge there are positions of honor and I have one of them. If people now hear about me it will be because of the prominence I have been given by the one ahead of me. For no other reason. Indeed it is good.

I am not able to utter a word of importance. This, the one who invited me, knew very well and yet, behold! he continued with his desire to bring me life. I was living in a most miserable manner and he brought me into connection with true living! It is good.

If our thoughts are loyal and sincere, we were told that it would be possible to really obtain life. Such a person it is who has brought his child here, his dearly beloved one, so that he might obtain life, that he might live long. And I, who have nothing to say, who, assuredly, can secure long life for no one, have been brought here in such a connection because they had compassion upon me! I bless you, O footsteps of the road in which the Medicine Rite men have trod, and I intone for all of you a life-engendering song of greeting!

The person ahead of me has already told you all there is to say. Since all has thus been said I who follow after will confine my actions to the intoning of the mourning song. Here it is. I greet you, I greet you! (mourning song)

North now walks around the lodge until he reaches the south side. There he stops and speaks:

N O R T H : I greet you, you who sit here as Host; I greet you who sit in the First Seat; I greet you ancestors, all of you, who are standing here with me. I greet, likewise, the seat that has been designated for me to sit in. I greet the bear. It will be impossible not to hit him under the armpits. I greet you, too, kinsmen in my group. I send my life-engendering greeting to you for having brought me into connection with life. It is about this which I wish to talk to you, ancestors. (song)

All now go to their seats in the north and sit down. Almost immediately North rises again, goes to Ancestor-Host, offers him some tobacco and speaks:

N O R T H : Hãhã, I greet you. For each one of the seats there is to be a pipeful of tobacco. This is what Earthmaker created for us. A handful of this tobacco I shall now offer you and after you have accepted it, puff it upon yourselves. Here it is. I greet you!

Then he gives Ancestor-Host the tobacco.

A N C E S T O R - H O S T : I thank you. I greet you.

N O R T H : We send our greetings to you, ancestors.

North and the members of his band go to their seats and sit down. Now West and his band enter the lodge. They go around it once and when they come to the east end, the place from which they had started, they stop and West speaks:

W E S T : I greet you, you who sit here as Host; I greet you who sit in the First Seat; I greet you who impersonate the North; I greet you ancestors, who are standing here with me.

Those ahead of me have already said all that is to be said. Besides, I am not capable of saying anything. All that I could conceivably do would be to repeat the same words of thanks over and over again. I really cannot tell you anything. I never could do anything. I shall therefore send you, as a greeting, a minor song. That will be my speech. I greet you. I bless you, O footsteps of the Road in which Medicine Rite men of yore have trod, and I intone for all of you, a life-engendering song of greeting. Following the steps of the one ahead of me I came here. What I was told to say, that I have said. Now let us pour our tears for the ghost of the departed. Let us beseech him to leave behind for us the life that was still his due and which he did not use. Ancestors, we greet you, we greet you! (mourning song)

Then West walks around the lodge until he comes to the west side. There he stops and speaks:

W E S T : Ancestors, I greet you. I greet you, O seat in the west, seat of the Island-Anchorer, the one I am to impersonate. Truly I send my greeting to you. I greet, too, the life with which I am to be connected and the new sitting-place designated for me and mine. They say it is impossible to miss the bear in the lair, the armpits imprinted with life. By this shooting shall we feel that we have obtained life. In return let me start up a song in lieu of words. I greet you. (song)

Then West and the members sit down. Immediately after West rises, takes some tobacco and, walking around the lodge to the seat of Ancestor-Host, speaks:

W E S T :   Hāhā, I greet you. A small handful of tobacco has been sent to me so that we can become strengthened. For you have I desired it in return for your compassion. Ancestors, I greet you.

West returns to his seat. South and his band, accompanied by Ghost and his band, now enter. They make the complete circuit of the lodge until they come back to the eastern end, near the entrance. There they stop and South speaks:

S O U T H :   I greet you, you who sit here as Host; I greet you, you who sit here impersonating the East; I greet you, you who sit here impersonating the North; I greet you, you who sit here impersonating the West; I greet you, you who are here impersonating Ghost.

The time for the delivering of speeches has now come to me. I send forth my greeting to all of you, from the first to the last one, to each one individually. They have blessed me with this seat, the seat of an Island-Anchorer, a seat not made for weaklings to occupy. Yet, in spite of the fact that they knew my unfitness, they did this because they desired me to be brought into connection with life. The most important of all seats is this one they, in their kindness, have designated for me! It is good.

I shall tread in the very footsteps made by the Medicine Rite members and thus be connected with the life these possess. Beyond, there in the lodge, lies the appointed destination, the stopping-place in the South. And all this is for me, me, ignorant, incapable of saying anything! Yet knowing this they yet blessed me.

A good and esteemed member of the Medicine Rite has sustained a loss. At once he remembered what his relatives had impressed upon him, words to which he had listened. 'If I sustain a loss,' they said to me, 'do not, because your heart is sore and evil, drop tears upon our grandmother, Earth.' So, as he thought of his very own, the one he had lost, he remembered their words and his thoughts were not evil when he wept.

'Up above where the creator dwells there let me cast my thoughts,' he said to himself. Soon, very soon, light and life were visible to him. Then the creator told him to try to obtain the gifts possessed by the spirits, by all of them. So he sent his thoughts out again, deep into

219

our grandmother, Earth. As far and deep as it had gone into the earth, that far they now returned and were made visible to him. His older relatives had told him of the true life he would obtain by doing this and how thankful and grateful he would feel towards them for having enabled him to seize hold of it.

Now as the day for the Rite approached, all he had been doing was to be left behind; the evil hairs, the uncleanliness, the ill-temper, the unkind words, the evil dreams.[10] All that was evil and bad, he was to discard tonight. So the elders spoke to the bereaved man.

But now the Road of the Medicine Rite members has come into view, their footprints are visible. I send a life-begetting greeting to them. What we are about to do and say here will give all those who are with me strength. Thus will it be, I was told.

And, now my friend, it is your turn. We came in together, we have walked around the lodge together. We must now prepare to take our seats. I greet you, ancestors, I greet you. (entrance song)

G H O S T :   I greet you, you who sit here as Host; I greet you who sit here impersonating the East; I greet you, you who sit here impersonating the North; I greet you, you who sit here impersonating the West; I greet you, you who sit here impersonating the End-of-the-Road. As many as are here to be blessed, all of you, each in turn, I greet.

I greet you, my friend. I have no words of blessing such as were told you. All I can ask is that you have compassion upon me and then I can step into the blessings you have obtained. Would that I could send you a real greeting! All those who are with me and their seat, have been blessed. Let me, in my turn, now send a greeting to my friend over there where-the-sun-straightens, he whom they call South. His seat I now greet. The bear cannot be missed by our missile. Deep, up to his very arm, he is imprinted with life.

Soon we shall sit in our seat. I greet that seat in which I shall soon sit! May it be blessed! So did our ancestors speak. But now I must start up a song. The tear-pouring has returned. Ancestors, I greet you, I greet you! (mourning song) s o u t h : I greet you, you who sit here as Host; I greet you, you who sit here in the First position; I greet you, you who sit here impersonating the North; I greet you, you who sit here impersonating the West; I greet you, you who sit here impersonating Ghost; I greet you, you who sit here impersonating the One-at-the-end-of-the-Road. All those who have come to be blessed, I greet you all, I greet you all!

Hāhā, ancestors, we greet all of you. It is good. Let me be the one to say it is good so that no one else will have to say it for me. If, within our heart, we feel that what is done here is good, then we will gain real life. Thus did our compassion-seeking ancestors speak. 'Only so,' they insisted, 'only through this Rite can you obtain true life for yourselves.' Again and again they enjoined us to pay attention to this Rite, particularly to the *hoki'una* [the main ceremony]. Through it a man can gain possession of life.

This ceremony belongs to Earthmaker. It is a ceremony full of hardships, hardships and trials, difficult to overcome. But if we persist patiently, if we are willing to stand the rigors of the cold, if we are willing to have our finger-joints become pulverized,[11] in short, if we are really willing to endure sufferings in order to obtain true life, then be assured, we can obtain it.

Earthmaker created this ceremony for us. For the people of old, the speeches and actions were as difficult as they are for us. But they surmounted the difficulties and we in consequence are the recipients of the blessings they then obtained. Earthmaker loved us and, for that reason, we have been brought into connection with life. We are thankful and grateful indeed, more in fact that we can express. Let the depth of our thankfulness and gratitude be proportional to the new life that has been vouchsafed to us.

There where-the-sun-straightens, there is the South Island-Anchorer, the one I am to impersonate. It is one of the foremost seats and yet I have been permitted to represent it! It is good. In gratitude, I send a life-engendering greeting to the Road, the Road of the Medicine Rite members. I greet you. (song)

g h o s t : I greet you, you who sit as our councillor; I greet you, you who impersonate the One-who-sits-in-the-East; I greet you, you

221

who impersonate the One-who-sits-in-the-North; I greet you, you who impersonate the One-who-sits-in-the-West; I greet you, you who impersonate the One-who-sits-at-the-End-of-the-Road.

I send my greetings here within the lodge. One can never have enough of such life-engendering greetings, our elders always told us. And so I extend them. He and his people who occupy the seat at the End-of-the-Road, the seat of honor, thought that there were two [12] of us. I send a life-engendering greeting to him and his people.

You know I have absolutely nothing to say except to beg you, ancestors, to have compassion upon me. May I not trouble you too much! I have only one song with which to greet you. I shall try it. Ancestors, I greet you, I greet you! (song)

G H O S T : Now that I have finished my song, we shall immediately proceed around the lodge until we stand before the seat in which we are to sit.

I greet you, O seat, in the manner I have been told to do.

S O U T H : I greet you, you who sit here as Host; I greet you, you who sit here in the First position; I greet you, you who sit here impersonating North; I greet you, you who sit here impersonating West; I greet you, you who sit here impersonating Ghost; I greet you, you who sit here impersonating the one at the End-of-the-Road. All those who have come to be blessed, I greet you all, I greet you all.

There are four life-blowing spirits, the ones-who-sit-at-the-corners-of-the-island, who throw their breath upon us in speech.[13] The last one, where-the-sun-straightens, is the smallest and youngest but on the other hand, he is the most famous and the one in control of the greatest quantities of life. Where he sits no darkness can overtake him and no evil winds can come walking upon him. His lodge is placed in the light, in the shimmering light of a perfect day. It is said that, as he made his way toward the Creation-Lodge, he was arrayed in the great power of light and life that comes from Earthmaker. Four steps he made toward the Creation-Lodge and he already stood at its entrance. Then he entered and walked right to the end of the lodge. There was no lack of light as he walked in. Then those within, put their thoughts together and the light sparkled and was immediately suffused throughout the lodge. Now he turned toward the right and walked around the lodge until he came to the point from which he had started.

As he walked along the Road of the lodge, at the very first place he stopped, the light that accompanied him was most pleasant to behold. Then as he continued along the Road to the seat in the south, the light that accompanied him became brighter with every step and suffused itself through the lodge.

He-whom-we-call-our-nephew, Hare, sat in his place and felt proud of the means-for-obtaining-life [14] he had brought into existence.

Thus did our grandfathers speak. But I, I am an old pity-inspiring man, I am quite unable to speak or act as they did. What I say would only be a source of embarrassment to you, so all I ask is that you have compassion upon me, O ancestors! The Road, too, I greet. Ancestors, we greet you, we greet you!

s o u t h : I greet you, you who sit here as Host; I greet you, you who sit here in the First position; I greet you, you who sit here impersonating North; I greet you, you who sit here impersonating West; I greet you, you who sit here impersonating Ghost; I greet you, you who sit here impersonating the one at the End-of-the-Road. All those who have come to be blessed, I greet you all, I greet you all. The seat of South, I greet. It is said that this seat is greater in dispensing life than the others. There, straight ahead of me, I see my destined place.

I greet you, you who sit here as Host; I greet you, you who sit there in the First position; I greet you, you who sit here impersonating North; I greet you, you who sit here impersonating West; I greet you, you who sit here impersonating Ghost; I greet you, you who sit here impersonating the one at the End-of-the-Road. All those who have come to be blessed, I greet you all, I greet you all. I send my greeting and blessing to the seat in which my younger relative and those with him will soon be sitting and in which they will feel themselves brought into connection with life. Ancestors, we greet you, we greet you. Let us then start up our song. We greet you. (song)

Ancestors, I greet you.

South is still standing in front of his seat.

S O U T H : You who sit over there impersonating the Rite-Giver, the Host, I greet you; you who sit over there impersonating the One-who-was-First, I greet you; you who sit over there impersonating North, I greet you; you who sit over there impersonating West, I greet you; you who sit over there impersonating Ghost, I greet you. I greet you all, ancestors.

There before me is the seat of the South one, the bear and his lair. Imprinted with life it extends before me. I know, however, that he cannot be missed by my missile and that in a moment I and mine will be sitting down. So I send the seat a greeting and blessing after which we shall immediately take our seats. I have done. (song)

They all sit down. Almost immediately after, South rises again, takes some tobacco and walks to Ancestor-Host. He stops in front of his seat and speaks:

S O U T H : Hāhā, ancestors. You have made the life-beseeching offering, tobacco, come to me and I will now return a small handful of it to you. Thus shall we all, each of us, be strengthened, we have always been told. In the past when I did so the tobacco was always accepted with pleasure. I send my greetings to you, to you!

This last greeting is made in a very loud voice. South now returns to his own seat. Immediately after, Ghost rises, greets those present and then sits down. Everyone has now taken his proper seat and the ceremony proper begins. Ancestor-Host rises and speaks:

A N C E S T O R - H O S T : You who sit over there impersonating the One-who-was-First, I greet you; you who sit over there impersonating North, I greet you; you who sit over there impersonating West, I greet you; you who sit over there impersonating Ghost, I greet you; you who sit over there impersonating the End-of-the-Road, I greet you. I greet you all, ancestors. *ho-ho-o.*

Hāhā, my ancestors. It is good that you have consented to come

224

here and help me. I am extremely happy to contemplate your faces. However I am capable of telling you little indeed. The best I can do is to sing a minor dance-song. That is all that remains for me. I have been expecting you and shall therefore begin at once with this minor dance-song. I beg you to have compassion upon me and that you fill up my cup of life. I beseech you to place it in front of me. Let my words indicate my gratitude and thankfulness to you. Ancestors you know what it is we are seeking, life, true life. We beg all of you who can to rise with the leader. Ancestors, we thank you. (song)

All the leaders and the older members who have this privilege have come to Ancestor-Host's seat and are singing and dancing there. When the song is finished, Ancestor-Host speaks again:

A N C E S T O R - H O S T :   You who sit over there impersonating the One-who-was-First, I greet you; you who sit over there impersonating North, I greet you; you who sit over there impersonating West, I greet you; you who sit over there impersonating Ghost, I greet you; you who sit over there impersonating the End-of-the-Road, I greet you. I greet you all, ancestors. In a moment I shall take the announcer along with me and place it in front of He-who-sits-in-the-first-Seat. With it I shall bring the life-beseecher, tobacco. Ancestors, I greet you.

The drum is now brought to He-who-sits-in-the-first-seat. He gets up and extends his greeting.

E A S T :   You who sit over there impersonating the Rite-Giver, the Host, I greet you; you who sit over there impersonating North, I greet you; you who sit over there impersonating West, I greet you; you who sit over there impersonating Ghost, I greet you; you who sit over there impersonating the End-of-the-Road, I greet you. I greet you all, ancestors. Let us all express our thankfulness now through the life-beseecher, tobacco. As for myself I have nothing to say, absolutely nothing to say, so I shall proceed at once to fill my pipe and let my breath emerge from my throat in speech. (song)

As soon as the song is finished he goes to the fireplace, turns to the left, the east, and pours out a handful of tobacco. Then he does the same for the north,

225

the west and the south. When he has concluded this, he lights his pipe and puffs some tobacco-smoke first toward the east, then towards the north, the west and the south. All now begin to smoke. When they have finished Ancestor-Host returns to his own seat next to that of the initiate. The greetings now make the round of the lodge. East continues:

E A S T : The words of my ancestors have reached me as well as their desire to be blessed. Now I shall induce them to try to obtain life, to place life before their own people by puffing, to obtain life by means of their mouth.

East now tells all the participants to smoke. First, each one is to fill his pipe. North is the first to speak:

N O R T H : You who sit over there impersonating the Rite-Giver, the Host, I greet you; you who sit over there impersonating the One-who-was-First, I greet you; you who sit over there impersonating West, I greet you; you who sit over there impersonating Ghost, I greet you; you who sit over there impersonating the End-of-the-Road, I greet you. I greet you all, ancestors. I will now fill my small pipe immediately and, having filled it, send my greetings to you.

W E S T : You who sit over there impersonating the Rite-Giver, the Host, I greet you; you who sit over there impersonating the One-who-was-First, I greet you; you who sit over there impersonating North, I greet you; you who sit over there impersonating Ghost, I greet you; you who sit over there impersonating the End-of-the-Road, I greet you. I greet you all, ancestors. In a moment I shall fill my little pipe with a handful of tobacco, the life-beseecher, for which all of us are so anxiously waiting.

G H O S T : You who sit over there impersonating the Rite-Giver, the Host, I greet you; you who sit over there impersonating the One-who-was-First, I greet you; you who sit over there impersonating North, I greet you; you who sit over there impersonating West, I greet you; you who sit over there impersonating the End-of-the-Road, I greet you. In a moment I shall fill my little pipe with a handful of tobacco, the life-beseecher, for which all of us are so anxiously waiting.

s o u t h : You who sit over there impersonating the Rite-Giver, the Host, I greet you; you who sit over there impersonating the One-who-was-First, I greet you; you who sit over there impersonating North, I greet you; you who sit over there impersonating West, I greet you; you who sit over there impersonating Ghost, I greet you. I greet you all, ancestors. In a moment I shall fill my little pipe with a handful of tobacco, the life-beseecher, for which we are all so anxiously waiting.

East now speaks again.

e a s t : You who sit over there impersonating the Rite-Giver, the Host, I greet you; you who sit over there impersonating North, I greet you; you who sit over there impersonating West, I greet you; you who sit over there impersonating Ghost, I greet you; you who sit over there impersonating the End-of-the-Road, I greet you. I greet you all, ancestors. I have nothing to tell you, absolutely nothing. Since the drum, the announcer, has been passed on to me, I shall intone a song. If we could but get hold of our relative, the announcer, it would give us new strength. We would be attaching ourselves to life. So let me do what I was told to do and let a life-engendering greeting be passed on to you. A song, too, I shall soon commence.

When the song starts you will see a man whispering to another person. Do not jump to conclusions and think he is speaking about you.[15] Actually, he will be speaking of how to obtain true life. I greet you all.

East and the one helping him now sing and when he is finished he walks over to where the one impersonating North is sitting and speaks:

e a s t : I greet you. You should now be ready to prepare four shells. I greet you.

n o r t h : I send you my greetings in return. I am prepared.

North now selects those who are going to help him specifically. Secretly each one whispers to the other. Each of the persons designated takes a shell and puts it in his mouth. Then they sit quietly and wait.

East now walks over to West and, whispering, tells him he is to have four life-obtainers, four shells ready to show publicly. He expresses his thanks and greets him. West selects those who are to help him and they prepare themselves by putting shells in their mouths and sit and wait. Then East goes to Ghost and finally, to South. Both select their helpers and all prepare for the coming ceremony by placing shells in their mouths.

Throughout this whispering and talking other members are singing.

East, having returned to his own place, now rises and speaks:

E A S T : You who sit over there impersonating the Rite-Giver, the Host, I greet you; you who sit over there impersonating North, I greet you; you who sit over there impersonating West, I greet you; you who sit over there impersonating Ghost, I greet you; you who sit over there impersonating the End-of-the-Road, I greet you. I greet you all, ancestors. All those seeking blessings each one, in turn, we greet.

For those belonging to my band sitting here we shall try to have life become apparent. Four shells we shall show publicly, as many as four. You-who-impersonate-North, your task it shall be to select four very expert shell-watchers.[16] What before was being whispered secretly now can be told publicly. You are all to get ready so that we can soon get up and begin our performance.

N O R T H : I thank you. I send my greeting to you.

E A S T : You, too, West, are to select four expert shell-watchers. Publicly you may do so. I wish you to listen.

W E S T : I feel happy and grateful at what you have said. I send you my greeting, I send you my greeting!

E A S T : You, too, Ghost, are to select four very expert shell-watchers. Publicly you may do so.

GHOST :   I feel happy and grateful at what you have said. I send you my greeting, I send you my greeting!

EAST :   And you, who impersonate He-who-sits-at-the-edge-of-the Island, four shells you can make visible. That is what I desire you to do.

SOUTH :   I am very proud of what you have told me. I thank you and send my greeting to you.

Then East with three men rises and starts around the lodge. As they approach North he rises and speaks:

NORTH :   Let us follow them, I and you three.

As they approach West, West rises and speaks:

WEST :   Let us follow them, I and you three.

As they approach Ghost, Ghost rises and speaks:

GHOST :   Let us follow them, I and you three.

As they approach South, South rises and speaks:

SOUTH :   Let us follow them, I and you three.

And so they march around the lodge preceded by East with three men and followed respectively by North, West, Ghost and South, each of them with three assistants. When they have reached the eastern end of the lodge, East stops and speaks.

EAST :   You who sit over there impersonating the Rite-Giver, the Host, I greet you; you who sit over there impersonating North, I greet you; you who sit over there impersonating West, I greet you; you who sit over there impersonating Ghost, I greet you; you who sit over there impersonating the End-of-the-Road, I greet you. I greet you all, ancestors. I have little to say and I shall not even try to say that. Perhaps tomorrow I shall be able to say something worth listening to. At least I shall try to do so. The time has now arrived where we are all anxiously waiting to participate in the ritual-drama[17] itself. One song, however, I shall start up and recount an incident.

Two men spoke to me. The first one said that he would insert the most important shell inside of me, put it firmly under my heart. 'You will never be able to see it,' he told me. 'I have lived by it, grandfather,' he said to me. The other man said that he, too, was going to insert the shell firmly under my heart. If I wanted to make it become visible and work for me in the lodge that, too, I would be able to accomplish. I would not be able, however, to have any success with it outside the lodge[18] nor would I be able to obtain life in that manner. In a place like this, in the lodge, I can send it out and when it returns it will bring life to me. And so I shall use the shell to strengthen and help my own kinsmen and those who are assisting me. That is what I wished to tell you.

This shell shall make life visible for us.[19] When we send it out we shall feel that we are really connected with life. Yet when it returns to us it will be a life, tangled and confused.

This then, is what I wanted to tell you, ancestors sitting around this lodge. All of you, I beg you, concentrate your thoughts upon me and mine, upon all of us. (song)

While East is singing, he walks to the west end of the lodge ejaculating 'yoho-o-o-o-o, ya-a-a-a, ya-a-a-a-a, ya-a-a-a-a, ho-ho-ho.' *Arrived at the east he stops and talks:*

E A S T :   You who sit over there impersonating the Rite-Giver, the Host, I greet you; you who sit over there impersonating North, I greet you; you who sit over there impersonating West, I greet you; you who sit over there impersonating Ghost, I greet you; you who sit over there impersonating the End-of-the-Road, I greet you. I greet you all, ancestors.

I do not wish to imply that those in the center are of lesser importance than my grandson at the end, but I shall call upon him to tell us of how he obtained that for which he is now so grateful and so thankful.

s o u t h :   You who sit over there impersonating the Rite-Giver, the Host, I greet you; you who sit over there impersonating the One-who-was-First, I greet you; you who sit over there impersonating North, I greet you; you who sit over there impersonating West, I greet you; you who sit over there impersonating Ghost, I greet you. I greet you all, ancestors.

What I have to say is this. Two men, my superiors, made me follow them. They assured me that here in the lodge I would be able to make the shell become visible. In all sincerity they told me this and in all sincerity I believed them. For that reason it is I wish to make this statement for myself and for those with me. Ancestors, I greet you. (song)

South now walks toward the east end of the lodge ejaculating 'yoho-o-o-o-o, ya-a-a-a, ya-a-a-a-a, ya-a-a-a-a, ho-ho-ho.' When he arrives at the east end he stops and East speaks again:

e a s t :   Ancestors, I greet you, each one in turn. In a moment I shall make my attempt. Do you all concentrate your minds on what I am attempting to obtain. Make your thoughts like mine. However, if you wish, you can do what now is to be done, individually. I shall not wait for anyone. Ancestors, I thank you.

I am now going to take the birdskin pouches to Ancestor-Host so that I can cough up the shell in his presence. Do you all do the same.

They now arrange themselves around the fireplace in a semi-circle with their birdskin pouches on the ground before them. East speaks:

e a s t :   I shall now begin and attempt to obtain true life for myself and mine. When you have done the same and are finished you must extend a life-engendering greeting to all of your kinsmen. Let us begin and remember, I shall wait for no one.

All now sit down on their knees before the birdskin pouches. With great effort they force the shells out of their throat and let them fall on the pouches. Then they pick them up as well as the shells. Each person remains kneeling as before while East speaks:

231

E A S T : Ancestors, I greet you. In a moment I shall raise up this light and life. Nor will I wait until you have been relieved of the shell.

East jumps up and begins walking around the lodge. The others follow behind him. When they have made the circuit of the lodge four times, they stop at the east end in front of Ancestor-Host. Each of the sixteen people carries his shell in one hand and his birdskin pouch in the other. Immediately after they have come to a halt in front of Ancestor-Host's seat, they place the shell in their mouths and swallow it. As each person swallows the shell he falls to the ground almost instantaneously as if dead. They must fall to the ground in a certain order, East and his group first, then North, etc. In a few moments, as if with great effort, they cough up their shells, rise to their feet, 'load' their birdskin pouches and begin making the circuit of the lodge. As they approach Ancestor-Host, on the fourth circuit, just near the entrance, East shouts:

E A S T : I am now going to shoot!

He begins the shooting of the shells and the others follow, strictly in turn. Four members of Ancestor-Host's Band are shot, four of East's and North's, two of West's, two of Ghost's and two of South's.

After he has shot his shell and been shot in turn, East continues singing and dancing around the fireplace. Any number of individuals, provided they have that privilege, can come and join him. On this particular occasion there were four gourd-holders and one drummer.

As each man is shot he falls instantaneously to the ground as if dead. Then he gets up and follows the others who have been shot and recovered. Whenever a person is shot he must shoot some one in return. Before a person takes his place in the march around the lodge, he must, for a moment, stand still at his seat.

When the marchers reach the east end of the lodge, East stops and speaks:

E A S T : I am now about to carry the drum to the next leader. You who sit here impersonating the Host Band, I greet you; you who sit here impersonating the East Band, I greet you; you who sit here impersonating the North Band, I greet you; you who sit over here impersonating the West Band, I greet you; you who sit here impersonating the Ghost Band, I greet you; you who sit over here impersonating the End-of-the-Road Band, I greet you. I greet you all, all of you.

232

The instrument-that-announces, the messenger, I shall now move on forward. Would that I could say anything of value to you. What, however, we can do, I and my people, is to seize firmly with our hands the materials that will give us strength, to seize hold of life, to feel ourselves in connection with life. Even if to the point of annoyance, we are going to try to contact the spirits and to imitate them. We will follow and obey them after we have taken a firm grip on the life they control. Then, we will be happy and contented.

All now begin making the circuit of the lodge slowly. They sing a song at the fireplace before they start. Then they stop at South's place and sing a song there. Continuing, they stop at the fireplace again and sing a song and then stop at South's place and sing the final song.

When the songs are finished they make four circuits of the entire lodge ejaculating 'wahihihi, wahihihi, wahihihi, eho-ho-o' and stop at North's seat. Just before ejaculating eho-ho-o, the drum and the gourds are placed in front of North's band. Then East and his band walk to their seat. Before he sits down, East speaks again:

E A S T : You who sit over there impersonating the Rite-Giver, the Host, I greet you; you who sit over there impersonating North, I greet you; you who sit over there impersonating West, I greet you; you who sit over there impersonating Ghost, I greet you; you who sit over there impersonating the End-of-the-Road, I greet you. I greet you all, ancestors.

Hehe, ancestors, have compassion upon me! I am in no way your equal. The force of our walking past you must have swept dust into your eyes, must have fanned you.[20] Some knowledge I possess, but my elders told me that I would feel myself connected with far more knowledge and would have had far more freedom if I had bought four times as many privileges. However, I was unable to do so. All I can do, therefore, is to stand about going through motions, talking and shouting before I do anything. Mere nothings, such have these actions of mine amounted to. Ancestors, I greet you. Have compassion upon me!

All now sit down. Meat, berries, wild potatoes, etc. are now brought to East to be given to Ancestor-Host. East receives them and speaks:

233

E A S T :   You who sit over there impersonating the Rite-Giver, the Host, I greet you; you who sit over there impersonating North, I greet you; you who sit over there impersonating West, I greet you; you who sit over there impersonating Ghost, I greet you; you who sit over there impersonating the End-of-the-Road, I greet you. I greet you all, ancestors.

I have but little to say. Those of my relatives who have the right to give feasts have brought this food for you. May it be acceptable! I was told that it might be so. I, myself, was able to obtain very little indeed but that was the best I could do, little as it is. This is what I wish to tell you, my kinsmen. Ancestors, I greet you all.

East now takes the presents and gives them to Ancestor-Host. East speaks:

E A S T :   Nephew, you who are sitting here, and all your dear relatives, accept this little gift that I have been able to acquire. Compared to what you have placed at my disposal, this constitutes a very small life-beseeching gift that I now proffer you. It is all I have, however. Do accept it and, with it, this present of tobacco. I greet you.

A N C E S T O R - H O S T :   I thank you and send my greetings to you.

North now rises and speaks:

N O R T H :   You who sit over there impersonating the Rite-Giver, the Host, I greet you; you who sit over there impersonating the One-who-was-First, I greet you; you who sit over there impersonating West, I greet you; you who sit over there impersonating Ghost, I greet you; you who sit over there impersonating the End-of-the-Road, I greet you. I greet you all, ancestors.

From my relatives sitting behind me, the lesser feast-givers, I will now gather together the life-beseeching gifts in order to present them to Ancestor-Host. In spite of their insignificance I hope they will be completely acceptable to him. Ancestors, I greet you.

Then he carries the presents of food to Ancestor-Host and speaks:

NORTH : It is little, indeed, that I am placing before you. Yet it is all I have. You have already blessed me and I hope you will continue to do so in spite of my unimportance. Our feast-givers are offering you this life-beseeching gift, this food. It is all we have been able to obtain. May it be of some value to you! That it would be I have always understood from my elders. However it be, this is all we have been able to procure. Ancestors, I greet you.

North now returns to his place and sits down.
West now rises and speaks:

WEST : You who sit over there impersonating the Rite-Giver, the Host, I greet you; you who sit over there impersonating the One-who-was-First, I greet you; you who sit over there impersonating North, I greet you; you who sit over there impersonating Ghost, I greet you; you who sit over there impersonating the End-of-the-Road, I greet you. I greet you all, ancestors.

I shall now gather the life-beseeching gifts in order to present them to Ancestor-Host. In spite of their insignificance I hope they will be completely acceptable to him. Ancestors, I greet you.

West now carries the presents of food to Ancestor-Host and speaks:

WEST : It is little indeed that I am placing before you. Yet it is all I have. You have already blessed me and I hope you will continue to do so in spite of my unimportance. Our feast-givers are offering you this life-beseeching gift, this food. It is all we have been able to obtain. May it be of some value to you! That it would be I have always understood from my elders. However it be, this is all we have been able to procure. Ancestors, I greet you.

West now returns to his place and sits down. Ghost now rises and speaks:

GHOST : You who sit over there impersonating the Rite-Giver, the Host, I greet you; you who sit over there impersonating the One-who-was-First, I greet you; you who sit over there impersonating North, I greet you; you who sit over there impersonating

West, I greet you; you who sit over there impersonating the End-of-the-Road, I greet you. I greet you all, ancestors.

I shall now gather the life-beseeching gifts in order to present them to Ancestor-Host. In spite of their insignificance, I hope they will be completely acceptable to him. Ancestors, I greet you.

Ghost now carries the presents of food to Ancestor-Host and speaks:

G H O S T :   It is little indeed that I am placing before you. Yet it is all I have. You have already blessed me and I hope you will continue to do so in spite of my unimportance. Our feast-givers are offering you this life-beseeching gift, this food. It is all we have been able to obtain. May it be of some value to you! That it would be I have always understood from my elders. However it be, this is all we have been able to procure. Ancestors, I greet you.

Ghost now returns to his place and sits down.
  South now rises and speaks:

S O U T H :   You who sit over there impersonating the Rite-Giver, the Host, I greet you; you who sit over there impersonating the One-who-was-First, I greet you; you who sit over there impersonating North, I greet you; you who sit over there impersonating West, I greet you; you who sit over there impersonating Ghost, I greet you. I greet you all, ancestors.

My small band has been able to get together a few things. I, myself, however, have not been able to procure anything. In fact, I, myself, am actually in need of food. If I get anything to eat it will be from the little food I have gathered together for you. It is the meat of one of the wild animals roving about here. That is one of the few things I have succeeded in securing. In addition, however, as my elders enjoined upon me, I have secured some of the walkers-on-light as we call them, birds, some vegetables, some nuts, some fruits, some tree-sap (maple-sugar?). That much I have obtained and a kettle of that food I shall now present to you. What I have brought together is what children might collect. But here it is. I place it before you.

South now takes the presents of food to Ancestor-Host and speaks:

236

S O U T H : I greet you, ancestors. I have brought you a gift worthy only of children. But it is all I have. I offer it to you, together with tobacco. I beg you to accept it and bless me. Ancestors, I greet you.

South now returns to his seat and sits down.
  Ancestor-Host now rises and speaks:

A N C E S T O R - H O S T : You who sit over there impersonating the One-who-was-First, I greet you; you who sit over there impersonating North, I greet you; you who sit over there impersonating West, I greet you; you who sit over there impersonating Ghost, I greet you; you who sit over there impersonating the End-of-the-Road, I greet you. I greet you all, ancestors. *Hehe*, ancestors, have compassion upon me.

It is good. What I and mine have craved, you have granted me in full measure. You have, by your actions and your gifts, caused me to be thankful. You have placed before me a liquid means-of-asking-for-life, have filled our bowls to the brim. It is good.

What I have to offer you in food and drink is not of an unusual kind nor will it, I fear, be adequate. You will probably leave here hungry. It was our intention to prepare food and drink for the four great spirits sitting here, the Island-Anchorers. In spite, however, of our best endeavors you will find it lacking in every respect. Take this into account, ancestors, and, in spite of it, bless us, have compassion upon us. We will bring you the means-of-thankfulness and do you, in return, bless us. Ancestors, we greet you.

So much for ourselves. It is said, however, that we should put a separate kettle in the center of the lodge for the person who represents Ghost. Let him accept it without any second thought. That will be his gratitude and thankfulness.

Ancestor-Host now brings the others food.

A N C E S T O R - H O S T : You may begin to eat, East.

E A S T : You may begin to eat, North.

N O R T H : You may begin to eat, West.

W E S T : You may begin to eat, Ghost.

G H O S T : You may begin to eat, South.

All now eat. When the meal is finished North rises and speaks:

N O R T H : You who sit over there impersonating the Rite-Giver, the Host, I greet you; you who sit over there impersonating the One-who-was-First, I greet you; you who sit over there impersonating West, I greet you; you who sit over there impersonating Ghost, I greet you; you who sit over there impersonating the End-of-the-Road, I greet you. I greet you all, ancestors.

Everything that East has said so definitely and clearly, I wish to repeat. In addition, I wish to extend my greeting to you in a song that I am about to start up. My elders told me that I should be proud to possess such a song. Together with it, the announcer, our relative, the drum, will proclaim a message that we must take hold of firmly so that we can be strengthened. Ancestors, I greet you. (song)

N O R T H : Ancestors, I send my greetings to you. In a moment I shall start up a minor dance-song. That will be my speech. (song)

East now speaks again:

E A S T : You who sit in the place of the feast-giver, Ancestor-Host, I greet you. All our ancestors sitting here in the shade of the Medicine Rite lodge, under its protection, possess various kinds of privileges.[21] Some have the privilege of singing certain songs. Let them release their breath in that way and bring you blessings. Others have the power of making their birdskin pouches become alive and make certain squeaking noises. Let those who can, permit their birdskin pouches to speak and squeak.

Remember, also, that one of our Rite members has died and that if we move about frequently and actively, possibly the feeling of desolation and mourning of the bereaved will be deadened. Do not, there-

238

fore, sit here and watch one another but let everyone move about in lively fashion. Let them make use of all the privileges they possess. Let even those who are taking the place of him who has died, join in lustily. Heed my words, listen carefully to what I am telling you.

All now proceed to North's place and dance and sing there. Then they go to the fireplace. There the members of North's band sing while the others dance around them. After the singing North speaks:

N O R T H : You who sit over there impersonating the Rite-Giver, the Host, I greet you; you who sit over there impersonating the One-who-was-First, I greet you; you who sit over there impersonating West, I greet you; you who sit over there impersonating Ghost, I greet you; you who sit over there impersonating the End-of-the-Road, I greet you. I greet you all, ancestors.

Our grandfathers are about to move the announcer to the next person. May my relatives take hold of this messenger of ours, the drum, and thereby strengthen themselves! May their sisters who have bought the privilege raise their voices in song! Let all who can, come and help us. Ancestors, we greet you! (song)

North and his helpers now walk around the lodge until they come to West's seat. There North stops and speaks:

N O R T H : You who sit over there impersonating the Rite-Giver, the host, I greet you; you who sit over there impersonating the One-who-was-First, I greet you; you who sit over there impersonating West, I greet you; you who sit over there impersonating Ghost, I greet you; you who sit there impersonating the End-of-the-Road, I greet you. I greet you all, ancestors. As we walk around the lodge the force of our movements will probably sweep dust into your eyes. Forgive us and do not withhold your blessing from us for that reason. Remember, we are not your equals. Ancestors, we greet you.

North and his assistants now begin making four circuits of the lodge ejaculating 'wahihihi, wahihihi, wahihihi, wahihihi.' On the fourth circuit of the lodge the 'wahihihi' is uttered very fast and the drum and gourds are placed in front of West's band. Then North speaks again:

N O R T H :   You who sit over there impersonating the Rite-Giver, the Host, I greet you; you who sit over there impersonating the One-who-was-First, I greet you; you who sit over there impersonating West, I greet you; you who sit over there impersonating Ghost, I greet you; you who sit over there impersonating the End-of-the-Road, I greet you. I greet you all, ancestors.

As we walk around the lodge the force of our movements will probably sweep dust into your eyes. Forgive us. Remember we are not your equals. What I have been doing here is not anything of my own volition.[22] They are actions that have been enjoined on us. So, too, if I stamp the ground [23] before your seat, Ancestor-Host, that likewise is a time-honored custom. This is not the place to do anything of one's own volition. It is not right. My stamping on the ground in front of you, Ancestor-Host, is, I know, a waste of effort for I did not buy it properly nor am I doing it correctly. All that I am trying to do is to seize hold of life for my relatives that they may be strengthened thereby and that their lives may be lengthened. It is an indication of my thanks and gratitude to you. Ancestors, have compassion on us, bless us. We send forth our greetings to you.

West standing at his own seat speaks:

W E S T :   Those who spoke before me have said all there is to be said. There is nothing that I can add. Ever since I was informed that the givers of this performance had had me in their minds, ever since then I have had a feeling of thankfulness in my heart. But to-day is the first time that I am permitted to express this thanks publicly, in words.

When I came in here I felt as if I were entering the Creation-Lodge. The life-engendering greeting I extend to you is but a small measure of my overwhelming thanks, for my gratitude to you, for the blessing you have bestowed upon me. If I could say anything I would, but when I try to say anything I find myself repeating the same thing over and over again. That is, of course, not what I wished to do.

The announcer has been moved on to my relatives and to me, so that we can take hold of the drum firmly and thus feel that we have

240

been brought into connection with life. Here is our messenger. I greet you. (song)

W E S T :   Now that this song is finished I shall start up a minor dance song. Here it is. (dance song)

West and his assistants now proceed to the fireplace where they sing, dance and shoot one another with the sacred shell. Standing at the fireplace, West now speaks:

W E S T :   You who sit over there impersonating the Rite-Giver, the Host, I greet you; you who sit over there impersonating the One-who-was-First, I greet you, you who sit over there impersonating North, I greet you; you who sit over there impersonating Ghost, I greet you; you who sit over there impersonating the End-of-the-Road, I greet you. I greet you all, ancestors. All those who have been blessed each one, in turn, I greet.

Shortly, I shall carry the announcer to Ghost's seat there to the left of me. Since I have nothing to say I will start up some songs for you at once. (four songs)

W E S T :   Ancestors, you have made me feel unbelievably proud of myself. I feel extremely happy and exhilarated. But now I must lead my people around the lodge. As we march around it, the shuffling of the feet, the shaking of the gourds, the striking of the drum, all these actions will cool your face as we sweep by. Ancestors, in no way are we your equals, but, still, do have compassion upon us, bless us. We send you a life-engendering blessing, ancestors.

As soon as I have finished my song I shall lead my people in their march around the lodge. I greet you. (song)

West and his assistants now begin to make the circuit of the lodge slowly. They sing a song at the fireplace before they start. Then they stop at South's place and sing a song there. Continuing, they stop at the fireplace again and sing a song there and then stop at South's place and sing a final song.

When the songs are finished they make four circuits of the entire lodge ejaculating 'wahihihi, wahihihi, wahihihi, eho-ho-o,' and stop at Ghost's seat. Just before ejaculating 'eho-ho-o,' the drum and the gourds are placed in front of Ghost's band. Then West and his assistants return to their own seat. Before sitting down, West speaks again:

w e s t :   You who sit over there impersonating the Rite-Giver, the Host, I greet you; you who sit over there impersonating the One-who-was-First, I greet you; you who sit over there impersonating North, I greet you; you who sit over there impersonating Ghost, I greet you; you who sit over there impersonating the End-of-the-Road, I greet you. I greet you all, ancestors. All these who have been blessed, we greet, each one in turn.

We are not your equals, ancestors. I have really nothing to say. Besides, all that was to have been said has already been said. I am extremely proud, however, that you have asked me to come here. If I stamp upon the ground and shake my feet in front of you, Ancestor-Host, I do it well aware of the fact that I have no right to this privilege. Undoubtedly you know that. But I wished so keenly to obtain added life for my relatives! That is why I have seized hold of our messenger so avidly. It was to give them strength.

Long ago I visited four old men and they told me what I had to do to gain this privilege of stamping on the ground. I was to make a four-fold payment to them. But I was unable to do so. Ancestors, I greet you.

Ghost now rises and speaks at his own seat.

g h o s t :   You who sit over there impersonating the Rite-Giver, the Host, I greet you; you who sit over there impersonating the One-who-was-First, I greet you; you who sit over there impersonating North, I greet you; you who sit over there impersonating West, I greet you; you who sit over there impersonating the End-of-the-Road, I greet you, I greet you all, ancestors!

In the old days they used to say that whenever a man put himself in a pitiable condition, he would be blessed. Furthermore, that if one is not able to pay anything, one can at least extend a life-engendering greeting. That which our elders and ancestors said in the distant past, every utterance they made in the distant past, all this has come into my power.

Tonight I am well-clothed with the blessings given me and, in return, I extend to all those sitting here, a life-engendering greeting. To the initiate, He-for-whom-we-seek-life, I further extend this

242

greeting and add my words and thoughts to what the others have already said. For that member of the Medicine Rite who has sustained a loss, the members are continuing the well-honored customs. Winters have followed winters, generations, generations, yet they still do it. The bond between the bereaved and the Medicine Rite still exists. But the smoke still lies thick within the lodge of the bereaved one.[23] He sees no light, no life. That he may see the light again, is our prayer to you. Here are the life-beseechers! Accept them!

Let us now take stock of what our ancestors left behind them for us when they departed and let us see how much of that life they left behind, still their due, we can obtain through dance, through the ministrations of our feet. As for speeches, you have already said everything that was to have been said, so let us proceed with the Tear-Pouring ceremony. Ancestors, we greet you, we greet you! (mourning song)

G H O S T :   Ancestors, we send forth our greetings to you. Soon we shall make our appeal to the ghost of the departed and beseech him to put at our disposal the life he left behind him still unused. This we would like to obtain by our cries and our prayers. Thus we should act I was told. And thus do I act. (completion song)

G H O S T :   You who sit over there impersonating the Rite-Giver, the Host, I greet you; you who sit over there impersonating the One-who-was-First, I greet you; you who sit over there impersonating North, I greet you; you who sit over there impersonating West, I greet you; you who sit over there impersonating the End-of-the-Road, I greet you, I greet you. I greet you all, ancestors!

Let me start up a dance song for you. To all of you present I send a life-engendering greeting. Of these one can never have enough, my ancestors told me. And, after extending these greetings, let me start up the dance song at once. I extend my voice in greeting you. Ancestors, I greet you, I greet you!

Those entitled to, now come to Ghost's seat and sing and dance there. Then they proceed to the fireplace where they continue their dancing and singing

243

and where they shoot the sacred shells at one another. They are joined there by members from the other bands.

When the shooting is over, Ghost, facing east but still at the fireplace, speaks again:

G H O S T : You who sit over there impersonating the Rite-Giver, the Host, I greet you; you who sit over there impersonating the One-who-was-First, I greet you; you who sit over there impersonating North, I greet you; you who sit over there impersonating West, I greet you; you who sit over there impersonating the End-of-the-Road, I greet you. I greet you all, ancestors.

The messenger and his goods are now to be passed on to the next person. I am but a weakling myself and can do nothing but still I am proud of having been permitted to do this. Since I have very few words at my command let me start up a song and at the same time, send you a life-engendering greeting. (song)

Ghost and his assistants now begin making the circuit of the lodge slowly. They sing a song at the fireplace before they start. Then they stop at South's place and sing a song there. Continuing, they stop at the fireplace again and sing a song and then stop at South's place and sing the final song.

When the songs are finished, they make four circuits of the entire lodge, ejaculating 'wahihihi, wahihihi, wahihihi, eho-ho-ho,' and stop at South's seat. Just before ejaculating 'eho-eho-ho' the drum and the gourds are placed in front of South's seat. Then Ghost and his band walk to their seat. Before he sits down, Ghost speaks again:

G H O S T : You who sit over there impersonating the Rite-Giver, the Host, I greet you; you who sit over there impersonating the One-who-was-First, I greet you; you who sit over there impersonating North, I greet you; you who sit over there impersonating West, I greet you; you who sit over there impersonating the End-of-the-Road, I greet you. I greet you all, ancestors.

I am not a Rite member of importance and I must have swept dust in your eyes as I and mine swished in front of you. Indeed I must have made you sleepy. However, ancestors, have compassion upon us and bless us! You have given my ancestors and myself reason to be proud, for none of us were ever leaders. Yet, in spite of all this,

244

I have been enabled to get a firm grip on the announcer and I feel that I have been brought into connection with life. It is here they say, that one passes life from one person to the other. And now we have passed life on to He-who-impersonates-the-End-of-the-Road. Our steps dragged along, to be sure, and we just barely managed to push it on to him. Ancestors, we greet you, we greet you!

South now rises and speaks:

S O U T H : You who sit over there impersonating the Rite-Giver, the Host, I greet you; you who sit over there impersonating the One-who-was-First, I greet you; you who sit over there impersonating North, I greet you; you who sit over there impersonating West, I greet you; you who sit over there impersonating Ghost, I greet you. I greet you all, ancestors!

He-who-sits-in-the-First-Place, as well as North, West and Ghost, have all passed on to me now the duty of speaking and, with it, have passed on to me, life. I welcome the opportunity of seizing the announcer, of securing a firm grip on life in this way, without the need of saying a word. I will repay it, after sending you a life-engendering greeting, by starting up a song. The members of the Rite, gathered here, have concentrated their minds upon the initiate, He-for-whom-we-seek-life.

Now the desire to obtain life is not anything you can compel people to have. You must come to it yourself. All I can do for He-for-whom-we-seek-life is to repeat the customary words. This is all I can say to him. (song)

S O U T H : You who sit over there impersonating the Rite-Giver, the Host, I greet you; you who sit over there impersonating the One-who-was-First, I greet you; you who sit over there impersonating North, I greet you; you who sit over there impersonating West, I greet you; you who sit over there impersonating Ghost, I greet you. I greet you all, ancestors!

I have very little to tell you. Instead of talking I will start up a minor dance song. Here it is.

245

All those of South's band who are qualified, sing and dance at South's seat. When this is over they go to the fireplace where they continue their singing and dancing, and, in addition, shoot the sacred shells at one another. Three kinds of songs are used. When they have finished them, members of Ancestor-Host's band replace them and continue the singing and dancing. Sometimes East, North, West and South will make a complete circuit of the lodge and then return to the fireplace before stopping. Finally, South, still standing at the fireplace, speaks again:

S O U T H : You who sit over there impersonating the Rite-Giver, the Host, I greet you; you who sit over there impersonating the One-who-was-First, I greet you; you who sit over there impersonating North, I greet you; you who sit over there impersonating West, I greet you; you who sit over there impersonating Ghost, I greet you. I greet you all, ancestors!

A small seat you have reserved for me but, nevertheless, I send a life-engendering greeting to you. I shall soon return the messenger, the drum, to the middle of the lodge. For my unimportant relatives I am going to seize hold of this messenger firmly so that they may be strengthened and feel themselves, likewise, in connection with life. A song, too, I shall try to start up for, of words, I have absolutely none at my command, none. And now, ancestors, have compassion upon me and bless me! (four songs)

South, standing at the west end of the lodge, speaks again:

S O U T H : You who sit over there impersonating the Rite-Giver, the Host, I greet you; you who sit over there impersonating the One-who-was-First, I greet you, you who sit over there impersonating North, I greet you; you who sit over there impersonating West, I greet you; you who sit over there impersonating Ghost, I greet you. I greet you all, ancestors.

As soon as the song is finished I will lead the singers around the lodge. Before that, I beseech you, ancestors, have compassion upon us and bless us. We are, indeed, in no way, equal to you. Hence our prayer. (song)

All now begin making the circuit of the lodge slowly. They sing a song at the fireplace before they start. Then they stop at South's place and sing a song there. Continuing, they stop at the fireplace again and sing a song and then stop at South's place and sing the final song.

When the songs are finished they make four circuits of the entire lodge ejaculating 'wahihihi, wahihihi, wahihihi, eho-ho-o,' and stop at the fireplace. Just before ejaculating 'eho-ho-o,' the drum and the gourds are placed in front of the fireplace.

After the drum has been brought to the fireplace, South returns to his seat. East now rises and speaks:

E A S T :   You who sit over there impersonating the Rite-Giver, I greet you; you who sit over there impersonating North, I greet you; you who sit over there impersonating West, I greet you; you who sit over there impersonating Ghost, I greet you; you who sit over there impersonating the End-of-the-Road, I greet you. I greet you all, ancestors!

I will not sit down any longer for we are now to remain standing; everyone has just been told. That is all I have to say. I send my greetings to you.

N O R T H :   You who sit over there impersonating the Rite-Giver, I greet you; you who sit over there impersonating the One-who-was-First, I greet you; you who sit over there impersonating West, I greet you; you who sit over there impersonating Ghost, I greet you; you who sit over there impersonating the End-of-the-Road, I greet you. I greet you all, ancestors.

I will not sit down any longer for we are now to remain standing; everyone has just been told. That is all I have to say. I send my greetings to you.

W E S T :   You who sit over there impersonating the Rite-Giver, I greet you; you who sit over there impersonating the One-who-was-First, I greet you; you who sit over there impersonating North, I greet you; you who sit over there impersonating Ghost, I greet you; you who sit over there impersonating the End-of-the-Road, I greet you. I greet you all, ancestors.

I will not sit down any longer for we are now to remain standing;

everyone has just been told. That is all I have to say. I send my greetings to you.

G H O S T : You who sit over there impersonating the Rite-Giver, the Host, I greet you; you who sit over there impersonating the One-who-was-First, I greet you; you who sit over there impersonating North, I greet you; you who sit over there impersonating West, I greet you; you who sit over there impersonating the End-of-the-Road, I greet you. I greet you all, ancestors.

I will not sit down any longer for we are now to remain standing; everyone has just been told. That is all I have to say. I send my greetings to you.

S O U T H : You who sit over there impersonating the Rite-Giver, the Host, I greet you; you who sit over there impersonating the One-who-was-First, I greet you; you who sit over there impersonating North, I greet you; you who sit over there impersonating West, I greet you; you who sit over there impersonating Ghost, I greet you. I greet you all, ancestors.

I will not sit down any longer for we are now to remain standing; everyone has just been told. That is all I have to say. I send my greetings to you.

All now get up and greet one another. East speaks again:

E A S T : I am afraid that whatever I were to say now would only annoy you, so let me merely send you a life-engendering greeting and express my deep feeling of gratitude and thankfulness for what you have done from the beginning of the ceremony until now. I greet you. (song)

Let me now pass the means-of-thankfulness to North.

N O R T H : You who sit over there impersonating the Rite-Giver, the Host, I greet you; you who sit over there impersonating the One-who-was-First, I greet you; you who sit over there impersonating West, I greet you; you who sit over there impersonating

248

Ghost, I greet you; you who sit over there impersonating the End-of-the-Road, I greet you. I greet you all, ancestors.

In a moment I shall give voice to my thankfulness, in a little speech, a song. With that I greet you and pass on the means-of-thankfulness to West.

W E S T :   You who sit over there impersonating the Rite-Giver, the Host, I greet you; you who sit over there impersonating the One-who-was-First, I greet you; you who sit over there impersonating North, I greet you; you who sit over there impersonating Ghost, I greet you; you who sit over there impersonating the End-of-the-Road, I greet you. I greet you all, ancestors. With a small speech of thankfulness I now greet you. Ancestors, I greet you. (song)

I now pass on the means-of-thankfulness to Ghost.

G H O S T :   You who sit over there impersonating the Rite-Giver, the Host, I greet you; you who sit over there impersonating the One-who-was-First, I greet you; you who sit over there impersonating North, I greet you; you who sit over there impersonating West, I greet you; you who sit over there impersonating the End-of-the-Road, I greet you. I greet you all, ancestors. With a small speech of thankfulness I now greet you. Ancestors, I greet you. (song)

I now pass on the means-of-thankfulness to South.

S O U T H :   Ancestors, all of you who are present here, I greet you. With one song I shall greet you. (song)

While they are singing they march toward the entrance. Just before they reach it, they stop singing and suddenly ejaculate 'wahihihi, wahihihi, wahihihi, wahihihi.' *Then they pass out of the lodge.*

PART FOUR

THE RITUAL OF REWARDS

Shortly before sunrise Ancestor-Host with two assistants and the initiate, East with two assistants, North with two assistants, and, at least, one member of West's and South's band, leave the ceremonial lodge where the Rite is being performed and make their way to a secluded place in the brush. There an oval-shaped space has been specially cleared for them. The whereabouts of this place is a carefully guarded secret known only to the people actually participating in the ceremony to be given there. No order is observed in the march to this place until it is actually reached. Then, however, all fall in line, East and his assistants leading, followed by North and his assistants, by the representatives of West and South and by Ancestor-Host, his two assistants and the initiate.

As soon as the line is formed, East, singing, and followed by the others, circles the space four times. At the end of the fourth circuit, they all turn around and face east. North then does the same thing. Still standing at the west end of the cleared space and facing east, Ancestor-Host now speaks:

ANCESTOR-HOST : We send our greetings to you, ancestors who are sitting here; we send our greetings to every one of you. I am now about to prepare the Road for He-for-whom-we-seek-life. This is the Road laid out by He-whom-we-call-our-nephew, and the initiate cannot fail to stay in it. For him there will be neither falling nor standing, illness nor death. The spirits created this Road for us and He-for-whom-we-seek-life will stand in it firmly, will step into it, into life, firmly, today. He who travels along this Road, if he has lived properly and if he has been virtuous, will discover that our grandmother, Earth, has been observing him and that she will extend her broad breasts to him and to us. What I tell you is absolutely true, dependant, however, upon whether the spirits have seen you leading a virtuous existence.

Try then, I beg of you, to act virtuously in your travels along the

250

Road upon which you are now to enter. If you walk along it properly it will benefit you greatly. I, myself, shall now step into this Road at a walking pace. Let everyone here follow me as I pass my seat, the seat of one of those who sits at the edge of the island. Indeed, as I enter and continue my walk I shall be walking past the door where the Island-Anchorers, the Four Directions, actually dwell. Hāhā, ancestors, let us start. I greet you. (song)

Then all enter and walk around the inside of the cleared oval space four times. Before sitting down, conversation is permitted between the participants. Ancestor-Host speaks again.

A N C E S T O R - H O S T : All who are standing here, I greet you. When I sit down and begin I will be reenacting what Earth-maker himself did.

He sits down and the others follow his example. Shortly after, Ancestor-Host, accompanied by the initiate, rises, circles the enclosure, and finally stops in front of East. Ancestor-Host speaks, addressing East.

A N C E S T O R - H O S T : Hāhā, You-sitting-there-in-the-first-Place, and you others, gathered around here, I greet you.

I am going to let my son have a place in your midst and after he sits down I shall send forth a life-engendering greeting to all our ancestors, yours and mine, who long since have lain mixed and mingled with the earth. You, too, relatives who have accompanied me, to you, too, I send a life-engendering greeting and I beseech all those who are present, to have compassion upon you and bless you.

Your ancestors, undoubtedly, have passed on to you, excellent utterances, spirit-utterances, appropriate for good and virtuous living. Do not keep these from my son, I beg of you, do not be selfish or niggardly with them. Remember, he is standing here, weeping.

Ancestor-Host now greets East and, almost immediately begins to speak to him again.

A N C E S T O R - H O S T : I greet you, all of you present here. My son and yours, begs you not to be selfish or niggardly with the excellent speeches that your ancestors have left behind for you.

251

He sends his greetings to you, standing before you, weeping. Of a very special blessing is he thinking. Indeed, it is added life that he beseeches you to give him. Ancestors, I greet you. Let me hear your consent. Now we shall sit down.

Then a space is made between Ancestor-Host and East where the initiate can sit down. East now rises and speaks:

E A S T :   Grandson, I shall now tell you a story, a true story about what Earthmaker created. You must not, however, expect any great or wonderful tale . . .

Of the four worlds, Earthmaker is himself in charge of the first. There he lives. Of the second world, Trickster is in charge. There he has his lodge and there he lives in control of life. Of the third world Turtle is in charge. There he lives and there he has his lodge and there, also, he sits in control of the life bestowed upon him. Of the fourth world, He-whom-we-call-our-nephew, Hare, is in charge. There he has his lodge and there he sits in control of the life bestowed upon him.

Up above, it seems, a being was coming to consciousness. It would seem that he was in a lying position as he was thus coming to consciousness. 'How am I?' he thought to himself just as do the members of the Rite.[1] Then he had pity upon himself and tears poured from his eyes. He moved his right arm, then his left, his right leg, then his left. 'Will it be good, I wonder,' so he thought to himself.[2] He now took a piece of the fleshy part of his right side and commenced to stretch it till it became round and, from where he was sitting, he dispatched it downward.[3] He could see it. A pleasing light it produced.[4] Now, for the first time, he cast his eyes about toward the east.[5] The light lay there as if it were falling, limitless, lost in the distance, lost in the horizon of a world where no earth as yet existed.

Then he gazed toward the north and there, too, he saw the light as if it were falling, lost in the horizon of a world where no earth as yet existed. Then he gazed toward the west and, there, too, he saw the light as if it were falling, limitless, lost in the horizon of a world

252

where no earth as yet existed. Then he gazed toward the south and there, too, he saw the light as if it were falling, limitless, lost in the horizon of a world in which no earth as yet existed.

Up above the man-being sat and felt happy at what he had created.

Now once again he thought he would create something that was good. Thereupon he created a world for him to sit upon and live. Then a second world he created and then a third. There were thus three worlds. Finally, he formed a fourth one, a smaller one. He made it round and after he had finished it he thrust his thumb into it, and pressed it out to prevent it from bouncing up and down and to give it the shape it now has.[6]

There this fourth world lay, but it would not remain quiet. 'What shall I do to keep it quiet?' he thought. 'I wonder if I do the following whether that would be the way of making it quiet?' he thought to himself. So he formed four Island-Anchorers with his own hands and placed them in the four corners of the island-earth. One of them was placed in the east, where-the-light-comes-from and he sat there in that place in control of life. The second one was placed in the north, where-the-cold-comes-from and he sat there in control of very white life.[7] The third one was placed in the west, where-the-sun-sets and he sat there in control of life. The fourth one was placed in the south, where-the-sun-straightens. There he sat in control of the largest amount of life.[8]

Yet in spite of all this, the earth still was not quiet.

So once again, Earthmaker, with his own hands, formed four Island-Anchorers, four very white and awe-inspiring waterspirits. He placed them, all in a row, facing the east, right underneath our grandmother, Earth. Then he looked down to see if that had accomplished his purpose. But the island-earth still was not quiet.

So, once more, with his own hands, he formed four spirit-walkers, snakes, very white and awe-inspiring and placed them in between the four waterspirits in the east. Their tails were visible in the east and their heads were visible in the west, protruding from our grandmother, Earth. Yet the earth still kept on moving.

So, once again, the one sitting there, took a piece of the fleshy part of his right side, and with his own hands, he formed a very large sacred woman,[9] a female, and he dispatched her down toward the earth on which we dwell. She fell directly in the center below the seat of Earthmaker and our earth. As she came down crashing she split in two with tremendous noise. The light also split in two.[10] Then with crushing force she landed on our grandmother, Earth, along her whole length and settled at the corners. When Earthmaker looked to see the result, the earth was no different. It was still moving.

So, once again, with his own hands, he formed four very enormous trees with four branches and these he sent crashing down.

When they got to where the sacred woman had broken in two, they, likewise, broke in two, and the trees were scattered over the length and breadth of our grandmother, Earth.

There were all kinds of trees, very pleasant to look at. The leaves, too, were lovely and soon they took on their present appearance. Then Earthmaker looked down and, in addition, created smaller trees and leaves. 'That will be good,' he thought.

Once, again, he formed something, blue-stemmed grass, to be a covering for our grandmother, Earth. With his own hands he made it. It had four branches. Down below he sent it and when it came to where the previous ones had split in two, it, likewise, split in two and scattering, covered our grandmother, Earth. From it originated all the various medicinal herbs and grasses. Then Earthmaker looked again and, what he had created, had finally become quiet. Without movement it was.

Pleasant it looked, this newly created world. Along the entire length and breadth of the earth, our grandmother, extended the green reflection of her covering and the escaping odors were pleasant to inhale. 'This it is, this is the right way,' Earthmaker thought to himself.

Now, once again, Earthmaker formed an object. He took some dirt and made a man. When he had finished the man he spoke to him. But the man remained quiet. He pondered over the matter and concluded that the man could not hear him. So he stuck his finger in his own ear and then worked it into the man's ear and thus the latter could hear.

254

Then he spoke to him again. This time the man moved and Earth-maker realized that he had heard him. But he could not see. So Earthmaker touched his own eyes and then the eyes of the man and he could see.

Then Earthmaker spoke again to the man. This time he turned around but did not answer. He could hear and he could see him but he was not able to speak. Then Earthmaker put his finger into his own mouth and then into that of the man. Then the man knew how to speak yet did not succeed in saying anything for he did not know what to say since he had neither a mind nor a heart.

Then Earthmaker took some dirt and a portion of his own body, mixed and rolled them together, made a heart and gave it to the man. Then he spoke to him and the man talked to him quietly with a nice, strong voice.

He now took this man and hurled him from above toward the earth. When he came to the center below Earthmaker, there where the others had split into pieces, there he too, split open and was scattered. Thus arose all the different peoples and languages found on our grandmother, Earth [11] . . .

That is all I wished to tell you.

E A S T :   The time has now come for me to release certain information to the initiate. It is indeed time for me to tell it to him, and I shall. I greet you . . .

Earthmaker created a pouch from the skin of the otter, a pouch that was to be our guide.[12] Now the otter that Earthmaker created appeared suddenly in the middle of the ocean, in the east. There he built a lodge only for life. Into it no form of death could enter.

Earthmaker concentrated his mind upon the otter and the otter said to his old wife, 'Earthmaker has decided that Hare is to go in search of life for his uncles and his aunts.' Thereupon otter started to walk toward the Medicine Rite lodge. First, however, he approached his fireplace and circled it four times. As he did this his lodge began to sparkle with light and life. Only after the light had become greatly intensified did he leave his lodge and go out. He made four steps toward the water and then he walked in it. Finally he dived down to the bottom of the water. When he came up he had brought some sand with him. Suddenly an island emerged out of the water.[13]

Once more he strengthened himself with the power he possessed and dived into the water. When he emerged he had a kingfish in his mouth. Using the bear, his seat, as a plate,[14] he imprinted the middle of the kingfish's body with life.[15] Four times he bit into the intestines of that fish and with each bite, life and light were lengthened.[16] Then the otter's wife took hold of the very white bones that still remained on the plate and imprinted them with additional light and life.

Both of them now proceeded to walk on the water, and the ocean, large and turbulent as it had been before, became as calm and quiet as water in a small dish.[17]

On top of the water the otter walked until finally he stepped out on to the shore. There he rested. Once again he strengthened himself with the power he possessed and again dived into the water together with his wife. When they emerged they had between them four children.

Again the otter dived into the water and when he emerged he had in his mouth a very old, gray kingfish. Again he made the bear his plate and, starting for the kingfish, bit into the middle of its body and smeared it with light and life.[18] Four times he bit and snatched at it and with each bite he lengthened the light and life. Then, together with his wife, he took ahold of a piece of the kingfish again and the plate became marked and smeared with exceedingly white life and light. Thus it was.

Both now proceeded to walk toward the Creation-Lodge. After otter had taken four steps, he thought he would try his shell [19] so he shot at a very large tree he encountered and when he came up to the tree to look at it, he saw that he had struck right into the center of the core.[20] He was greatly pleased with himself.

Again he continued his walk toward the Creation-Lodge. After taking four steps he shot at a very old, awe-inspiring rock. When he

256

came up to it he saw that he had struck right at its very center. He was greatly pleased with himself and he recovered his shell.

As he proceeded still further along the road, he noticed the protruding edge of some white clouds. Immediately he shot at it and he struck it right in the very center.[21] He was greatly pleased with himself and he recovered his shell.

Now, for the fourth time, he tried it and shot into the Creation-Lodge and at the object which stands in the very center of the lodge, the unopposable.[22] When he got there he found his shell right in the middle of the fire.[23] Indeed he was pleased with himself . . .

Feast-giver, Ancestor-Host, I greet you. All who are present here, I greet you.

As soon as East ends North begins:

N O R T H :   Feast-giver, I greet you, You-who-sit-in-the-first-position, I greet you; all you others sitting here, I greet you. What I am going to tell you now is nothing really unusual. Nothing of that kind can you hear from me. What I am going to tell you relates to sacred utterances and you must listen to them. If you will abide in every respect by what I am now going to speak about to you, you will enable the initiate to live to a normal old age.

Now thus is it our custom to speak to one another with regard to this matter:

Grandson, never doubt this Road. If you doubt it you will be unhappy and cause yourself injury. If, on the contrary, you have full trust in it and do well, you will be greatly benefited by it. It is about this Road that I am going to speak to you now. I am going to begin by telling you of the manner in which you must start out.[24]

As you travel along this Road the first obstacle upon which you will come, will be a ravine extending, on both sides, to the very end of the world. It will seem to you impossible to cross at any place. Yet when you get there stop and think to yourself, 'Grandfather told me I would be able to cross it no matter how impossible it seems.'

Plunge through it courageously and you will soon find yourself on the other side. You will not fail.

Comment

This means death. It means that some day, as you have been traveling along the path of life, you will lose a child. Then thoughts of death will assail you. You, too, will want to die. But, if you pay attention to our teachings, you will be able to overcome your grief; you will be able to plunge right through this ravine and find the road of the Medicine Rite Lodge on the other side. If, however, you become completely disheartened and you make no attempt to cross the ravine, if you are frightened and dismayed and dwell upon your hardship too greatly and too long, here you will find your own grave.

N O R T H :   Continue along the road. After you have crossed the ravine you will find the footsteps of the Medicine Rite men who have gone before you. They will be plainly visible and clearly outlined. Step into them firmly and your heart will feel good. Then go right along. Soon you will come upon a seemingly impenetrable brushwood of brambles and thorns and weeds. Passing through or circumventing it will appear utterly impossible. Then stop and think to yourself, 'Grandfather told me I would be able to pass through, no matter how impossible it seemed.' Plunge through courageously and soon you will find yourself on the other side; the brambles and thorns will be behind you.

Comment

My nephew, this forest of brambles and thorns means death. It signifies that death has come across your path again. Someone whom you greatly love has died, someone almost as close to you as your wife. You will again become disheartened and thoughts of death will again assail you. But if you pay attention to the teachings of the Medicine Rite Lodge, you will gain the strength to endure this trial and ovecome these obstacles. If, however, on the contrary, you be-
258

come discouraged and frightened and dwell upon your grief too strongly and too long, here you will find your grave.

N O R T H :   Continue along the road. As you travel it, evil little birds will constantly din their noise into your ears and cast their excrement upon you. The excrement will stick to your body. Be careful not to brush it off. Pay no attention to what they do. If you were to take too much cognizance of their actions, you might possibly forget yourself and suddenly brush off their defilement. Yet that, my nephew, is wrong. Not in such fashion is the true life attainable.

Comment

My nephew, let me tell you the meaning of these evil birds. By joining the Medicine Rite you have indicated to the world that you wish to lead an upright life. As usual, however, no sooner have you become a member than the work of the evil tattlers and the malicious will begin. They will point out that before joining the Rite you had done things contrary to its teachings. Let it be so. Say some bird's excrement does fall upon you? What of it? Is that sufficient reason for brushing it off without thought? Some evil-minded ones might even say that you had once maligned the Medicine Rite, that you had said it possessed no merit. What of it? That is not sufficient cause for you to blurt out, 'Who said that?' and lose your temper. Keep your silence and hold your peace. That is much better.

N O R T H :   Continue along the road. As you travel it you will come to an enormous fire encircling the entire world. So close will it be to you that your face will almost be scorched. Nowhere will there be a spot where you can cross or evade it. When you reach this fire, again remember what your grandfather told you and plunge right through. Immediately you will find yourself on the other side. Nothing will have happened to you. On the other side you will come upon the footprints of the Medicine Rite men who have gone before you.

Comment

This fire, nephew, means death. This fire means that your wife has died. Endure your loss as bravely as you can. You must not get discouraged. Indeed, this will be the worst grief that you will ever suffer. And what will make it so difficult to bear is that it came without warning. You may have been living happily and carefree and then death struck. And so, you and your children will find yourself sitting there alone. Now, of all times, must you remember what your grandfather said and what he taught you to do. Now, of all times, must you pull yourself together and be undismayed. For if you dwell upon your hardship too strongly and too long, this will indeed be your grave. Then truly will your children be alone. So plunge straight through, plunge straight through!

N O R T H : Continue along the road. No obstacles will be in view. Then, suddenly, almost before you are aware of it, tremendous, perpendicular bluffs will rise up in front of you, bluffs you cannot scale nor circumvent. There you will come to an abrupt stop. But, my nephew, think of what your grandfather told you and then without any effort you will suddenly find yourself on the other side, safe and unhurt.

Comment

Do you know what these bluffs mean, my nephew? They mean death. The Road of life along which you are traveling, will find you without companions. You will be alone, quite alone. All, all are gone, those you have loved, your relatives, your friends. Sadly you will think to yourself, 'Why, for what purpose, do I continue to live?' Your heart will yearn for death. Nephew, nephew, here will you indeed need courage, here will you indeed need strength of mind and firmness of heart! Yet you must persevere. Over this, the most difficult of all the obstacles on the Road, over this it is imperative that you triumph. Now remember what you have to do. Keep in the footprints of the Medicine Rite men and then you will be safe. Bear this in mind: the teachings of the Rite are the only Road. Only if you adhere to them can you surmount this greatest of all obstacles and find the footprints of the Medicine Rite men ahead of you.

N O R T H :   Continue along the Road. Soon you will see a hill in the distance. When you have reached the foot of it, sit down, eat and rest. You will receive bear-meat mixed with spirit-food and the spirit-food will vibrate with light and life. After you have consumed it, climb to the top of the hill and look behind you. No one will be following you, but you will see many people in front of you.

Comment

This hill, nephew, means that you have arrived at that period in life where, because of your loyal adherence to the teachings of the sacred Rite, you will be continually partaking of feasts. Invitations will be extended to you from all sides. The Road full of people in front of you, represents the Medicine Rite men who have passed before you. No one is behind you because you are now about to enter on this new Road, the Road of the old and revered members of the Medicine Rite.

N O R T H :   Continue along the road. After a while you will see another hill. It will be set in beautiful scenery and all around it will be scattered red stones. When you come to the foot of the hill sit down, rest and eat. You will find food there and it will be served in a greasy kettle. When you have finished, ascend to the top of the hill. Look about then. You will see some people behind you and the number of people in front of you will have decreased.

Comment

The countryside through which you are passing will be better than that through which you passed after you descended from the first hill. What is meant here is that you will be better taken care of. More feasts will be extended to you and greater respect paid you.

261

N O R T H : Continue along the Road. It will be pleasant country. In the distance another hill will loom in sight. Walk toward it briskly. On all sides you will see bulrushes and red willows growing in abundance and over this most delectable of lands there will be scattered everywhere gifts for you to accept and to enjoy. At the foot of the third hill you must sit down, rest, and eat the food presented to you. After you have eaten it, ascend to the middle of the hill. There you must sit down and rest again. A reddish haze will lie across the land. After you have rested a while, climb to the top and look about you. There will now be many people behind you and but a few ahead.

Comment

This is the meaning of what you have heard, nephew. The red haze spreading over the land as you stopped halfway on the hill, signifies the Indian Summer. You have reached that period in life where you tire easily and your eyes have become dim. The bulrushes and the red willows mean that your hair has become grizzled. The men you see in front of you are the older members of the Medicine Rite, few in number now. They will help you by inviting you to participate in feast after feast. Those behind you, now very large in number, are the younger members of the Medicine Rite. They will invite you to feasts so that they can enlarge their knowledge of the Rite.

N O R T H : Continue along the Road. The countryside will be more beautiful and pleasant than before and you will see white poplars growing on all sides. In the distance another hill will loom. When you come to its foot you will have to sit down and rest. You will find food there. After you have rested and eaten, begin the ascent of the hill. It will not be easy and you will have to stop and rest four times before you arrive at the summit. When you have reached the top, look around you. No one will be ahead of you and many will be following. The place from which you had started at the beginning, seemingly a long time ago, will now appear very close as if you had started but recently.

Comment

This means, nephew, that by the time you get to the fourth hill you will be so feeble that you will have to rest four times before you can reach the top. The fact that you see no one in front of you signifies that you have become the oldest member of the lodge.

N O R T H : Continue along the Road. After a while you will come to an oval lodge and a man will speak to you and say, 'Grandson, how did you behave throughout your life?' Humbly you must answer, 'I do not know.' And then he will say again, 'Grandson, it is good. I know how you have acted. Come take some of this food.' He will place four dishes with food in them before you and you must take a spoonful from each dish. After you have swallowed the fourth spoonful your body will take on the appearance of a dog or a flea. By this I mean that because of your great age your body will not only be thin and flat but your ribs will have caved in.

Now the person to whom you have been speaking is the spirit in charge of the Medicine Rite.

Then, nephew, you will become unconscious for a short time. You will die but you will then continue on the Road as a spirit and quite unaware of your death. Close to you, on all sides, you will find the staffs of the members of the Rite. There you will find the ladders which you must ascend, the trees. There are two of them, one on the right and one on the left. That on the right is a tree twisted beyond description and very slippery because of the incessant rubbing it has endured. That on the left is a red cedar, polished and smooth from wear and tear and greasy and filthy from repeated handling. You must seize hold of these trees firmly and, by means of them, ascend. The country to which you have now come is the home of Earthmaker. It has been especially provided by Earthmaker for the members of the Medicine Rite. From now on this will be your home.

Soon you will be escorted to a long lodge where you will find all those of your relatives who belonged to the Medicine Rite and who adhered faithfully to its teachings. As you enter the lodge, grown up

263

man that you are, you will be passed from one person's lap to the other.

After you have stayed in this lodge for a little time, the attendants of Earthmaker will come for you and bring you to his presence. You will see him face to face. He will speak to you and he will tell you that you have done well and that as recompense he will permit you to be born into the world of men again whenever and wherever you wish.

A N C E S T O R - H O S T :   This then, O nephew, is the Road. Along this you must travel. Today, a young man, you are about to begin the journey which another has just ended.

As soon as North finishes his story the initiate is instructed in the technique of shooting the shell and falling to the ground as if dead. He is particularly warned against losing confidence in the Rite. They give him a shell to swallow and then cough up. When he has acquired the desired efficiency in swallowing the shell and throwing it up, East speaks to him:

E A S T :   Grandson, you have done well for yourself. It is good. *You have seen the shell.* Remember you must put it in your mouth and under your tongue wherever it seems best. Never swallow it.

When people shoot one another, they do not really die. In a moment you will be shown how to act so that you can do it well. The time is now at hand when you can see people go through these various actions. The more proficient you become, the more you will succeed in helping yourself.

Earthmaker called what they are doing here the Creation. In the very beginning they really used to kill one another but, nowadays, they are doing it as you see us do it.[25] Through this Rite we can succeed in shedding our skin, in living a second life. It is our only place of refuge, our only hope. That is why they enjoin one another to perform the Rite well and live up to its tenets. Only, in this way, be assured can real life be secured and can a person become happy. Thus have the members of the Rite always encouraged one another to act and behave so that they will attain to the good life as long as the world lasts.

264

This, too, remember. Never tell anyone about this Rite. Keep it absolutely secret. If you disclose it the world will come to an end. We will all die.[26] That is why our ancestors were always opposed to betraying the secrets of the Rite.

It is said that once two friends decided to test a slave. They waylaid him near the brush where this part of the Medicine Rite was being performed. Grabbing him they exclaimed, 'Tell us what is taking place here. If you don't, we will kill you. If you tell us, we will let you go free.' But the slave replied, 'Go on and kill me. I died a long time ago.[27] Never shall I tell you. Kill me if you wish.' Then they let him go free and one of the two friends said to the other, 'Didn't you say he would speak? But you see he didn't.'

So you see, grandson, why we forbid members ever to reveal the secrets of the Rite. Only misery and catastrophe would result from such conduct. Earthmaker himself assured us that happiness and good fortune will come to us only if we keep silent about these matters. Into the very bowels of our grandmother, Earth, must we project this information, so that by no possible chance can it ever emerge into daylight. So secret must this be kept. Forever and ever must this be done.

The leaders now take a blanket and spread it on the ground. Then they place the initiate upon it and shoot him, showing him how to fall down and pretend to be dead, and gradually to come back to consciousness and get up. As soon as he had become proficient in these matters they stopped and thanked him.

N O R T H : You have done well, grandson. When anyone learns as quickly as you have done that is a sign that he will live to a ripe old age. Anyone who is slow at learning it and does not persist until he has acquired proficiency, that is an indication that he will not live long.

With these words of North they all file out and make their way back to the Medicine Rite lodge just when the morning ceremonies are about to begin there. Ancestor-Host and his assistants have left sometime before.

PART FIVE

THE RITUAL OF LIFE, DEATH AND REBIRTH

The Medicine Rite lodge. Ancestor-Host is sitting inside the lodge with the members of his band. The members of the other bands are outside arranged, roughly, in the order in which they will enter. When he has finished certain songs, Ancestor-Host begins to speak:

A N C E S T O R - H O S T : Relatives, I greet you. Our ancestors are waiting for us. Let us therefore not delay and let us begin our prayers and appeals for life at once, together with He-who-sits-First. What he says we must try to imitate. Yet to imitate and repeat what our distant ancestors said at the very beginning, that, of course, is impossible. Again, we greet you, ancestors. Soon the messenger will make himself audible. Our words will be what he announces. I greet you.

The drum is now struck four times, slowly at first, then rapidly. At the fourth stroke, East and his band enter, make a circuit of the lodge and stop at the east end. Then East speaks:

E A S T : Ancestor-Host, you who sit here as Feast-giver, and those with you, I greet you all. It is good. Have pity and compassion upon us. Miserable and pity-inspiring we have come here. That you must see. I am not the equal of the other members of the Rite yet I know you will try to give us some of your own life so that I and mine can really feel that we are alive. If, today, I am truly in possession of such life, it is because of your efforts.

Indeed it is good and I mean this when I say so. I am not being polite or hypocritical. My mind and heart testify to the fact that I am now, for the first time, really living. This is the kind of living our ancestors of old always talked about; this is what they must have meant.

266

My dear nephew, the great Island-Anchorer in the east, whose impersonator I am, took four steps as he traveled toward the
Creation-Lodge. With his fourth step he reached the entrance of
the Creation-Lodge, an entrance that had no way of being closed.
Yet, in spite of its being open, no spirit-weakling could have gone
through it. Where-the-light-comes-from, the East Island-Anchorer,
he indeed could enter, for the creator had placed him in charge of
abundant life. He was clothed with all this power of life and he made
this life his own body.

He entered and walked to the fireplace whose circumference was
like a road extending along the whole length of the world. By the
force of his walk he imprinted the middle of the lodge with life,
smeared it with life. He made the air absolutely still so that the day
became perfect.

He who travels on the Road he laid down, never will he stumble
or fall; death will not come to him. The Island-Anchorer spoke to
those within the lodge about this life he had brought with him and
which had become transformed into a perfect life. It was a perfect
day. Like cobwebs the clouds swayed to and fro. Yet so still was the
air that one wondered what force it was that made them move.

Ancestors, I send forth my greetings to you.

Now, however, let me greet and bless you with a song. It is an
insignificant greeting, I know, but it has come down from my ancestors. Besides, I have nothing else to give. All I am endeavoring to do
is to supply myself with enough blessings. This is what we have
always been told to do. So, ancestors, here is the song, the blessing-
greeting, that I am about to begin. I greet you all. (song)

*East and his assistants now walk to the west end of the lodge. There they
stop and East speaks:*

E A S T :   Nephew, you who sit here as Feast-Giver, Ancestor-
Host, I greet you. I greet you, likewise, who are standing here with
me. The seat which I shall occupy in the east is not one that can be
occupied by a weakling. That bear-seat, prepared for me so that I
might impersonate the Island-Anchorer, where-the-light-comes-

from, cannot be missed, for it is imprinted and smeared with life. That is to be the seat of my band and of myself. I send a life-engendering greeting to that seat which will bring me into connection with life! Ancestors, we send forth a greeting, a greeting. (song)

E A S T :   Nephew, you who sit here as Feast-Giver, Ancestor-Host, I greet you. You, too, I greet, all of you who are standing here with me. In a moment I shall send a life-engendering greeting to the seat in which I and my insignificant relatives are going to sit. I send forth my greeting to you.

All now sit down. Shortly after, East rises again and after circling the lodge, steps in front of Ancestor-Host. He has some tobacco with him.

E A S T :   I greet you. That which we regard as life, a handful of tobacco, the life-requester, we bring back to you. It will strengthen each of us, they say. So now I am bringing back to its source, a small handful of tobacco. I send forth my greeting to you.

A N C E S T O R - H O S T :   With it we have been blessed. Ancestors, I send forth my greetings to you, to you!

North now enters and walks around the lodge until he comes to East's place.

N O R T H :   You who sit here as Feast-Giver, Ancestor-Host, I greet you; you who sit in the seat of the First-One, I greet you; you who are standing here with me, I greet you all.

I am not talking to you without purpose. What I am going to tell you I mean sincerely. Would that I could speak like the one occupying the First Seat! Unfortunately I know nothing and what I say is simply a matter of form. However, I will try to say something, something truthful. Probably the only thing I shall accomplish by my talking is to make you fretful and uneasy. I do not like to speak. I feel nervous and shy here.

When we tread in the footprints of a member of the Rite long since dead, may the footsteps we take strengthen us!

They have made me think that I am the impersonator of the Island-Anchorer, of the one who sits at the edge of the island in the

268

north. With pride they have filled me. Indeed I am very, very proud. If I only knew how to say anything, gladly would I say it. In fact I would talk a great deal.

'Remember,' so I was told, 'that if, in times to come, you are ever invited to the Medicine Rite and have nothing to say, you will stand there in the midst of everyone like a fool!' If I had only listened to their counsels and advice I would have been anxious to have had such an occasion as this come to me. But I did not listen and so I have nothing to say. And this, again, my elders told me: 'If you do not listen to us, when a blessing like this one comes to you, you will be quite unable to say a word. Then the best thing you can do is to use a song of thankfulness.'

This is what I wished to tell you, this is what I mean. A life-engendering greeting I send you! A life-engendering greeting, likewise, I send to the Road. I bless it and I bless the Creation-Lodge and the feasters sitting within it. Ancestors, I send forth my greetings to you, I send forth my greeting to you! (song)

North now walks to the west end of the lodge. There he stops and speaks:

N O R T H : Ancestor-Host, you who sit here as Feast-Giver, I greet you; you who sit here in the First Seat, I greet you; all those standing here with me, I greet. The bear-seat reserved for me in the North, it will be impossible for me to miss. It is imprinted and smeared with life. There one is connected with very straight, vertical life. When I have finished this song, then I shall make my way to this straight, vertical life. I greet you all. (song)

North now walks to his own place, stops there and speaks again:

N O R T H : Ancestor-Host, you who sit here as Feast-Giver, I greet you; you who sit here in the First Seat, I greet you; all present here, I greet, each one in turn. In a moment I shall send a life-begetting greeting to the seat in which my relatives and I are going to sit. But, before that, we shall take back to Ancestor-Host, the tobacco, the life with which we are to be brought into connection when we sit down. We send forth our greetings to you.

269

You have had a wonderful life reach me and this life which you brought into connection with me, I now pass back to you. Thus both of us possess it and both of us are given added strength. I beg you to puff this life upon yourself. I greet you.

West now enters, walks around the lodge until he comes back to the place where he entered and then speaks:

W E S T : Ancestor-Host, you who sit here as Feast-Giver, I greet you; you who sit here in the First Seat, I greet you; all those standing here with me, I greet. You have had us blessed. It is good. The message has reached me here from the far past just as the life-engendering greetings have been handed down from the distant past to the present. Here I am actually within the Medicine Rite lodge and I am really extending life-engendering greetings to people and not simply doing it in my imagination!

He who preceded me has said everything that can be said. I cannot speak like him for I am not his equal. I am therefore afraid to say anything lest I make mistakes. Truly I do not feel able to say anything. However a few words I would like to say—to send a life-begetting greeting to the Road and to start up a life-engendering song-greeting. Here it is. Ancestors, I greet you all. (song)

West now goes around the lodge until he reaches the west end. There he stops and speaks:

W E S T : Ancestor-Host, you who sit here as Feast-Giver, I greet you; you who sit here in the First Seat, I greet you; all those standing here with me, I greet.

In the west, in that direction, lies my bear-seat. It will be impossible to miss this seat for it is imprinted and smeared with life. I send a greeting to the life with which I am to be connected, the Creation-Lodge and to all those present. I greet you all. (song)

West now goes and stands before his own seat. Then he speaks:

W E S T : Ancestor-Host, you who sit here as Feast-Giver, I greet you; you who sit here in the First Seat, I greet you; all those

270

standing here with me, I greet. I, again, send a greeting to the seat where my relatives and myself are soon to sit down and where they will feel themselves in connection with life, where we are to live and increase. Ancestors, I send forth my greetings to you.

West and his group now sit down. Shortly after West rises and walks over to Ancestor.

W E S T : I greet the life with which I am to be brought into connection. You have had a wonderful life reach me and that life which you brought into connection with me, I now pass back to you. Thus both of us possess it and both of us are given added strength. I beg you to puff this life upon yourself. I greet you.

Ghost now enters and walks around the lodge until he returns to the place from which he started. Then he speaks:

G H O S T : Ancestor-Host, you who sit here as Feast-Giver, I greet you; you who sit here in the First Seat, I greet you; you who sit in the North, I greet you; you who sit in the West, I greet you; all present here, I greet, each one in turn.

What those preceding me have said covers everything. I am quite unable to tell you anything more. All I know is that those who invited me here blessed me and had compassion upon me. If I were to talk, all I could do would be to repeat the same word over and over again. I do, however, possess a short song and this I can send to you, as a greeting. Here it is. (song)

Ghost now goes to the west end of the lodge and speaks:

G H O S T : Ancestor-Host, you who sit here as Feast-Giver, I greet you; you who sit here in the First Seat, I greet you; you who sit in the North, I greet you; you who sit in the West, I greet you; all present here, I greet, each one in turn.

The seat that has been reserved for me I greet. It is impossible to miss this bear-seat, they say. I greet the seat with which I am to be connected as impersonator. Ancestors, I greet you. (song)

Ghost now goes and stands in front of his own seat:

271

G H O S T : Ancestor-Host, you who sit here as Feast-Giver, I greet you; you who sit here in the First Seat, I greet you; you who sit in the North, I greet you; you who sit in the West, I greet you; all present here, I greet, each one in turn.

I greet the seat in which my relatives and I are to sit, shrunk very much though it is, the place where we are to live and increase.

Ghost now walks over to Ancestor-Host and addresses him:

G H O S T : Ancestor-Host, you who sit here as Feast-Giver, I greet you; you who sit here in the First Seat, I greet you; you who sit in the North, I greet you; you who sit in the West, I greet you; all present here, I greet, each one in turn.

I greet you. You have had life reach me and this life which you brought into connection with me, I now pass back to you. Thus both of us possess it and both of us are given added strength.

South now enters and walks around the lodge until he comes to the place from which he started. Then he speaks:

S O U T H : You who sit over there impersonating the Rite-Giver, the Host, I greet you; you who sit over there impersonating the One-who-was-First, I greet you; you who sit over there impersonating North, I greet you; you who sit over there impersonating West, I greet you; you who sit over there impersonating Ghost, I greet you. I greet you all, ancestors.

What those preceding me have said covers everything. I am unable to tell you anything more. All I know is that those who invited me here, blessed me and had compassion upon me. If I were to talk, all I could do would be to repeat the same word over and over again. I do, however, possess a short song and this I can send to you as a greeting.

In the south, where-the-sun-straightens there lies a seat, the one at the corner of the island, belonging to one of the great Island-Anchorers. It is connected with life.

It is good. As a result of this honor I really feel that I have now

272

been brought into connection with life. The Island-Anchorer at the south made his thought extend down here. He fixed his mind firmly upon the Creation-Lodge and dispatched it to the lodge on the fourth night. Whoever is seeking for life, when the time comes, will concentrate his mind on the initiate.

Towards the Creation-Lodge the Island-Anchorer walked and all the life-giving powers that Earthmaker had put in control of him, he wrapped around himself. They became his body. Then he entered the Creation-Lodge and started toward the Road. As he entered it and walked along the Road, life and light accompanied him and, great as had been the light before, now it began to sparkle throughout the whole lodge with still greater splendor.

Ancestors, I greet you. With a song I shall now send you a life-engendering greeting. (song)

South now walks to the west end of the lodge and speaks:

S O U T H :   You who sit over there impersonating the Rite-Giver, the Host, I greet you; you who sit over there impersonating the One-who-was-First, I greet you; you who sit over there impersonating North, I greet you; you who sit over there impersonating West, I greet you; you who sit over there impersonating Ghost, I greet you. I greet you all, ancestors.

To the seat reserved for me in the south, the seat where I shall be the impersonator, I send my greeting. This bear-seat where I shall be the impersonator, cannot be missed. I greet it. I greet all those present. (song)

South now standing in front of his own seat, speaks:

S O U T H :   You who sit over there impersonating the Rite-Giver, the Host, I greet you; you who sit over there impersonating the One-who-was-First, I greet you; you who sit over there impersonating North, I greet you; you who sit over there impersonating West, I greet you; you who sit over there impersonating Ghost, I greet you. I greet you all, ancestors.

I send a life-engendering greeting to the seat, shrunk very much,

273

in which my relatives and I are going to sit. And now we are going to start for this seat. I send forth my greeting to you.

South and his band sit down. Shortly he rises again and walks over to Ancestor-Host.

S O U T H :   I greet you. You have caused life to come to me and this new existence which you have brought into connection with me, I now pass back to you. Thus both of us possess it and both of us are given added strength.

Ancestor-Host now gets up and speaks:

A N C E S T O R - H O S T :   You who sit over there impersonating the One-who-was-First, I greet you; you who sit over there impersonating North, I greet you; you who sit over there impersonating West, I greet you; you who sit over there impersonating Ghost, I greet you; you who sit over there impersonating the End-of-the-Road, I greet you. I greet you all, ancestors.

Let me say this to you as I rise up. It is for me that you have done this, the one thing I desired. All night you have kept me with you and what I longed for, you have granted me. I have a dance song waiting for you and as soon as I sit down I will continue talking, holding the life-beseecher in my hand. But now, the announcer is about to become audible. Ancestors, I greet you. (song)

Ancestor-Host, his assistants and those privileged to, first sing and dance alone but, after a short time, privileged people from other bands join them. When the singing and dancing is finished, Ancestor-Host speaks again:

A N C E S T O R - H O S T :   The announcer, the life-be-seecher, I am now about to pass on to the one in the east and whenever he feels ready he can start. I greet you all.

Drum and gourds are now placed in front of East's seat. East rises and speaks:

E A S T :   You who sit over there impersonating the Rite-Giver, the Host, I greet you; you who sit over there impersonating North, I greet you; you who sit over there impersonating West, I greet you;

274

you who sit over there impersonating Ghost, I greet you; you who sit over there impersonating the End-of-the-Road, I greet you. I greet you all, ancestors. The announcer has been passed on to me and with it has come the realization of a new life. I like it.

I have been placed here at the front yet there is nothing that I can accomplish. Still, ancestors, I beg of you, have compassion upon me and bless me! Something, I assure you, I shall try to do.

He-whom-we-call-our-nephew, Hare, secured a new life for us. This is the kind of life we have today. . . .

When He-whom-we-call-our-nephew, Hare, had secured this life for us, the Creation-Lodge was completely full. There were members of all the different kinds of spirits when the ceremonies in that Creation-Lodge started.

When the creator looked down upon it, that which he had created, lay there calm and quiet. Those who were within were centering their thoughts upon the center of the lodge. The light was shimmering and sparkling, a perfect day.

Now the creator pondered and thought to himself, 'These spirits should have something on which to center their thoughts, something good.'

Accordingly, Earthmaker took a piece of flesh from the right side of his body and, with his own hands, moulded a man,[1] a nice one. Then he gave him a nice voice. He painted his body, making the top of his head yellow. Finally, he inserted in this man true life and hurled him down below him. Whenever the man hit the center of the worlds that had been created, the entire atmosphere trembled and shook. Four days he came tumbling down and as he reached each of the worlds, he went right through it, at the center.

He did not even stop when he arrived at our grandmother, Earth, but crashed right through her with tremendous force. At the place where Earthmaker had put a waterspirit, even there it was not very quiet.[2] Right at the side of the waterspirit which Earthmaker had placed at this spot by the force of his thoughts,[3] the man fell.

The waterspirit became aware of him at once. The man was very thankful. Like one of those that bestow (?) life, he thought he was. Then the waterspirit worked over the man with his own hands and great as had been the life Earthmaker had put in his charge before, the waterspirit increased it still further.

The waterspirit was not going to be at the Creation-Lodge so Earthmaker sent the man to him that he could add his powers. Indeed this waterspirit increased the powers of this man and he also painted his face blue.

The man started for the Creation-Lodge. He took four steps and then gave a whoop. His voice became audible.

Here the drum is struck once.

As he walked along, he swept away all that was clinging to the tops of the trees, growing on our grandmother, all the debris. As he walked along he swept away all the bad and evil secretions that collect everywhere on our head and on our skin, as well as the thrown-off remnants of spring's leaves and blossoms. Everything was swept clean and with this cleaning there came an increase of light and life.

Now the man took the second of his four steps and, for the second time, he gave a whoop. Again his voice became audible.

Here the drum is struck once.

As he walked along over the whole length of our grandmother, Earth, there suddenly appeared, on all the trees, white spots, blossoms. Like condensed vapor, like frost, they seemed.

Then he took the third of his four steps and, once again, he gave a whoop and, once again, his voice became audible.

Here the drum is struck again.

As he walked along, it became green over the whole length of our grandmother, Earth. All the many trees had green leaves and they were pleasant to behold.

Then he took the fourth of his four steps and, again, he gave a whoop and light and life burst right through the Creation-Lodge and into the object that stands in the center of the lodge. His voice was, indeed, audible.

Here the drum is struck again.

And then over this whole earth, throughout the length and width of our grandmother, everything became green. Our grandmother thus received her proper hair, her proper covering. The trees too, all of them, everywhere, had all their buds.

There in the center of the lodge stood the blaze of fire. The man spun this blaze around so that nothing could blow it aside. Then he spun the Creation-Lodge around by the force of his words and the pole in the center became unbendable.[4]

As he was doing these things, the light and life within the Creation-Lodge began sparkling with ever increasing brilliance. When he was finished, the day had become perfect. Not the slightest breath of wind could be felt and as cobwebs swayed above, one wondered by what force they could be floating.

Then the announcer became truly audible and distinct. Throughout the whole creation could be heard the utterance of that man. Those sitting within the lodge could hear it and, up above, the source of this creation, he could be heard. Throughout the whole length and breadth of the universe, that far, could that man be heard. Up above where Earthmaker dwells, he could be heard. There Earthmaker sat happy. . . .

Ancestors, I greet you. The messenger will now make his appearance. I shall send you a life-engendering greeting through a song. That is what I mean. Here it is. Ancestors, you who are present here, all of you I greet, each one in turn. (song)

East, at his own seat, speaks again:

E A S T :   You who sit over there impersonating the Rite-Giver, the Host, I greet you; you who sit over there impersonating North, I greet you; you who sit over there impersonating West, I greet you; you who sit over there impersonating Ghost, I greet you; you who sit over there impersonating the End-of-the-Road, I greet you. I greet you all, ancestors.

I shall now start up a small dance song. Here it is. Ancestors, all who are here, I greet you.

East, his assistants and those of his band privileged to do so, now sing and dance. After a while they are joined by others who have similar privileges. When they have finished Ancestor-Host speaks again:

ANCESTOR - HOST : You who sit over there impersonating the One-who-was-First, I greet you; you who sit over there impersonating North, I greet you; you who sit over there impersonating West, I greet you; you who sit over there impersonating Ghost, I greet you; you who sit over there impersonating the End-of-the-Road, I greet you. I greet you all, ancestors.

I beg you to have compassion upon me and bless me and I hope you will do what I ask of you now. All those who concentrated their minds upon this Rite, did so in order to bless me and help me. I, in turn, have sent a life-engendering greeting to you for the blessing you have brought me and the objects with which you showed your pity for me. But indeed, even more and more would I have you bless me! I extend a greeting to all of you!

All of Ancestor-Host's band now get up and walk around the lodge touching the heads of those they pass with their otterskin pouches and exclaiming, 'I greet you,' as they do so. The initiate, at the same time, goes to the fireplace and stands in front of it. After the members of Ancestor-Host's band have again taken their seats, Ancestor-Host joins the initiate at the fireplace. Then he speaks again:

ANCESTOR - HOST : Ancestors, I greet you. We are asking for life for one who is seeking it. I am about to prepare a seat for him, one in which his forebears once sat. That is the seat in which he presently will sit. Ancestors, I greet you, I greet you.

Then Ancestor-Host addresses the initiate directly.

ANCESTOR - HOST : My son, that about which I am going to speak to you, that about which I am going to give you counsel, to that I hope you will listen, and that, I hope, follow.

The people who are gathered here, all of them, are likely to exclaim when they hear these words, 'Why, he will not listen to you!' having, justly, no confidence in my knowledge. But I know you will listen. By listening you will greatly benefit yourself.

Earthmaker gave us this life of the Rite. It is truly the only kind of life that exists. No other is comparable to it. In order to make this life secure, from the depths of the earth, he obtained for us a black

278

stone, a chief, one who was in charge of all the other stones. This stone is quiet, calm and sedate, and is very, very heavy. 'This you are to have as your heart,' Earthmaker said. 'Then you will never be superficial, never will you lack firmness. Your faith will be as steady as this black, heavy stone.'

Love everyone whosoever he be. Never steal. Never fight. Take care of your conscience.[5]

Take care of your own people and of yourself so that you may live long.

Take care of the 'woman to whom you are married. Be good to her. Never treat her badly. Remember, our grandmother is a woman and she will hear of it.[6] Never mistreat a woman, I counsel you.

Stop drinking. I prohibit it for four years.[7]

The creator formed a tree that was the chief of trees and placed it in the middle of the earth.[8] It was a tree that could not be split with one's teeth. You must bite into that tree now but you must not make marks on it with your teeth.

Stop chewing.

If you obey me in all these things then the old members of the Rite, long since dead, will place you on this Road. So do try and perform everything well and efficiently. If you do so then that much more life will you obtain for yourself. Hãhã, Ancestors, I greet you.

Ancestor-Host now speaks to the whole group.

A N C E S T O R - H O S T :   I spoke to our son about a stone and about a tree. The stone I shall now hold to his mouth so that his faith will be like it, hard and firm. When I say I am holding this stone to his mouth, I mean the same as his heart. Ancestors, I greet you. (song)

Ancestor-Host now escorts the initiate to the west end of the lodge. As he walks around the lodge he holds on to the tail of the otterskin pouch. At the west end of the lodge the initiate is being prepared for the shooting.

The presents are now arranged. Twelve blankets are spread out on the ground like a carpet from the western end of the lodge toward the east, and a bolt of calico is placed on top of it. The initiate sits at the head of the carpet at the west. Ancestor-Host now walks around the lodge until he comes to East. When he stops in front of him, he touches his head in greeting. When he is ready, he speaks:

A N C E S T O R - H O S T :   I have already told you the small and unimportant presents I am going to give you. You are to receive clothing enough for the upper half of your body from the initiate, as well as blankets and half the calico on top of these blankets. These you are to take with you to your seat to the left, there where-the-sun-rises. I greet you with them. Ancestors, I greet you.

E A S T :   I greet you, I greet you!

Ancestor-Host walks over to North and speaks:

A N C E S T O R - H O S T :   Ancestors, I greet you. I wish to speak to you about something I have in mind for you. You are to receive clothing enough for the lower part of your body from the initiate, as well as six blankets and one half of the bolt of calico on top of the blankets. I greet you with them. Ancestors, I greet you.

N O R T H :   I greet you, I greet you.

Ancestor-Host walks over to West and speaks:

A N C E S T O R - H O S T :   Ancestors, I greet you. I know I have little with which to bless you. It may even be less than that. By your presence here you have shown compassion upon me, yet I ask you to bless me again. And here are my offerings to you—approximately twenty three yard strips of calico. This is my greeting to you. I am as one barehanded in my treatment of you. Indeed, I have invited you without being able to give you anything in return. But I hope you will forgive me and bless me again as you have already done. Ancestors, I greet you.

Ancestor-Host walks over to Ghost and speaks:

A N C E S T O R - H O S T :   I greet you, Ghost. However little those in the west will throw off for you, do you accept it with

280

thanks. What our forefathers told you that the ghost should ask of the spirit he controls, that you have, I am sure, already asked him. I beg you to mention this for me so that the ghost may pay heed to it when he reaches his destination. I greet you. Indeed, I greet you. Ancestors, I greet you all, I greet you all.

Ancestor-Host walks over to South and speaks, touching his head as he greets him:

A N C E S T O R - H O S T :   What I am going to bless you with is small and utterly inadequate in view of the fact that I have been begging you to bless me and have pity on me. Here are twenty yards of calico lying in the middle of the lodge. With that I greet you. Do not think it too little. Bless me, I beg of you! I am a poor, compassion-seeking man. They told me always to have pity on people. Do you, then, also have pity on me! I greet you.

Ancestor-Host sits down. East and North walk around lodge and stop at the east end. East speaks:

E A S T :   This is to be the giving of true life to the initiate, He-for-whom-we-seek-life. Thus our forefathers have said. Ancestor-Host recognized this fact and that is why he has so keenly desired this Rite for his dearly beloved son. We have, likewise, thereby achieved for ourselves, a minimum of life. Today, at noon, what Ancestor-Host so truly longed for, will be accomplished and I will bring life, a long life, to the young man by directing a shell toward him.

Trickster, it is said, once, long ago, spoke to Hare, and said, 'My friend, did not Earthmaker give you something to bring here?' 'That is, indeed, true and what Earthmaker entrusted to me I have right here.' He had hidden it in his chest. Then he coughed a little and a black hawk [9] with gray back was forced out of his throat. The back of this bird was sparkling with light and life. There the bird reposed in Hare's hand.

What Trickster and Hare accomplished, this I also desire to obtain for the initiate, for He-for-whom-we-seek-life, to try to encourage him to look for life. Today is the life-designated time.

I have no more to say. I hope I have not annoyed those present with my words and now I shall pass the means-of-thankfulness on to the next person. I greet you all, I greet you all.

North speaks:

N O R T H :   There is nothing to add to what the one in front of me has said. I, too, desire to obtain life for the initiate. That is what I wish to tell him.

It is said that Hare spoke to his friend Turtle and asked him, 'My friend, did not Earthmaker, when he sent you here, entrust you with some object?' 'What he gave me I have right here,' answered Turtle. Then he coughed and from his breast was brought up a black hawk with sharp wings. And then, round and full was the light, the life, that now became visible. So perfect was the atmosphere that the smoke took on the form of rings.

This is what I wished to say to He-for-whom-we-seek-life, the initiate. This is the life-designated day. Ancestors, I greet you.

And now, like the one who sits in the First Place, East, I wish to intone an unimportant song for you just as he did when he passed on his song to me. Here it is, my small song.

East speaks:

E A S T :   We are to concentrate our mind on the initiate, on He-for-whom-we-seek-life. I shall intone a song for him and present it to him so that, at some future time, he will recognize it in the Creation-Lodge.[10] But even in this kind of a lodge he can make use of it if he is asked to do so and he is so inclined. (song)

East speaks again:

E A S T :   Let the song be started at once so that I can pass on to the one ahead of me the means-of-thankfulness.

North speaks:

N O R T H :   I, too, will try a song. I, too, will present the initiate with one. Although I am giving him very little indeed, nevertheless, I will continue with this song. As long as I am alive, that long, will I and mine sitting here in the North and whose original occupant I am impersonating, concentrate our minds and hearts on He-for-whom-we-seek-life. Ever my thoughts will be for him. This song that I now intone is an expression of my sincere desire that he receive a full life. Indeed, indeed, this is my intense wish. (song)

East and North now start for the west end of the lodge, ejaculating 'ya-a-a, ya-a-a' as they shuffle along. They stop in front of the initiate who is sitting at the head of the spread-out blankets. East speaks:

E A S T : I shall try to bring you life. If you concentrate your minds upon the initiate it will be accomplished. Just keep your thoughts fixed upon him and the ceremony, and I shall succeed in bringing you life. I greet you all.

North speaks:

N O R T H : Ancestors, I greet you. I also, O ancestors, beg you to concentrate your minds upon the ceremony now to be performed. Ancestor-Host and his people have personally purchased two pieces of calico and allowed us to cough the shells upon it.[11] This he did out of respect for the shell so that it could fall upon a proper and good cushion. When we drop the shell upon this calico it will thus be because of Ancestor-Host's sacrifice. So should it be, for the shell is a very holy missile.

They drop their shells upon the calico, then pick them up and walk around the lodge. The shells are now swallowed and they walk to the east end of the lodge again. Here East speaks:

E A S T : Ancestors, I greet you. We have been centering our minds upon He-for-whom-we-seek-life, the initiate. And now I shall proceed to blow, far away from him, all the bad dreams and visions he may ever have had. I am going to blow, far away from him, all the evil thoughts that ever ran through his mind. Only the good and true life shall I permit to emerge. I am ready, and now I shall attempt, as best I can, to blow far away from him, all those things that should never have been around him. I greet you.

North speaks:

N O R T H : I, too, desire him to live. That is the thought within my mind. Exactly so do I wish it. Ancestors, I greet you.

Both East and North now hold the otterskin pouch in position for shooting. Then they jerk it forward, fully outstretched, four times, ejaculating each time 'dje-ha-hi, dje-ha-hi.' Now they point it, in succession, first toward the east, then the north, then the west and then the south, each time ejaculating 'e-ho-ho-ho.' This done, they put the shell in the otterskin pouch, run rapidly toward the kneeling figure of the initiate and shoot him. He falls to the ground instantaneously as if dead. He is immediately covered with a blanket and two otterskin pouches are placed upon it. East and North, with four helpers, then take the blanket off the initiate and undress him. They gather up his clothes and take these and the presents of blankets and calico away. The initiate, somewhat shaky, is made to rise and conducted toward the seat reserved for him and made to sit down.

Now East speaks:

E A S T : Our ancestors, the people of old, knew of the life you were to receive and of the seat in which you were to sit. You cannot possibly fail to see this life. I greet you all.

All sit down. Soon East rises again and selects one of his followers he thinks might be good in the magicorotc [12] *part of the ceremony. This follower now rises and speaks:*

E A S T ' S   F O L L O W E R : You who sit over there impersonating the Rite-Giver, the Host, I greet you; you who sit over there impersonating the One-who-was-First, I greet you; you who sit over there impersonating North, I greet you; you who sit over there impersonating West, I greet you; you who sit over there impersonating Ghost, I greet you; you who sit over there impersonating the End-of-the-Road, I greet you. I greet you all, ancestors.

284

Willingly do I speak. Whenever a Medicine Rite member asks one to do something for him, one always accepts with pleasure and with fearlessness.

Let me first, however, send a life-begetting greeting to all those who are here in this lodge. If they are fond of you, you will undoubtedly live a long life. You can be equally certain that if those listening here do not like you, that you will not live a long life. One must, therefore, never reject the request of the leader ahead of you. When you do accept, however, do not do so with embarrassment or diffidence because you will have the right to use the privileges of such a Rite member.[13] What he likes, do for him and try to duplicate exactly the manner in which he performs those actions of his which he has handed over to you for the time being. Since he is my superior who has so honored me I shall show no diffidence. I, on my own, can really do nothing but what I can, I shall begin to do at once.

The spirits fixed their minds upon the Creation-Lodge that lay stretched out below them. They concentrated their minds upon the middle of that lodge. As a result, so it is said, light and life lay shimmering and resplendent upon the earth. From above, the creator looked down below him. His creation lay there quiet and serene and he was pleased with it, just as it was. Then he thought of how he might provide those there with something, some beings that would be good for them to associate with. So he took a piece of flesh from his body and, with his own hands, he formed a bird, an awe-inspiring eagle.[14] With its mate, he placed him on earth. As they came they produced light, shimmering and resplendent, and life.

Then he took another piece of flesh from his body and formed another bird, and its mate, a sparrow hawk.[15] It was awe-inspiring. He placed them in front of the first one. With it there came light and life. Much farther back now did the light, round and full, extend. The creator was pleased.

Now, for the third time, the creator took a piece of flesh from his right side and, with his own hands, made an awe-inspiring squirrel [16] and its mate and placed them on earth. The creator looked down

285

at the spot where he placed the squirrel and the squirrel appeared all curled up like a very red hot coal, a live coal; he appeared as round as a silver dollar. Then he became larger and the light and life shimmered and sparkled.

Then, for the fourth time, the creator took a piece of flesh from the right side of his body and, with his own hands, formed an awe-inspiring weasel[17] and its mate, and placed them where the others were. The weasel would not remain quiet and kept moving around and darting in every direction. Wherever he moved and darted there was light and life.

For the fifth time the creator took a piece of flesh from his body and, with his own hands, formed an awe-inspiring beaver[18] and its mate, putting them in control of light and life. At the spot where he placed them, light and life appeared and larger and larger became the area where it shimmered and sparkled. From one place to the other it spread.

Finally, for the sixth time, he took a piece of flesh from his body and formed an awe-inspiring otter[19] with its mate and placed them below. The light and life were pleasant to behold. The creator liked it and was happy. He had put all these animals, taken from his body and made with his own hands, in control of great amounts of light and life.

It was now time for these animals to make their way to the Creation-Lodge. Soon, from above, a bird with a very nice voice, made his appearance. The Creation-Lodge was located right below the middle of the cloud-expanse we behold. When the other birds got there they stopped and, entering the lodge, they made plates[20] of the bear-seats designated for them.

Now a white-haired animal appeared, an animal with horns, horns that were shedding. Right into the middle of the lodge the mark of his light and life extended. No sooner had this animal been discovered than he was grabbed by those within and, in a short time, the plates were filled with his bones. And now the light had shrunk perceptibly.

Now, for the second time, a white-haired animal with horns appeared, just above the tree-tops. He, too, stopped there at the lodge.

Light and life sparkled from the middle of his body. He, too, soon was in the plates. As soon as those within the lodge had seen him, they had seized him. When they were finished they left just the least little piece of his body on the plate so that he might have young ones again.[21] That much they left there.

As they entered the lodge, from the nostrils of the animals the creator had formed, sparks flew in every direction. They looked like fire.

The Creation-Lodge was now full, full to capacity, with all the different kinds of spirits and as the birds made their way in, the spirit occupants were frightened, frightened by the fire they seemed to be carrying in their mouths, the fire that sparkled from their nostrils.

Around the lodge they made their way just as we do today and sat themselves right behind He-whom-we-call-our-nephew, Hare. They sat there in a row. What they had in their nostrils swayed lightly to and fro as they were sitting there behind him. Then they spoke and they said, 'Hare, in such fashion will they call on us for help. He who imitates us well and efficiently, he who directs kind thoughts toward us, he shall obtain life, life as it was understood in the past.' . . .

Well, ancestors, I am tired of standing and of making you stand so. I beg of you, do have compassion upon me. This play,[22] this ceremony, causes me great anxiety. I was glad to do it for my leader, glad to work for him. And now I have amply expressed my thankfulness and gratitude. Ancestors, all those standing around me and that I am leading, I am finished with my requests from you. What I beseech you to do for me may it not be too difficult! That is all I ask. Ancestors, I greet you. (song)

As soon as he finished the song he walks once around the lodge and then stopping, speaks again.

E A S T ' S F O L L O W E R : Ancestors, I greet you. Those in the middle are only able to say 'I greet you.' By this, however, I do not mean to imply that they are of lesser importance nor do I mean

287

to doubt their ability. This play, this ceremony, causes me great anxiety. Ancestors, I send you my greeting, I send you my greeting!

Now he passes the greeting on from one person to the other until all have responded. Finally when it reaches South, he rises and speaks:

s o u t h : You who sit over there impersonating the Rite-Giver, the Host, I greet you; you who sit over there impersonating the One-who-was-First, I greet you; you who sit over there impersonating North, I greet you; you who sit over there impersonating West, I greet you; you who sit over there impersonating Ghost, I greet you. I greet you all, ancestors!

The leader has asked me to do some work for him and I gladly comply. He assured me that this would bring me into connection with life and it is just this life for which I have been yearning. I do not intend to annoy you much and shall simply say what I have to say.

The one before me spoke about the birdskin pouches. He talked about them excellently, far beyond my powers to imitate. Yet let me continue. . . .

He-whom-we-call-our-nephew, Hare, had brought together, at the gathering-place, all the good spirits, those from above, those on the earth and those below the earth and, now that they were crowded into the lodge, all of them, he began speaking to them:

'It is in connection with life that we are gathered here, that we might obtain a good, a true one. To secure that is our purpose.'

The lodge was full to capacity with spirits; crowded, in fact, they lay there. As far as one could see the spirits were spread, sitting around the center of the lodge and onward. The light lay in shimmering cobwebs over the center of the lodge.

Far up above, the region from which the Creation-Lodge had come, sat the creator and he looked down upon them. The lodge lay there just as he had planned it. Pleased, he sat there, contemplating his own handiwork. There it lay extended, quiet and serene.

As he sat pondering, it occurred to him that he should give the spirits there assembled, some new gift, something they still lacked.
288

So he took a white cloud and a blue cloud, rolled them together and produced something very beautiful indeed. This he sent down, hurling it from above, down toward the Creation-Lodge. Then the light was stretched out and lengthened and all the evil clouds, everyone of them, were scattered and forced out beyond the confines of the earth.

Thus did the creator produce a perfect day. The light looked like the spreading web of a spider and, as it waved to and fro, one wondered by what force it could be moving.

Near the Creation-Lodge the otter was standing, the least and last of the birds the creator had formed. This the creator knew and this the otter knew as well. The white cloud and the blue cloud which had been mingled and combined into one, fluttered right above the top of the lodge.[23] The otter went to meet it. He seized it. In the east the light and life trembled and shook. When he recovered consciousness [24] and arose, he started immediately along the route that we all take, the Road of the Lodge.

Around he hastened until he came to the center of the lodge, snorting as otters do. That which had come from above he now forced up. Into light and life it had become transformed. Towards this object he now hastened. Then he moved it on to the next one and so it passed from one individual to the other until every one of the spirits lay there provided with light and life. . . .

And thus has it come back to me. A large quantity of light and life has come back to me, just as it was told me it would happen.

However, I must tell you something again. Two men made me follow them. The first one inserted a shell into me. Tightly and firmly he inserted it. The second one said to me, 'Inside the lodge I shall insert this shell into you. If you concentrate your mind upon it, you will most certainly succeed.'

I am now concentrating my mind upon this shell as I said I would. I shall concentrate my mind upon it not only for myself but for all the others. Ancestors, I greet you. (song)

East now goes to the fireplace and speaks:

EAST : You who sit over there impersonating the Rite-Giver, the Host, I greet you; you who sit over there impersonating North, I greet you; you who sit over there impersonating West, I greet you; you who sit over there impersonating Ghost, I greet you; you who sit over there impersonating the End-of-the-Road, I greet you. I greet you all, ancestors.

I have little to say and I shall not even try to say that. Perhaps to-morrow I shall be able to say something worth listening to. At least I shall try to do so. The time has now arrived where we are all anxiously waiting for the ritual-drama itself. One song, however, I shall start up but before I do let me recount an incident.

Two men spoke to me. The first one said that he would insert the most important shell inside of me and put it firmly under my heart. 'You will never be able to see it,' he told me. 'I have lived by it, grandfather,' he said to me. The other man said that he, too, was going to insert the shell firmly under my heart. If I wanted to make it become visible and work for me in the lodge, that I would be able to accomplish. I would not be able, however, to have any success with it outside the lodge nor would I be able to obtain life in that manner. In a place like this, in the lodge, I could send it out and when it returns it will bring life to me. And so I shall use the shell to strengthen and help my own kinsmen and those who are assisting me. That is what I wished to tell you.

This shell shall make life visible for us. When we sent it out we felt we were connected with existence. Yet when it returned to us it was a life, tangled and greater.[25]

This, then, is what I wanted to tell you, ancestors sitting around this lodge. All of you, I beg you, concentrate your thoughts upon me and mine, upon all of us. (song)

While East is singing he walks to the west end of the lodge ejaculating 'yoho-o-o-o-o, ya-a-a-a, ya-a-a-a-a, ya-a-a-a-a, ho-ho-ho.' *Arrived at the east he stops and talks:*

EAST : You who sit over there impersonating the Rite-Giver, the Host, I greet you; you who sit over there impersonating North, I greet you; you who sit over there impersonating West, I greet you;

you who sit over there impersonating Ghost, I greet you; you who sit over there impersonating the End-of-the-Road, I greet you. I greet you all, ancestors. I do not wish to imply that those in the center are of lesser importance than my grandson at the end and I shall call upon him to tell us of how he obtained that for which he is now so grateful and so thankful.

s o u t h : You who sit over there impersonating the Rite-Giver, the Host, I greet you; you who sit over there impersonating the One-who-was-First, I greet you; you who sit over there impersonating North, I greet you; you who sit over there impersonating West, I greet you; you who sit over there impersonating Ghost, I greet you. I greet you all, ancestors.

What I have to say is this. Two men, my superiors, made me follow them. They assured me that here in the lodge I would be able to make the shell become visible. In all sincerity they told me this and in all sincerity I believed them. That is the reason I wish to say this for myself and those with me. Ancestors, I greet you. (song)

South now walks toward the east end of the lodge ejaculating 'yoho-o-o-o-o, ya-a-a-a, ya-a-a-a-a, ya-a-a-a-a, ho-ho-ho.' When he arrives at the east end he stops and East speaks again:

e a s t : Ancestors, I greet you, each one in turn. In a moment I shall make my attempt. Do you all concentrate your minds on what I am attempting to obtain. Make your thoughts like mine. However, if you wish, you can do what now is to be done, individually. I shall not wait for anyone. Ancestors, I thank you.

I am now going to take the birdskin pouches to Ancestor-Host, so that I can force up the shell in his presence. Do you all do the same.

They now arrange themselves around the fireplace in a semi-circle with their birdskin pouches on the ground before them. East speaks:

e a s t : I shall now begin and attempt to obtain true life for myself and mine. When you have done the same and are finished, you should extend a life-engendering greeting to all of your kinsmen. Let us begin and, remember, I shall wait for no one.

All now sit down on their knees before the birdskin pouches. With great effort they force the shells out of their throat and let them fall on these birdskin pouches. Then they pick them up with the shells. Each person remains kneeling as before while East speaks:

E A S T : Ancestors, I greet you. In a moment I shall raise up this light and life. Nor will I wait until you have been relieved of it.

East jumps up and begins walking around the lodge. The others follow behind him. When they have made the circuit of the lodge four times, they stop at the east end in front of Ancestor-Host. Each of the sixteen people carries his shell in one hand and his birdskin pouch in the other. Immediately after they have come to a halt in front of Ancestor-Host's seat, they place the shell in their mouths and swallow it. As each person swallows the shell he falls to the ground almost instantaneously as if dead. They must fall to the ground in a certain order, East and his group first, then North, etc. In a few moments, as if with great effort, they cough up their shells, rise to their feet, 'load' their birdskin pouches and begin making the circuit of the lodge. As they approach Ancestor-Host on the fourth circuit, just near the entrance, East shouts:

E A S T : I am now going to shoot!

He begins the shooting of the shells and the others follow strictly in turn. Four members of Ancestor-Host's band are shot, four of East's and North's, two of West's, two of Ghost's and two of South's.

After he has shot his shell and been shot in turn, East continues singing and dancing around the fireplace. Any number of individuals, provided they have that privilege, can come and join him. On this particular occasion there were four gourd holders and one drummer.

As each man is shot he falls instantaneously to the ground as if dead. Then he gets up and follows the others who have been shot and recovered. Whenever a person is shot, he must shoot some one in return. Before a person takes his place in the march around the lodge, he must, for a moment, stand still at his seat.

When the marchers reach the east end of the lodge, East stops and speaks:

E A S T : I am now going to carry the messenger to He-who-impersonates-the-North. There I shall place it. There are so many speeches and actions, so many ceremonies in this Rite of our ancestors that it is difficult to attain proficiency in all of them. But my grandfather told me, "Try hard, nevertheless, to attain this profi-
292

ciency!' When I told him that I simply could not attain it, he said, 'Remember that these speeches, this talk, represents life.' What those forefathers of ours did and said was accomplished by their enduring hardships and sufferings. This is what my grandfather wished to impress upon me.

You know that I am an ignorant person and if you gain anything through listening to me that is due entirely to the speeches themselves, not to me. My grandfather told me, 'Grandson, if you do not listen to what I am telling you, when it is your turn to take care of the means-of-thankfulness, you will be standing before all the others, making weak attempts at coughing; you will stand there scratching your head in bewilderment. But even if, grandson, you are frequently deficient and inadequate, try and say something anyhow even if it is not quite the right thing' . . .

The original Island-Anchorer who sat in the east position possessed a messenger and something called that-which-stands-within-the-lodge,[26] given to him by Earthmaker. This latter object was stained black with age. Then he took this messenger, rattled it and started along the path with his hair waving.[27] Great as had been the light and life before, now it became greater. He-who-stands-in-the-middle-of-the-lodge, the unopposable, before this a twisting blaze, now became straight and the small hazy white clouds, all the evil ones, were swept away from the Road as the Island-Anchorer in the east made his way. Thus was evil demolished.

Then, again, for a second time, did he shake his rattle as he passed along and all the different spirits near the fire, the entire Road he swept clean of evil. He-who-stands-in-the-middle-of-the-lodge, the unopposable, the unbendable, rose up in a straight blaze. Great as had been the life and light in the lodge before, now it became that much greater.

For a third time, he now started around the Road, shaking the messenger. He-who-stands-in-the-middle-of-the-lodge, the unbendable, the unopposable rose in a straight blaze upward in sight of the multitude of spirits assembled there. Like old men near death they looked.

293

Finally, for a fourth time, he started around the Road, shaking the messenger. Again, He-who-stands-in-the-middle-of-the-Road arose in a straight blaze. This time the blaze extended as far as the home of the creator. The Creation-Lodge, the multitude of spirits within it, everything there, was resplendent with life and light. Quiet and serene lay the lodge and the creator became satisfied and pleased. No wind marred that light and the spiders were threading their webs undisturbed on that perfect day. . . .

But, now, to return to what those ahead of me have asked for the initiate, He-for-whom-we-seek-life. Indeed, I too, am trying to obtain for him the life-beseechers; I, too, desire to call upon the life-beseechers to aid him. If I perform my part well and sincerely, I know this can be accomplished. The leaders have assured me that if I sit here in front and if I get myself properly excited and enthusiastic then, at my command, the wind will blow from the direction I designate. They told me that if I correctly imitate and emulate the wind-position which I occupy, whatever I say, I can accomplish. If I perform my part in the *hoki'una* well, if I keep my mind on the initiate, if I stand humbly with tobacco in my hands, making my offering, then I shall be heating our grandfather for all the original spirits. What I have been saying and what I have been doing, it is all for one purpose, to secure and insure life for the initiate, for He-for-whom-we-seek-life.

But I have been keeping you waiting for too long a time. I greet you ancestors. (song)

East sings four songs as he walks around the lodge, at the east, the north, the west and the south. Finally he stops at North's seat and speaks:

E A S T :   You who sit over there impersonating the Rite-Giver, the Host, I greet you; you who sit over there impersonating North, I greet you; you who sit over there impersonating West, I greet you; you who sit over there impersonating Ghost, I greet you; you who sit over there impersonating the End-of-the-Road, I greet you. I greet you all, ancestors.

I have been honored and made to feel proud. Would that I could stamp the ground in dancing like Ancestor-Host! The leaders of the four seats assured me that I would be able to perform all the actions that they did if I performed my part in the Rite correctly and that I would myself become the leader on the Road, the leader of the dancing, and obtain the right to place the drum and pass the means-of-thankfulness from one person to the other. Ancestors, I beseech you, have pity on me! I greet you, everyone in turn. (song)

All now begin making the circuit of the lodge slowly. They sing a song at the fireplace before they start. Then they stop at South's place and sing a song there. Continuing, they stop at the fireplace again and sing a song again, and then stop once more at South's place and sing the final song.

When the songs are finished they make four circuits of the lodge ejaculating, 'wahihi, wahihihi, wahihihi, eho-ho-ho' and stop at North's seat. Just before ejaculating 'eho-ho-ho,' the drum and gourds are placed in front of North's band.

N O R T H :   I thank you. It is good that you have made this come to me. Ancestors, I send forth my greetings to all of you, to all of you.

East has now returned to his own place. Before sitting down he speaks:

E A S T :   You who sit over there impersonating the Rite-Giver, the Host, I greet you; you who sit over there impersonating North, I greet you; you who sit over there impersonating West, I greet you; you who sit over there impersonating Ghost, I greet you; you who sit over there impersonating the End-of-the-Road, I greet you. I greet you all, ancestors.

The little I can say will annoy you, I am afraid, for I am not your equal. Yet, for the little I am saying, I beg you to have compassion upon me and bless me. I fear that I have been fanning your faces as I walked around the lodge, that I have been sweeping dust into your eyes. Still it was with a humble and contrite spirit that I spoke, always having in mind the hope of being brought into connection with life. I know that my performance was not good. If I presumed, in fact, to say or do anything, that was because I felt so proud at being invited here that I did not know how to refuse. So do not pay much attention to my efforts, sorry as I naturally am that you must think this way of me. This much let me say however. I did the best I could. Ancestors, I do beg you to have compassion upon me and let this request for pity and compassion hold for all of us. I greet you, each one in turn.

E A S T : You who sit over there impersonating the Rite-Giver, the Host, I greet you; you who sit over there impersonating North, I greet you; you who sit over there impersonating West, I greet you; you who sit over there impersonating Ghost, I greet you; you who sit over there impersonating the End-of-the-Road, I greet you. I greet you all, ancestors.

Hehe, ancestors, have compassion upon me! I am in no way your equal. The force of our walking past you must have swept dust in your eyes, must have fanned you. Some knowledge I have but my elders told me that I would have been able to connect myself with far more knowledge and would have had more freedom if I had bought four times as many privileges. However, I was unable to do so. All I could do was to stand about and go through useless motions, talking and shouting before doing anything. Mere nothings, such has it amounted to. Ancestors, I greet you. Have compassion upon me!

All now sit down. Meat, berries, wild potatoes, etc. are now brought to East to be given to Ancestor-Host. East receives them and speaks:

E A S T : You who sit over there impersonating the Rite-Giver, the Host, I greet you; you who sit over there impersonating North, I greet you; you who sit over there impersonating West, I greet you; you who sit over there impersonating Ghost, I greet you; you who sit over there impersonating the End-of-the-Road, I greet you. I greet you all, ancestors.

I have but little to say. Those of my relatives who have the right to give feasts have brought this food for you. May it be acceptable. I was told that it might be. I, myself, was able to obtain very little indeed. It is, however, the best I could do, little as it is. This, my kinsmen, is what I wish to tell you. Ancestors, I greet you all.

East now takes the presents and gives them to Ancestor-Host. East speaks:

E A S T :   Nephew, you who are sitting here, and all your dear relatives, accept this little gift that I have been able to acquire. Compared to what you have placed at my disposal, these are indeed small life-beseeching gifts that I now proffer you. It is all I have however. Do accept it and, with it, this present of tobacco. I greet you.

A N C E S T O R - H O S T :   I thank you and send my greetings to you.

North now rises and speaks:

N O R T H :   You who sit over there impersonating the Rite-Giver, the Host, I greet you; you who sit over there impersonating the One-who-was-First, I greet you; you who sit over there impersonating West, I greet you; you who sit over there impersonating Ghost, I greet you; you who sit over there impersonating the End-of-the-Road, I greet you. I greet you all, ancestors.

From my relatives behind me, the lesser feast-givers, I will now gather together the life-beseeching gifts in order to present them to Ancestor-Host. In spite of their insignificance I hope they will be completely acceptable to him. Ancestors, I greet you.

Then he carries the presents of food to Ancestor-Host and speaks:

N O R T H :   It is little indeed that I am placing before you. Yet it is all I have. You have already blessed me and I hope you will continue to do so in spite of my unimportance. Our feast-givers are offering you this life-beseeching gift, this food. It is all we have been able to obtain. May it be of some value to you. That it would be I have always understood from my elders. However it be, this is all we have been able to procure. Ancestors, I greet you.

North now returns to his place and sits down.
  West now rises and speaks:

W E S T :   You who sit over there impersonating the Rite-Giver, the Host, I greet you; you who sit over there impersonating the One-who-was-First, I greet you; you who sit over there impersonating North, I greet you; you who sit over there impersonating Ghost, I greet you; you who sit over there impersonating the End-of-the-Road, I greet you. I greet you all, ancestors.

I will now gather the life-beseeching gifts in order to present them to Ancestor-Host. In spite of their insignificance I hope they will be completely acceptable to him. Ancestors, I greet you.

West now carries the presents of food to Ancestor-Host and speaks:

W E S T :   It is little indeed that I am placing before you. Yet it is all I have. You have already blessed me and I hope you will continue to do so in spite of my unimportance. Our feast-givers are offering you this life-beseeching gift, this food. It is all we have been able to obtain. May it be of some value to you! That it would be I have always understood from my elders. However it be, this is all we have been able to procure. Ancestors, I greet you.

West now returns to his place and sits down. Ghost now rises and speaks:

G H O S T :   You who sit over there impersonating the Rite-Giver, the Host, I greet you; you who sit over there impersonating the One-who-was-First, I greet you; you who sit over there impersonating North, I greet you; you who sit over there impersonating West, I greet you; you who sit over there impersonating the End-of-the-Road, I greet you. I greet you all, ancestors.

I will now gather the life-beseeching gifts in order to present them to Ancestor-Host. In spite of their insignificance, I hope they will be completely acceptable to him. Ancestors, I greet you.

Ghost now carries the presents of food to Ancestor-Host and speaks:

G H O S T :   It is little indeed that I am placing before you. Yet it is all I have. You have already blessed me and I hope you will continue to do so in spite of my unimportance. Our feast-givers are offering you this life-beseeching gift, this food. It is all we have been able to obtain. May it be of some value to you! That it would be I

298

have always understood from my elders. However it be, this is all we have been able to procure. Ancestors, I greet you.

Ghost now returns to his place and sits down.
  South now rises and speaks:

S O U T H :   You who sit over there impersonating the Rite-Giver, the Host, I greet you; you who sit over there impersonating the One-who-was-First, I greet you; you who sit over there impersonating North, I greet you; you who sit over there impersonating West, I greet you; you who sit over there impersonating Ghost, I greet you. I greet you all, ancestors.

My small band has been able to get together a few things. I, myself, however, have not been able to procure anything. In fact I am actually in need of food for myself. If I get anything to eat it will be from the little food I have gathered together for you. It is the meat of one of the animals roving about here. That is one of the few things I have succeeded in securing.

However, as my elders enjoined upon me, I have, in addition, secured some of the walkers-on-light as we call them, birds, some vegetables, some tree-sap (maple-sugar?). That much I have obtained and a kettle of food will I present. What I have brought together is what children might collect. But here it is. I place it before you.

South now takes the presents of food to Ancestor-Host and speaks:

S O U T H :   I greet you, ancestors. I have brought you a gift worthy only of children. But it is all I have. I offer it to you together with tobacco. I beg you to accept it and bless me. Ancestors, I greet you.

South now returns to his seat and sits down.
  Ancestor-Host now rises and speaks:

A N C E S T O R - H O S T :   You who sit over there impersonating the One-who-was-First, I greet you; you who sit over there impersonating North, I greet you; you who sit over there impersonating West, I greet you; you who sit over there impersonating Ghost,

I greet you; you who sit over there impersonating the End-of-the-Road, I greet you. I greet you all, ancestors.

Hehe, ancestors, have compassion upon me. It is good. What I and mine have craved, you have granted in full measure. You have caused me to be thankful by your actions and your gifts. You have placed before us a liquid means-of-asking-for-life, have filled our bowls to the brim. It is good.

What I have to offer you in food and drink is not of an unusual kind nor will it, I fear, be adequate. You will probably leave here hungry. It was our intention to prepare food and drink for the four great spirits sitting here, the Island-Anchorers. In spite, however, of our best endeavors you will find it lacking in every respect. Take this into account, ancestors, and still bless us and have compassion upon us. We will bring you the means-of-thankfulness and do you, in return, bless us. Ancestors, we greet you.

So much for ourselves. It is said, however, that we should put a separate kettle in the center of the lodge for the person who represents Ghost. Let him accept it without any second thought. That will be his gratitude and thankfulness.

Ancestor-Host now brings the others food.

A N C E S T O R - H O S T :   You may begin to eat, East.

E A S T :   You may begin to eat, North.

N O R T H :   You may begin to eat, West.

W E S T :   You may begin to eat, Ghost.

G H O S T :   You may begin to eat, South.

All now sit down. Meat, berries, wild potatoes, etc. are now brought to East to be given to Ancestor-Host and the invitation-sticks are also returned to him.

When the meal is finished West and South take down the calico intended for themselves and then walk to their seats. West rises almost immediately and walks to the east end of the lodge and speaks:

300

w e s t :   You who sit over there impersonating the Rite-Giver, the Host, I greet you; you who sit over there impersonating the One-who-was-First, I greet you; you who sit over there impersonating North, I greet you; you who sit over there impersonating Ghost, I greet you; you who sit over there impersonating the End-of-the-Road, I greet you. I greet you all, ancestors. . . .

Earthmaker created human beings with a certain length of life, to attain an age where they would fall to pieces.

Now the first time he heard their voices they were singing.

The second time he heard their voices they were singing.

The third time he heard their voices they were singing.

Then the singing stopped. 'What is the matter?' he thought to himself. But he did not look down toward the earth. Had he done so he would have seen them standing, with their minds directed toward him, Earthmaker, and their faces turned toward heaven, pleading.

When he heard their voices for the fourth time, they were crying.

Their thoughts were turned fervently toward him and they were, most pitifully, beseeching him for help.

'How can this be?' he thought to himself. 'I thought I had endowed them with an abundance of life.' So he cast his eyes down below and, as he did so, *Herecgunina* and his attendants, as well as the wicked spirits and their attendants, those on earth, those above the earth and those below the earth, were digging their sharp teeth and claws into us. Weeping, they appealed to Earthmaker. 'We tried to found a village, we tried to obtain food. But we never succeeded in founding a village. The evil ones would not permit us to. That is why we are crying for succour to you, Earthmaker, why our thoughts turn toward you.'

Earthmaker heard them and knew that their words were true. He knew, also, that, if this continued, there would be nothing moving on earth, that mankind would be extinguished. So he began pondering upon what he might do to better his creation. Finally, after some thought, he decided upon what to do.

From below, he took a part of that on which he was sitting and, with his own hands, he made a man,[28] the very first one. He improved his heart and mind. A poor man he was.[29] Then he decided to send him to the earth. Before he hurled him downward he instructed him about what he was to do, that he was to make the earth a better, a safer, place for man to live in.

Flying and with great noise he was hurled down, his limbs whistling in the air. When he at last landed he thought to himself, 'How far, I wonder, have I come?' He looked at the earth as he turned himself over and recovered consciousness. He had been hurled head first but when he came to consciousness he was lying on his back.

Immediately he began traveling above the earth in every direction but yet accomplished nothing. As he stayed here on earth even the tiny little animals began to plague him.[30] So he sat there wondering what he could do, for he recognized that he was not their equal.

Up above where lies the sky we all see, again Earthmaker formed a man and he put him in charge of life. Turtle they called him; Turtle he was. He took him in his hands and improved upon him in such wise that at no part of his body was he vulnerable, no portion of his body contained death.[31] Then he provided him with a knife and turned him loose, and sent him forcibly down toward the earth. When he landed he found that the people were continuing their killings and he decided that he would accompany them. He thought they were doing it just as a game. 'For a short time I will go along with them,' he thought. So he accompanied them. He liked it so much that soon he was sweeping us human beings along in his destructive warpath, trampling upon us. But these actions of his were of no benefit to us. This he well knew.

This Earthmaker knew as well. So he formed Hare and he took him and placed him between his legs to speak to him and instruct him. This is what he told him, 'Hare, you are now to go to the earth. If you do not succeed, I shall have to remake my creation all over again.' He pointed out to Hare where the important evil spirits were to be found. Greatly he encouraged him as to what he was to do. 'Hare, if you do not succeed it will be very disappointing,' he impressed upon him, 'for the first two men that I sent to accomplish this task failed. Do you, then try your very best.' Then from above, downward toward the earth he sent him.

As Hare was falling downward toward the earth, repeatedly he kept thinking to himself,[32] 'I wonder what it will be best for me to do?' As soon as he struck the earth he saw his sister who was just then approaching her menstrual period. Yet he walked toward her and entered her womb. So at least, he thought. There he sat in her womb feeling crowded and worried for he heard our voices. Within the womb he sat anxiously. Then, after seven months, he burst out and was born. He injured his mother as he thus forcibly burst out from her and she died. And so it came about that never was he able to say 'Mother!' to any woman.

His grandmother took care of him and raised him. Morning after morning she would take him up and fondle him. Willingly and happily the baby would turn toward her. So it was the first morning. On the second morning again she picked up and fondled the child. Smiling all over he got on his feet. On the third morning she again picked up and fondled the child. Immediately he stood up on his feet and began speaking to her. Quiet and happy they were, the two of them. When the fourth morning appeared, once more she picked up the child and fondled it. Immediately he got up and walked over to the opposite side of the place where he had been sitting.[33]

Now the very first words he uttered were 'How are my uncles and aunts faring, grandmother?' 'Oh, there is nothing the matter with them,' she replied, 'they are doing well.' On the fourth day Hare began moving about in the lodge. Rapid and darting were his movements. As he was standing, he suddenly heard our voices. 'How are they prospering, my uncles and aunts, grandmother? Why are they uttering these words?' 'Oh there is nothing to say about them,' replied the grandmother, 'they are always like that, talking incessantly to no purpose.' But when he asked her the fourth time on the fourth day, she answered truthfully, 'Hare, your uncles and your aunts are in a most pitiable condition. That is why they are crying. Herecgunina [34] and his servants and all the evil spirits in general are maltreating them. When they humbly try to obtain the wherewithal of life, when they attempt to hunt for food, they never return from their hunting. The great evil spirits live upon the line of villages [35]

303

and their inhabitants. 'Grandmother,' exclaimed Hare, 'why did you not tell me this a long time ago?'

As soon as morning appeared Hare started out. First he went toward the east and killed the great evil spirit dwelling there, deprived him of the power of abusing human beings. Deep into the bowels of our grandmother, Earth, he thrust him. Then when it began to dawn, toward the left, toward the north, he traveled and killed the great evil spirit dwelling there, deprived him of the power of abusing human beings. Him, too, he thrust into the bowels of our grandmother, Earth. He thrust him so far down, tramped him so hard, that there could be no possibility of his ever emerging again. When the third morning arrived, he started out toward the left side, toward the west, and killed the great evil spirit dwelling there, deprived him of the power of abusing human beings. Him, too, he thrust into the bowels of our grandmother, Earth, thrust him so far down that there could be no possibility of his ever emerging again. And now, for the fourth time, he started out, this time toward the south. He killed the great spirit dwelling there, deprived him of the power of abusing human beings. Him, too, he thrust into the bowels of our grandmother, Earth, thrust him down so far that he could not possibly emerge again. Then he began covering the earth, throughout its full extent, everywhere. To the very rim of the island, to the seas, that far he traveled, so as to be certain that he had missed no evil spirit, that he had really killed them all, that he had really thrust them down into the bowels of our grandmother, that he had really deprived them, for all time, of the power of abusing human beings.

When he had completed all this, then he made a Road for himself extending from the east and around again. Four times he started and traveled in this Road and, after the fourth circuit, he stepped out and addressed his grandmother, saying, 'Grandmother, now my uncles and my aunts are going to be equal to me in the length of their lives!' 'No, no, what you say is impossible!' said Hare's grandmother. He turned to look at her. Part of her back was crumbling and caving in. 'My grandmother is like these evil spirits I have killed. She has a mind and heart like theirs.' So he thought to himself. 'And I

304

trusted her so implicitly, and now she is behaving like this to me! And all the time I thought she was telling me the truth!'

There he lay, Hare, and he felt sorrowful in his heart. He lay there outstretched, covered with his blanket, his feet extended toward the fireplace, sunk in thought. Then there came to him the thought that from now on, death would be the fate of all beings, wherever they lived.

Earthmaker, up above, became aware of Hare's plight so once more, he recalled to Hare's mind the purpose for which he had come and the thoughts that he should possess. Our grandmother, too, sat there pondering. She loved Hare and the human beings, what Hare had accomplished for them, and the great creation Earthmaker had brought into existence.

Suddenly Hare became wild with anger. 'Perhaps I, too, will be trampled under foot!' So he thought. Yet he realized that he could do nothing. Our grandmother, however, got up quickly and took her workbag in order to occupy herself with it. She was thoroughly frightened and was trying to do everything within her power to appease him. Finally she spoke to him:

'Grandson, my dear little one, what you have been musing about is true. Just in that fashion did Earthmaker form this earth. Too small he made it to enable all man's descendants, from one generation to the other, to stand on it. If there were no death there would be no place to move about in; it would be too crowded. Hard times, difficult times, would begin all over again for human beings. For that reason Earthmaker created the earth as he did. If there were no death human beings would all be miserable, people to be pitied. So do look at me, my dear little grandson, as I make something visible to you that will be of benefit to your uncles and your aunts. You are to bring them a religion, one in which they will succeed in attaining what they desire. My dear little Hare, I am telling you this to induce you to arise and give up your sorrow.'

Then Hare looked up without being noticed and, as he looked, he saw a very beautiful girl just passing into womanhood. Nevertheless, he remained as he was and refused to get up. Then for a second time, our grandmother said, 'My dear little grandson, please do get up!' But he refused. Then, again, he peeped in her direction and he saw a middle-aged woman facing the east. The hairs at the back of her neck were sprinkled with white. He looked toward the east and thought that, perhaps, something might happen so he did not get up. Again our grandmother spoke to him. 'Why do you not get up, my dear little grandson?' Hare remained as he was and again peeped in her direction and he saw a woman who had almost reached her normal years of life. A few hairs on her head were black, the rest not. 'Perhaps she will show me something more,' thought Hare and refused to get up. Then, for the fourth time, she said, 'Grandson, you were to get up. Why did you not do so?' But Hare remained as he was. Finally, he looked, once more, in the direction of the east and he saw her shaking nervously from old age, having almost reached the full extent of man's life. Her body looked like a flea in its thinness and her arm like the stem of a pipe. She was bald-headed and, on her head, she wore a swan. The hollow of her neck fell in soft folds of flesh. Indeed her skin fell in folds looking just like the feathers attached to a pipe.

Then He-whom-we-call-our-nephew threw off that which was covering him, arose and pushed away toward the north all the evil clouds [36] and life became, once more, pleasant and quiet and serene. Then, four times, he sent his greeting to our grandmother. After he had greeted her the fourth time, He-whom-we-call-our-nephew had reached extreme old age. His body had taken on the appearance of a flea and his arm looked like the stem of a pipe. There he stood in the east, carrying a cane with which to support himself under his chin and his head shaking from old age. 'Look, grandmother, just so will it be; so will I arrange it for my uncles and aunts. My uncles and my aunts, cannot, under any conditions, fail to obtain life, to live to extreme old age. . . .'

West and East now walk from east to west, West singing. When West reaches his seat he stops and speaks:

W E S T : You who sit over there impersonating the Rite-Giver, the Host, I greet you; you who sit over there impersonating the

306

One-who-was-First, I greet you; you who sit over there impersonating North, I greet you; you who sit over there impersonating Ghost, I greet you; you who sit over there impersonating the End-of-the-Road, I greet you. I greet you all, ancestors.

An offering as the expression of my gratitude, I shall now place in the back of the lodge. May this strengthen our relatives! And then we shall bestow a blessing on our leader so that he too may be strengthened. I greet you all.

West now sits down. South continues on from west to east, singing as he walks. When he comes to the east end of the lodge he stops and speaks:

S O U T H :   You who sit over there impersonating the Rite-Giver, the Host, I greet you; you who sit over there impersonating the One-who-was-First, I greet you; you who sit over there impersonating North, I greet you; you who sit over there impersonating West, I greet you; you who sit over there impersonating Ghost, I greet you. I greet you all, ancestors . . .

Now Hare got ready to construct a lodge for the spirits. He brought eight upright poles. Then he grabbed hold of our grandmother's breast and spread it out in the east.[37] Having done that, he threw the upright poles toward the east and bent them together. Together with the poles he had thrown, he placed something with which to tie them firmly, in the south. Then toward the east, he threw the spirit-walking soldiers [38] and they became objects to tie with. On the other side, in the direction where the sun travels, he threw the crawling soldiers [39] and they, too, became objects to tie with. On the side where the sun does not set, toward that side, he threw black rattlesnakes and they became objects to tie with. On the south side he threw long yellow snakes and they became objects to tie with. Straight upward, above the lodge he threw blue snakes. Finally he put two snakes on each side of the lodge pole at the entrance, a male on the right and a female on the left.

[Thus was the lodge constructed. On the south side Hare used long snakes and bull snakes as side poles and yellow snakes with which to tie them together, and on the north side of the lodge he used black snakes as side poles and rattlesnakes with which to tie them.] [40]

Hare now went out and brought some shiny-backed objects,[40a] stood them up and then sent them toward the east. The light became shut off and closed in. Now, the north side of the lodge he enclosed with black-haired animals.[41] Good spirit seats he thus arranged. On the south side he placed a white-haired animal.[42] Then, when he was quite ready, he threw these animals so that they spread out along the length of the lodge. On each side they were spread clear to the end. Thus did the spirit seats come into existence.

This done, Hare called upon his three friends to come and sit with him. They were Trickster, Turtle and our grandmother, Earth. These were the four who sat together when the spirits gathered in the Creation-Lodge.

Those who were to go out and extend the invitations were now selected. The first one was the very white walker-on-light, the very awe-inspiring, cackling-swan. From above he had come, and Earthmaker had placed abundant life in his control. He it was who left to walk on the light. When he returned, he made the circuit of the lodge four times. With each circuit the light and life became brighter. The toes of his feet were even and he stained and smeared the fireplace with light and life.

The second one to make the fourfold passage around the Island-Anchorers was a very blue-faced wolf. As he walked around the lodge, with each circuit of the lodge, the light and life became brighter. The third one to go out, came from below. He was a waterspirit and had been placed in control of abundant life so that when he walked life would be spread by him. Black-skinned he was and young, and he wore a belt of basswood bark. Four times he walked around the fireplace and the light and life became brighter with each circuit.

As the third messenger started to leave the lodge, the first one returned. He had left, a young person, but now his head was bare and his feathers and his hairs looked as if they had been pulled out. Very old, indeed he was. He made the circuit of the lodge and then stopped in the middle. 'Hare,' he said, 'when your uncles and your aunts are making their search for long life, upon me they shall call.

Thus will they look.' Then he shook himself and scratched up the ground in the four directions and he became as he had been on his departure, handsome and young.

Now the second messenger returned and entered the lodge. He who formerly had looked so youthful, had now reached the extreme of age. His head was bald. The hair on his body was sparse and a few scattered hairs stuck out along his back. The hairs on his feet they, too, were almost gone. He made the circuit of the lodge just as the members of the Rite do today and then stopped in the middle and spoke to Hare. 'Hare, your uncles and your aunts, when they go in search of life, should imitate me. If they do it well, if they keep this ceremony properly in their minds, let them call upon me. They cannot, then, possibly fail.'

Thus he spoke and, when he was finished there, in the middle of the lodge, he kicked up the earth in all four directions, scratched it and shook himself. Just as young as he had been before when he left, so now again that wolf became.

Now the third one returned, the one who had left as a young waterspirit, he who had come from below. As he entered age showed all over him. His head was bald and he looked like a worn-out moccasin. His neck was wrinkled. He walked around the lodge and then made his way to the center and addressed Hare as follows: 'Hare, your uncles and your aunts, when they go in search of long life, should imitate me. If they do it well, they cannot possibly fail. Let them call upon me.' Then he kicked up the earth in the four directions, scratched and shook himself. As he had been before he started, that young he became once more. . . .

South now walks from west to east singing. After he has come to his seat he stops and speaks:

S O U T H : You who sit over there impersonating the Rite-Giver, the Host, I greet you; you who sit over there impersonating the One-who-was-First, I greet you; you who sit over there impersonating North, I greet you; you who sit over there impersonating West, I greet you; you who sit over there impersonating Ghost, I greet you. I greet you all, ancestors.

An offering as the expression of my gratitude, I shall place in the back of the lodge. May this strengthen our relatives! And, now, we shall bestow a blessing upon our leader so that he, too, may be strengthened. I greet you all.

Then he sits down. North now rises and speaks:

N O R T H : You who sit over there impersonating the Rite-Giver, the Host, I greet you; you who sit over there impersonating the One-who-was-First, I greet you; you who sit over there impersonating West, I greet you; you who sit over there impersonating Ghost, I greet you; you who sit over there impersonating the End-of-the-Road, I greet you. I greet you all, ancestors.

He-who-sits-in-the-first-seat has talked about the messenger and has done it exceedingly well. I do not want to spoil his speech or the life he discussed so excellently, by any talk of mine. If he feels himself in connection with life and catches hold of it, then he will be stained with life. It is good that the messenger has been moved on to me.

I was told that one should never only have people in mind when one gets up to speak. Just to think of people, of the impression one makes on them or, on the contrary, to insinuate evil of them, that is not life. One must think of the spirits. It is on them that I have concentrated my mind completely. This ceremony of our forefathers cannot be secured by meaningless talking. Our utterances must be sincere.

I, myself, never took for granted what was said by anyone at large. I never was like that. What my superior said, that I took seriously and accepted.

What little I was taught and I learned, about that I shall now speak to you. The life-song that my forefathers used and passed on to me, one that I begged for, that life-begging I shall indulge in just as they told me. I shall now attempt a short greeting. This is my speech. Ancestors, I send forth my greetings to you, I send forth my greetings to you! (song)

N O R T H : Ancestors, a small dance song is about to be started and then a true song will be intoned. O, ancestors, I beg you to have compassion upon me and pity me! Ancestors, I greet you, I greet you! (song)

North dances and sings at his own seat with members of his band. Members of other bands properly privileged join them. When the dancing and singing are finished, they begin shooting at one another. When that is over they go to the fireplace and dance and sing there. North speaks again:

N O R T H : You who sit over there impersonating the Rite-Giver, the Host, I greet you; you who sit over there impersonating the One-who-was-First, I greet you; you who sit over there impersonating West, I greet you; you who sit over there impersonating Ghost, I greet you; you who sit over there impersonating the End-of-the-Road, I greet you. I greet you all, ancestors.

'Those within the lodge who have had compassion upon you and blessed me and you, meant what they said. Their object has been to obtain life for you, to make you feel that you who are present here have been brought into connection with life. Thankful and grateful you should be and you should present those within the lodge with this song in order to demonstrate it.' Thus did my elders speak to me. And it is this song that I shall use and, after that, the life-beseechers, the speeches.

The one thing, however, that upsets and frightens me is that my performances will irritate you, for I am not accomplished in the ways and actions of the Medicine Rite members. And yet we are to put ourselves in a pity-inspiring condition and beg for compassion, I have always been told. That is why I am again appealing to you to bring us into connection with life. Such, at least is my hope.

My elders once spoke to me and assured me that if I performed my part well and, if those present liked me, I would attain long life and that even if, on some previous occasion, I had erred I could still succeed, provided that I asked for life humbly and in a contrite spirit. And so I have tried to say a few insignificant things. I hope those within this lodge think I did well and that they like me enough to wish me long life.

Ancestors, I beg you to have compassion upon me. Do not dislike me. Remember, you, of all people, are supposed to be kind to others . . .

He who first occupied this seat in the north was accustomed to sweep away all evil with the gourd Earthmaker created for him and which he placed within this lodge, a gourd which was painted with white clay. North seized it and began shaking it. Like a young girl, at first, it looked, that gourd, like a young girl speeding along, with hair waving in the air. Then it was as if she had stopped suddenly. Again North struck these evil things and pushed them away, far away toward the north. That-which-stands-in-the-center-of-the-lodge began twisting itself straight.

Now for the second time, North shook his gourd and again, a figure was seen. It was as if a woman, in her middle years, her hair just beginning to turn white at the nape of her neck, it was as if such a woman, was speeding around the lodge. At the fireplace the light was trembling, life was trembling. That-which-stands-in-the-center-of-the-lodge began to shoot toward the sky in ever more straight and vertical flames.

Again, for the third time, North shook that messenger. As before, so now, again, it seemed as if a woman could be seen, a woman with long-horned hair, past the middle years of life, her hair partly white and partly black. There she was, speeding around the lodge. Suddenly she stopped. Greater and more perfect the light and life became, perfect sunshine prevailed. Straight, without any deviation or twisting, rose the flames from that-which-stands-in-the-center-of-the-lodge.

Then, again, for the fourth time, North began shaking his gourd, four times he shook it. Once, again, a figure was seen. It seemed as if a very old woman, her head bald, just a few coarse hairs at the back of her neck, as if such a woman was speeding along the lodge . . .

Such was the length of life that the spirits, assembled there, hoped to obtain for human beings.

Within that long lodge, all the spirits were sitting. The day was sunny and beautiful. All the evil clouds had been pushed far away toward the north, where the sun does not shine. It was, indeed, a perfect day. No breath of wind disturbed it.

Such is the beautiful life I desire for the initiate, for He-for-whom-we-seek-life. That is why I have come with these life-beseechers. Only thus, I knew, would I be able to obtain a life like that obtained by the one who originally sat in the seat I now occupy and whom I so earnestly wish to emulate. All the power I possess, all that was granted me, I have placed in my utterances and speeches so that I might obtain life. This is the way I was taught to speak. O, ancestors, all of you, do have compassion upon me and bless me. I greet you all, each one in turn! (song)

North makes the circuit of the lodge four times singing and then stops at South's position and speaks:

N O R T H :   You who sit over there impersonating the Rite-Giver, the Host, I greet you; you who sit over there impersonating the One-who-was-First, I greet you; you who sit over there impersonating West, I greet you; you who sit over there impersonating Ghost, I greet you; you who sit over there impersonating the End-of-the-Road, I greet you. I greet you all, ancestors.

I am now going to call upon a person who is as fast and proficient as myself. As soon as I finish my song he is going to lead. He will do his part well. All of us know that, because he bought the privileges he possesses from the older members here. So I shall close and ask you not to think ill of me for doing this.

Have compassion upon him and bring him into connection with life, for my follower has not, for some time, stepped into the Road as leader. Excuse him, therefore. Have compassion upon me ancestors, I beg you. Each one in turn I greet, I greet! (song)

North now makes the circuit of the lodge four times, ejaculating 'wahihihi, wahihihi, eho-ho-ho,' slowly at first then faster and faster. When he reaches his seat, he sits down.

N O R T H ' S   F O L L O W E R :   It is good that, once again, I am stepping into the Road. I hardly believed my leader would ask me to do this work for I am but a pitiable person trying to obtain

313

a modicum of life. But my leader has really made me feel that I am actively living. To him do I owe this. I know that I am incapable of doing anything of importance and that I shall only be sweeping dust into your eyes as I walk past you. I shall, however, try not to think of it. Have compassion upon me! Remember that I will be far in the rear, following you. Yet I do wish to do my part well and that is why, again, I appeal to all of you to bless me. Am I really a Medicine Rite member? I wonder. Ancestors, all of you present here, I greet, each one in turn!

West now makes the circuit of the lodge, stops at the east end and speaks:

W E S T :   You who sit over there impersonating the Rite-Giver, the Host, I greet you; you who sit over there impersonating the One-who-was-First, I greet you; you who sit over there impersonating North, I greet you; you who sit over there impersonating Ghost, I greet you; you who sit over there impersonating the End-of-the-Road, I greet you. I greet you all, ancestors.

He-who-sits-in-the-east talked to us about the messenger and about life and we were thus enabled to seize hold of life. Then they passed the announcer to North so that he, too, could seize hold of it. Now it has been passed on to me. Life, has been moved around the lodge until it reached me! It is good. For all my relatives who are here with me it means the same. This is as it should be and why I say it is good. I will be able to say very little, indeed, and that little I will repeat again and again. Yet this I cannot help and it will have to be my expression of gratitude and thankfulness. I know just a few words but I hope that something can be accomplished even by these, my very inadequate, utterances.

I was told that if you do this part of your work well, you can secure life, by such words alone, for some human being and strengthen him. The Island-Anchorer, the wind, who originally sat in the west position was in possession of great and abundant life. What he said when he talked about life was true and sincere in every respect. Him and what he said, do I wish to emulate and follow; him do I wish to impersonate. I cannot, of course, intone a song as the members of old

314

used to nor can I make my plea for life through songs as was done at the first performance of this Rite. My songs cannot accomplish this. I can, however, make our announcer step forward and those who taught me and others this Rite said that he will be listened to. They claimed that all those sitting around the lodge would take heed of it and that, even to Earthmaker, would our appeals reach. What we desire is that all hearken to him and be instructed. May all listen to it, may all thoughts be directed towards him, toward this messenger, the drum, who is now about to make himself heard! Ancestors, as many as have been blessed, I greet you, each one in turn! (song)

West now walks to his own place and speaks:

W E S T -: You who sit over there impersonating the Rite-Giver, the Host, I greet you; you who sit over there impersonating the One-who-was-First, I greet you; you who sit over there impersonating North, I greet you; you who sit over there impersonating Ghost, I greet you; you who sit over there impersonating the End-of-the-Road, I greet you. I greet you all, ancestors.

I shall now have a short song appear before you.

It will necessarily be a very short one, the kind, however, which I was instructed to use. For that reason I thought I might sing it. I know, of course, that I will not be able to sing it as real members of the Rite do but I hope, nevertheless, the members will like it. That is my reason for singing it. Ancestors, I greet you, I greet you! (song)

West and those of his band privileged to, sing and dance at West's position. They are joined, after a while, by members from the other bands. When the songs and dance are finished, they begin to shoot one another and when this is done they continue singing and dancing. Then they sit down. West rises shortly after, steps forward with the drum, and speaks:

W E S T : You who sit over there impersonating the Rite-Giver, the Host, I greet you; you who sit over there impersonating the One-who-was-First, I greet you; you who sit over there impersonating

North, I greet you; you who sit over there impersonating Ghost, I greet you; you who sit over there impersonating the End-of-the-Road, I greet you. I greet you all, ancestors.

The messenger is now to be passed along.

W E S T :   This is the religion that He-whom-we-call-our-nephew, Hare, obtained for us and by which we are to secure long life. I have listened to his injunctions, so I believe. But I am really not the kind of a person who can perform this Rite well. 'Speak frequently,' my elders told me. Willingly and gladly have I tried my best. They also told me to send life-begetting greetings. That, too, I have done. But I was not very successful, I fear.

How, indeed, could I be? I am, after all, a poor and miserable person, hardly able even to get myself the proper clothes. Throughout my life I have never had enough food. And yet, despite all, despite the fact that I was not wealthy, I knew that I had to join this Rite. Otherwise I would have constantly remained hungry and, in the end, succumbed. If the members of this Rite had not, in their generosity, compelled me to join, I would most assuredly, have been completely without clothing. I am still wondering why they honored me like this, why they took compassion upon me? What I have to say is not of much account. I am not a learned, nor a wise person. Rather, I am a foolish one.

What my father told me I did not listen to. I remember him saying to me, 'Dear son, this Rite is not one of these things that can be bestowed by one person upon the other merely because of the love one feels for him. It is not to be obtained merely by asking. Offerings must be made, privileges must be bought. You must be interested and you must want to learn.' Unfortunately, I did not want to learn. It is my own fault, consequently, if I am as I am.

My father cautioned me on this very point and told me I would have no one to blame but myself if I did not listen. 'Meaningless will be what you say and selfish. You will always be thinking about yourself. When the occasion arises for your impersonating a spirit, no one will listen to your insignificant speeches nor will they like them. Such will be your fate if you do not pay heed to my words.'

316

Thus spoke my father. But I still did not listen. Finally I said, 'I shall try.'

I know I have said very little but I did try and I hope that someone among the Rite members will like it. This is all I have to say. Ancestors, all of you who have been blessed, I greet you, I greet you!

West now walks around the lodge four times, stopping twice at the west and twice at the east end to sing. Before he finishes the last song, he stops at Ghost's position and speaks:

w e s t :   You who sit over there impersonating the Rite-Giver, the Host, I greet you; you who sit over there impersonating the One-who-was-First, I greet you; you who sit over there impersonating North, I greet you; you who sit over there impersonating Ghost, I greet you; you who sit over there impersonating the End-of-the-Road, I greet you.

As soon as I finish this song I am going to lead my followers back to their seat. Again, I assure you, that I am not the kind of person who can perform these actions correctly and it was only because I am a middle-aged individual and so proud of having been asked that I consented. Ancestors, I extend a life-begetting greeting to you, I greet you! (song)

West now makes the circuit of the lodge four times, ejaculating 'wahihihi, wahihihi, wahihihi, eho-ho-ho,' first slowly then faster and faster. When he reaches his seat he sits down. Soon he rises again and takes the drum and gourds, and places them in front of Ghost's seat and speaks:

w e s t :   You who sit over there impersonating the Rite-Giver, the Host, I greet you; you who sit over there impersonating the One-who-was-First, I greet you; you who sit over there impersonating North, I greet you; you who sit over there impersonating Ghost, I greet you; you who sit over there impersonating the End-of-the-Road, I greet you. I greet you all, ancestors.

Ancestors, I am indeed not your equal. I am, in fact, quite lost when I see how you perform this Rite. I never bought the privileges. I was advised to do so but I never did. I was not able to. Nevertheless, the leaders of the other bands had pity on me and kept me in their thoughts. They have made me unbelievably happy by what they have done for me. They have brought me into connection with life. This is what I always hoped would happen to me! Although I have not done well, I did what I could and feel connected with true life. Ancestors, have compassion upon me! Ancestors, I greet you, I greet you! (song)

Ghost makes one circuit of the lodge, stops at the east and speaks:

G H O S T :   You who sit over there impersonating the Rite-Giver, the Host, I greet you; you who sit over there impersonating the One-who-was-First, I greet you; you who sit over there impersonating North, I greet you; you who sit over there impersonating West, I greet you; you who sit over there impersonating the End-of-the-Road, I greet you. I greet you all, ancestors.

On one occasion some Rite leaders who had been blessed asked me, 'I wonder if it is true, if it will really be so, that we attain a great age?' I, too, was skeptical when I was very young before I had been blessed and before I had been brought into connection with life by these members of the Medicine Rite. Some people even said that no member of the Rite could give real assurance on this question. But I listened to them and I knew the members of the Rite were telling the truth. It is through them that I live; it is they who endeavored to make me live. It is good.

The leaders of the Medicine Rite used to say that if once you are blessed and if once you emulate the words and actions of those of long ago, then those who blessed you will see you following just behind them. They will see you walking and falling along the Road.[43] Then they will tell of how you have been blessed. If you ask for life in a humble spirit, people will have compassion upon you. That is how I came to be a member of the Rite, because people had compassion upon me, for I, myself, am incapable of saying anything. Yet if one cannot speak it is permissible to have a song represent one's life-begetting greeting. So, the older people used to say. With a song then I shall greet you. Enough of such greetings, they say, will make

318

up for other deficiencies. This is all I have to say. Ancestors, I greet you, I greet you!

Ghost now walks to his own place and speaks:

G H O S T : You who sit over there impersonating the Rite-Giver, the Host, I greet you; you who sit over there impersonating the One-who-was-First, I greet you; you who sit over there impersonating North, I greet you; you who sit over there impersonating West, I greet you; you who sit over there impersonating the End-of-the-Road, I greet you. I greet you all, ancestors.

The announcer will now make his appearance and with it there will be a song. In a moment I shall send a life-begetting greeting to all of you. Ancestors, I greet you, I greet you. (dance song)

Ghost and the members of his band so privileged sing and dance at his place. Members of the other bands join them after a while. When the songs and dancing are finished then they begin to shoot one another. When this is over they continue their singing and dancing and then sit down. Ghost rises, shortly after, steps forward with the drum and speaks:

G H O S T : You who sit over there impersonating the Rite-Giver, the Host, I greet you; you who sit over there impersonating the One-who-was-First, I greet you; you who sit over there impersonating North, I greet you; you who sit over there impersonating West, I greet you; you who sit over there impersonating the End-of-the-Road, I greet you. I greet you all, ancestors.

I shall now carry the announcer to the one ahead of me. He, I know, will be able to accomplish much for us with his utterances. I, myself, am completely unskilled in speech. What I can do is to start up some songs. Four times we shall stop to sing, aided by He-who-sits-at-the-End-of-the-Road, who will lead us. That is all I wished to say. Ancestors, I greet you, I greet you.

Ghost and his band, led by South, make the circuit of the lodge four times, stopping to sing twice in the east and twice in the south. Then the drum and gourds are brought to South's position. Ghost returns to his own position and speaks again:

319

G H O S T :   You who sit over there impersonating the Rite-Giver, the Host, I greet you; you who sit over there impersonating the One-who-was-First, I greet you; you who sit over there impersonating North, I greet you; you who sit over there impersonating West, I greet you; you who sit over there impersonating the End-of-the-Road, I greet you. I greet you all, ancestors.

If I wished to be blessed, my forefather long since dead, told me I would have to learn to say something worth while. Then the Rite members would send me a life-begetting greeting. The knowledge these ancestors left me, I will now make use of. I will try to fulfill my obligations and tell those assembled what they expect of me. . . .

Once, four men lived in a large oval lodge.[44] All day they talked, from morning until the setting of the sun. They were giving names to the various animals, to the various grasses and to the various trees. To all the animals, those above, those on land, those below the earth, those in the water, to all of them, these four brothers gave names. Even to the smallest insects names were given.

When they were finished the oldest brother did not feel well and the three others took care of him. About daylight he suddenly became absolutely quiet. The brothers waited for him to move but he did not move, not the least bit. He did not know how to move any more.

Then they took his body outside and placed it on a scaffold within reach and they went away immediately, for they did not wish to look at him. Their heads were wrapped in their blankets as they walked away. Only when they came to a secluded spot out in the country and were quite out of sight of the scaffold, did they uncover their heads.

As they sat there, one of them asked the oldest remaining brother, 'Brother, do you know what ails our oldest brother?' And this one answered, 'I am sorry to say it but I do not know.' Then the second one asked and he answered, 'I am sorry but I do not know.' Finally the youngest was asked and he answered, 'I do know, dearest youngest brother. I want all of you, however, to get ready and come with me now.' So they took the pipe of the dead brother, filled it, and left.

320

Weeping, they made their way towards the east. They had not gone far before they came to a large round lodge. They had already seen it from the distance. Their voices rose high in their weeping as they approached the lodge. It was one mass of light, this lodge, without the slightest trace of darkness. No evil winds blew upon it. They stood in front of what should have been the entrance, but there was no entrance. Everything was wide open.

They took the pipe and pointed it at the occupant but he would not smoke it. Then they spoke to him, 'Our oldest brother who was perfectly well, suddenly stopped moving some time ago and he has not moved yet.' 'Ah, ah, my friends, I am afraid I do not know what that means. You had better go on to the second man.' Thus he spoke.

Then they went away. When they looked at each other they were different in appearance from what they had been before they entered the lodge and they felt much more refreshed.

They did not go very far before they came to another round lodge, the lodge of the North Wind. Polished and shining was the edge of his lodge and over it all lay the most resplendent of white light. The brothers stood at what should have been the entrance, but there was no entrance. They entered and extended their pipe to the occupant. He would not smoke and in answer to their questions, said he did not know how to help them. 'Go on to the next one,' he encouraged them, 'he may know what I do not.'

Again they left. When they looked at their bodies they appeared fresher than before and they themselves seemed to have reached middle age.

Then the brothers made their way to the lodge of the great West Wind. There the light gleamed and sparkled as on a perfect day. No particle of darkness, none whatsoever, found its way there. No evil clouds, no storms walked across its path. More than resplendent was the light which lay spread out within that lodge. Where there should have been an entrance there was none. Everything lay wide open.

Then the brothers entered and spoke to the occupant. 'Our oldest brother has not moved and we do not know what has happened to him. That is why we have come here to see you.' Thus they spoke and pointed the pipe at him. But he would not smoke. 'I know nothing about it,' he said, 'go on to the next one.'

Weeping and gulping, they went on. They did not have to go far before they came to a lodge, one they had already seen from the distance. What they had seen before of large dwelling places seemed small in comparison with this large round lodge. When they reached it they seemed to have passed beyond the middle years of their life.

Weeping, they entered through an entrance that was wide open. Right into the lodge they went and extended their pipe. The occupant took it, smoked it and said, 'I know what you have come for and, yet, all I can say is that you be cheerful and happy of mind and heart. The way you have come, that path you must now retrace again. I will be there to welcome you.'

The three brothers greeted him. As they stood there they seemed in the last stage of life, all three of them. Little old men they were, wearing swans as headdresses.

Now they started for home. When they saw their own lodge the fire was still flickering and they felt that their brother must have been still keeping it up. They yearned greatly to see him. 'It must be he,' they said.

Then they entered the lodge, they saw the four spirits that they had just visited. Four times these men walked around the road of the lodge greeting one another. The one who sat in the very first place arose and spoke: 'Thus has Earthmaker ordained that human life should be, so has he created it. Death will exist.'

All four of them spoke in similar fashion. Finally the last one arose and speaking, said, 'Earthmaker ordained it thus and thus must it be. Within our grandmother, Earth, so deep that even the worms cannot get to him, so deep must you bury your brother.' . . .

This is what was said and this is what happened.

Ancestors, I send my greetings to you, I send my greetings to you.

South makes one complete circuit of the lodge, stops at the east and speaks:

s o u t h : You who sit over there impersonating the Rite-Giver, the Host, I greet you; you who sit over there impersonating the
322

One-who-was-First, I greet you; you who sit over there impersonating North, I greet you; you who sit over there impersonating West, I greet you; you who sit over there impersonating Ghost, I greet you. I greet you all, ancestors.

For the life-beseechers brought to me, I am indeed grateful and thankful. He-whom-we-call-our-nephew, secured a real life for us by means of this Rite which Earthmaker created. It is from the original Creation-Lodge that the speeches appealing for long life came, and it is by delivering these speeches properly and sincerely that we will be able to secure this life for ourselves and others. That is why our elders always encouraged us to learn some kind of speeches, to learn something that could be used here. I promised that I would try and that I shall now do, well aware of how unimportant it is. Here is what I have to say . . .

He-whom-we-call-our-nephew, Hare, asked our grandmother, 'Grandmother, did not Earthmaker have you bring something?' 'You, being a man, are wise, my dear grandson. Yes, Earthmaker, our father, did let me bring something. I have it right here.'

She opened the right side of her garment and displayed a nipple, a gift from Earthmaker. She seized hold of it. When she loosened her grip, behold! extremely white blossoms,[45] like life, sprouted from her breast and blossoms that looked like the ears of a beaver. When those present took their eyes off for a moment and looked again, branches appeared, one after the other. Soon a little boy with yellow hair [46] emerged. There she stood. When they looked at her for the third time, stocks appeared and, when they looked at her for the fourth time, there stood an old white-headed man—the life-be-seecher,[47] over-ripe and spent.

Now, once again, grandmother opened her garment, this time on the left side, and displayed a nipple. This she seized hold of and when she loosened her grip, behold! extremely white blossoms, life, sprouted from her breast. Then the leaves of the food of the spirits appeared and the branches. When those present turned their eyes away for a moment and then looked again they saw a young girl with yellow hair. When they looked a second time branches made their

323

appearance. When they looked for the third time there stood tobacco stalks and when they looked for the fourth time they saw a woman, full of years, head white and bald, her body like that of a flea and her arms like the stem of a pipe. There in the east she stood. Here was the food of the spirits, over-ripe and spent.

Now He-whom-we-called-our-nephew, Hare, prepared some untanned buckskin and, taking hold of it, stood up before those present in the lodge. In his hand he held some tobacco mixed with portions of the chief of trees,[48] and he spread this out in the middle of the lodge. All the spirits sat there anxious and tense with expectation, wondering which one of them would receive the tobacco, each one feeling that it should go to him. They thought that it would probably be given to the one in the east.

But, now standing up at the end of the lodge, on the right side, a very white-faced wolf[49] was ready to start his circuit of the lodge. He held in his hand that with which he was to smoke. He seized hold of the life-beseecher, filled his pipe and took a puff. Instantaneously he had attained the full measure of years; he had become an old man. Then he dug up the ground with his feet, kicking it first toward the east, then toward the north, the west and the south and howled 'hoho-ho-ho, hwa-hwa.' As he scratched the ground, with each scratch, he was transformed into his former appearance. Then he spoke: 'Hare, what I have just done, this, your uncles and your aunts must imitate and repeat when they go in search of long life. Anyone who does this properly and sincerely cannot fail. Anyone who has his thoughts truly fixed upon the obtaining of a long and full life, will attain it if they do as I have just done.'

All those present then held the pipe in their mouths. With each puff the light became increasingly brighter, life became increasingly greater. . . .

Well, ancestors, all who have been blessed, I greet you all. (song)

South now walks to his own place and speaks:

S O U T H :   You who sit over there impersonating the Rite-Giver, I greet you; you who sit over there impersonating the One-

324

who-was-First, I greet you; you who sit over there impersonating North, I greet you; you who sit over there impersonating West, I greet you; you who sit over there impersonating Ghost, I greet you. I greet you all, ancestors.

What He-who-sits-in-the-First-Seat was to tell us concerning life, he has finished. He now has seized hold of additional life through our messenger, the drum. North then moved life forward to West after he, too, had obtained life by seizing hold of the messenger. Finally West brought the life-beseecher to me, placed them before me. Thus West increased the quota of my years. The messenger through whom they strengthened their lives has come to me, and I now sit fully immersed in the life that was brought me. But not only to me, the leader of my band, has this happened. All my relatives, they too, have been brought into connection with life, a task we, ourselves, attempted in vain.

The messenger, stained and spotted with life, has come to me, the speeches imprinted with life have come to me. I and my relatives have seized hold firmly on them so that we might be strengthened thereby.

What we are performing here today is a ceremony given by one who gave voice to his thoughts and who desired to make a plea for long life. Because of their plea I shall now sing a few songs for the four Island-Anchorers.

My grandfather was given a song at the time he was blessed and the spirits spoke to him. The little he then obtained, they said, was to be put at the disposal of some dearly beloved child for whom his parents were seeking life, one who was about to be initiated into the Medicine Rite.

Willingly I shall now put that song at the disposal of those who are making their petition for life. Would that I were able to further their purpose by any words of mine! But I cannot obtain life for anybody in that manner. I have not done enough of anything. Yet, though I have no right to, I am going to attempt a little song that everyone can use for his most beloved one. So did my forefathers direct me. That is all I have to say.

All those assembled here who are blessed, I greet you all. (song)

South and those members of his band so privileged dance and sing at their own seat. After a while, members of the other bands join them. When the singing and dancing are over they all begin shooting at one another and when this is finished, they continue singing and dancing. As soon as this has stopped, South takes the drum and gourds to the fireplace and speaks:

s o u t h : You who sit over there impersonating the Rite-Giver, the Host, I greet you; you who sit over there impersonating the One-who-was-First, I greet you; you who sit over there impersonating North, I greet you; you who sit over there impersonating West, I greet you; you who sit over there impersonating Ghost, I greet you. I greet you all, ancestors.

It is the custom after the messenger has reached you and you have blessed others and been yourself blessed, to bring it back to the middle of the lodge. As you place it there, you are supposed to dig up the ground before Ancestor-Host.

I was told to seize hold of the messenger, the announcer, because it was moved on to me so that I might obtain life, something stained and imprinted with life. They told me that I was a man who could do it. But I am not. I am not able to walk in their track. They must have known this and yet they had compassion upon me. That is why, I feel, I should accept the life-beseecher and attempt to speak. But more than that, I owe it to the one who was instrumental in placing me in the seat in which I now sit, to say something. That I shall now try, although I cannot repeat accurately the knowledge I was given . . .

The Island-Anchorer of the South seized life, seized the messenger,[50] the one dwelling within the lodge, and shook it. Four times he shook it and suddenly there appeared a young woman dancing, with long hair almost touching the ground. Then he shook it again, four times, and all that was bad and evil, the evil dust and dirt, every speck of it, he pushed toward the north. The lodge looked clean. Then, for the third time, he shook the messenger, four times, and a woman suddenly appeared, one somewhat advanced in years, bald-headed. The spirits, all of them, from everywhere now began to sweep everything evil toward the north. The light sparkled and glit-

326

tered and He-who-stands-in-the-middle-of-the-lodge, the unoppos-able, sent his twisted flames straight upwards. All the evil clouds that were still there were pushed far to the north . . .

Ancestors, all of you, in turn, I greet!

South now makes the circuit of the lodge four times, stopping to sing twice at the west end and twice at the east. He stops in front of East and speaks:

s o u t h : You who sit over there impersonating the Rite-Giver, the Host, I greet you; you who sit over there impersonating the One-who-was-First, I greet you; you who sit over there impersonating North, I greet you; you who sit over there impersonating West, I greet you; you who sit over there impersonating Ghost, I greet you. I greet you all, ancestors.

I have now finished my songs and now I shall lead my followers back to their seat and mine. I know I am not your equal, ancestors, but I beg you, have compassion upon me nevertheless. Ancestors, I send forth my greeting to you, I send forth my greeting to you!

South and his followers now make the circuit of the lodge four times, ejaculating 'wahihihi, wahihihi, wahihihi, eho-ho-ho,' at first slowly but then faster and faster. When they reach their seat they all sit down, but South rises almost immediately and speaks:

s o u t h : You who sit over there impersonating the Rite-Giver, the Host, I greet you; you who sit over there impersonating the One-who-was-First, I greet you; you who sit over there imper-sonating North, I greet you; you who sit over there impersonating West, I greet you; you who sit over there impersonating Ghost, I greet you. I greet you all, ancestors.

I am not a true Medicine Rite member, so ancestors, you must have compassion upon me and forgive me for having swept dust in your faces as we walked past you shaking our grandmother.[51] Not shaking her as you can do it, however. Would that I could and thus feel myself really connected with life! I am not in control of enough power to do that well. As for this kicking up of the earth and other ritual actions these must be performed with proper authority[52] and only then will they be performed as our ancestors always did. If, however, a person possesses no such authority and does this, of his own free will, it will go badly with him; he will injure himself. So, I counsel you, therefore, buy some of these privileges tonight; make four payments, and then your mind will be at peace and you will never have to worry. Then you can indulge in these activities as often as you wish and enjoy yourself without nervousness.

This is what my elders told me. I followed their advice and I bought the rights to perform many of these actions. I paid four times for each of them as custom demanded. Had I been able to buy more, I would have. What my elders told me was excellent advice but, alas! I could not do it. Ancestors, as many as have been blessed, I greet you, I send my greetings to you.

East standing in his own place speaks:

E A S T :   You who sit over there impersonating the Rite-Giver, the Host, I greet you; you who sit over there impersonating North, I greet you; you who sit over there impersonating West, I greet you; you who sit over there impersonating Ghost, I greet you; you who sit there impersonating the End-of-the-Road, I greet you. I greet you all, ancestors.

I am speaking to those appointed to keep track of the shells. How have you been getting along? For my own seat I can tell you that each of the three leaders stationed here, has his shell. Ancestors, I greet you, I greet you!

N O R T H :   You who sit over there impersonating the Rite-Giver, the Host, I greet you; you who sit over there impersonating the One-who-was-First, I greet you; you who sit over there impersonating West, I greet you; you who sit over there impersonating Ghost, I greet you; you who sit over there impersonating the End-of-the-Road, I greet you. I greet you all, ancestors.

For our insignificant seat, four leaders and shell-experts were appointed. I report that one shell is missing. Ancestors, I greet you, I greet you!

328

W E S T :   You who sit over there impersonating the Rite-Giver, the Host, I greet you; you who sit over there impersonating the One-who-was-First, I greet you; you who sit over there impersonating North, I greet you; you who sit over there impersonating Ghost, I greet you; you who sit over there impersonating the End-of-the-Road, I greet you. I greet you all, ancestors.

For our insignificant seat, four shell-experts were appointed. I report that each leader has his shell. Ancestors, I greet you, I greet you!

S O U T H :   You who sit over there impersonating the Rite-Giver, the Host, I greet you; you who sit over there impersonating the One-who-was-First, I greet you; you who sit over there impersonating North, I greet you; you who sit over there impersonating West, I greet you; you who sit over there impersonating Ghost, I greet you. I greet you all, ancestors.

For our insignificant seat, four shell-experts were appointed. I report that two shells are missing. Ancestors, I greet you, I greet you!

E A S T :   You who sit over there impersonating the Rite-Giver, the Host, I greet you; you who sit over there impersonating North, I greet you; you who sit over there impersonating West, I greet you; you who sit over there impersonating Ghost, I greet you; you who sit over there impersonating the End-of-the-Road, I greet you. I greet you all, ancestors.

Since there are three shells missing, in order that each band may have the number allotted to it, I am providing the two bands that are deficient, with the shells they need. Ancestors, I greet you, I greet you!

East walks to the second position, the North, and shoots one person. This one falls to the ground instantaneously, then gets up, extends his greeting and takes his seat. East, thereupon, walks over to the South position and shoots two people. Both fall to the ground instantaneously and then get up, extend their greetings, and take their seats. When East is finished he returns to his seat. North now rises and speaks:

N O R T H : You who sit over there impersonating the Rite-Giver, the Host, I greet you; you who sit over there impersonating the One-who-was-First, I greet you; you who sit over there impersonating West, I greet you; you who sit over there impersonating Ghost, I greet you; you who sit over there impersonating the End-of-the-Road, I greet you. I greet you all, ancestors.

I am keeping the shell of He-for-whom-we-seek-life, the initiate, but I shall return it to him now so that he may obtain that new and long life I ardently wish him to have. Ancestors, I greet you, I greet you!

North walks to the newly initiated member and shoots him. He falls to the ground instantaneously, then gets up, extends his greeting and sits down.
Ancestor-Host now rises and speaks:

A N C E S T O R - H O S T : You who sit over there impersonating the One-who-was-First, I greet you; you who sit over there impersonating North, I greet you; you who sit over there impersonating West, I greet you; you who sit over there impersonating Ghost, I greet you; you who sit over there impersonating the End-of-the-Road, I greet you. I greet you all, ancestors.

Hãhã, ancestors, it is good. What I have asked you to do, you have indeed done. You have been most generous with all the speeches that bring life to people, bring them a new and happy life. You have indeed shown that you were not selfish. It is good.

Hãhã, ancestors. You have, throughout this ceremony, always had the new life before you when you spoke. I repeat; you have brought us all a good and adequate life. To me, particularly, have you brought additional years by your utterances. Now that the assembled spirits who came here are about to depart and leave me alone, I would like to tell you that even if our children and grandchildren play in the abandoned lodge afterwards when this ceremony is over, they will be strengthened by this. No harm will come to them.

I thank you for the kettles of food you have placed before me and for the life-beseecher, tobacco. All you were supposed to do, you have fulfilled magnificently. It is good.

330

All the blessings I asked of you, you have granted. All the blessings each one of those assembled here has asked, has been granted. It is good.

You came here in response to my invitation so that I might see your faces and I thank you. It is good.

I have lived as though I were one of the real spirits because of your forethought and consideration. My thankfulness overflows to you as I speak. Ancestors, all of you who have come here to ask for compassion, to ask for blessings, I greet you, I greet you, each one in turn!

East now speaks:

E A S T : You who sit over there impersonating the Rite-Giver, the Host, I greet you; you who sit over there impersonating North, I greet you; you who sit over there impersonating West, I greet you; you who sit over there impersonating Ghost, I greet you; you who sit over there impersonating the End-of-the-Road, I greet you. I greet you all, ancestors.

Let us all rise now for it is time to rise.

N O R T H : You who sit over there impersonating the Rite-Giver, the Host, I greet you; you who sit over there impersonating the One-who-was-First, I greet you; you who sit over there impersonating West, I greet you; you who sit over there impersonating Ghost, I greet you; you who sit over there impersonating the End-of-the-Road, I greet you. I greet you all, ancestors.

Let us all rise now for it is time to rise.

W E S T : You who sit over there impersonating the Rite-Giver, the Host, I greet you; you who sit over there impersonating the One-who-was-First, I greet you; you who sit over there impersonating North, I greet you; you who sit over there impersonating Ghost, I greet you; you who sit over there impersonating the End-of-the-Road, I greet you. I greet you all, ancestors.

Let us all rise now for it is time to rise.

331

G H O S T : You who sit over there impersonating the Rite-Giver, the Host, I greet you; you who sit over there impersonating the One-who-was-First, I greet you; you who sit over there impersonating North, I greet you; you who sit over there impersonating West, I greet you; you who sit over there impersonating the End-of-the-Road, I greet you. I greet you all, ancestors.

Let us all rise now for it is time to rise.

S O U T H : You who sit over there impersonating the Rite-Giver, the Host, I greet you; you who sit over there impersonating the One-who-was-First, I greet you; you who sit over there impersonating North, I greet you; you who sit over there impersonating West, I greet you; you who sit over there impersonating Ghost, I greet you. I greet you all, ancestors.

Let all of us, my relatives included, rise now for it is time to rise.

E A S T : You who sit over there impersonating the Rite-Giver, the Host, I greet you; you who sit over there impersonating North, I greet you; you who sit over there impersonating West, I greet you; you who sit over there impersonating Ghost, I greet you; you who sit over there impersonating the End-of-the-Road, I greet you. I greet you all, ancestors.

I take this opportunity to tell you how proud and grateful all of us here are for the sacrifices you gave us. As soon as we return home we will distribute them so that every one of my relatives will receive something he can wear, something by which he will be strengthened. This is what I wished to tell you.

I send a life-begetting greeting to all of you and assure you that the speeches, the advice, the counsel of the otterskin owners will not be a burden to us.

All assembled here in this lodge, to every one of you I send a life-engendering greeting! (song)

E A S T : To you who sit in the seat impersonating North, to whom the means of thankfulness was passed on, to you I send my greeting, to you, to you!

N O R T H :   To you, who sit in the First Position, to you who passed on to me the means-of-thankfulness, to you I send my greetings. To you, likewise, to all of you who gave us the sacrifices, I send my greetings. (song)

To you who sit in the seat over there impersonating West, to whom the means-of-thankfulness was passed on, to you I send my greetings, to you, to you!

W E S T :   To you who sit over there impersonating North, to you who passed on to me the means-of-thankfulness, to you and yours I send my greetings. (song)

To you who sit over there impersonating Ghost, to whom the means-of-thankfulness was passed on, to you I send my greetings, to you, to you!

G H O S T :   To you who sit over there impersonating West, to you who passed on to me the means-of-thankfulness, to you and yours, I send my greetings.

To you who sit over there impersonating the End-of-the-Road, to whom the means-of-thankfulness was passed on, to you I send my greetings to you, to you! (song)

S O U T H :   It is said that when the original occupant of this seat prepared to go out to walk, he took from his right side, a long-tailed wildcat, a very awe-inspiring one, an extremely white one, and placed it in front of him and on top of his head. With life he shod his feet. Thus apparelled with life, with the long-tailed wildcat in front of him and further enclosed in all the mighty powers the creator had given him and clothed with them, thus he stood there in all his majesty. Sacred and awesome his body had become.

Now he wriggled the bent tail of the wildcat and all the evil spirits, throughout the world, everyone of them, were swept away and pushed far to the north. The Creation-Lodge was swept clean. Life and light shimmered and glittered. He-who-stands-in-the-middle-of-the-lodge rose up straight in a blaze of fire. All the evil clouds were gone, all swept away far to the north. It was a perfect day, it was a

333

heart-satisfying life. The spinner stood there suspended and one wondered what could have been causing the fluttering of his web.

The very first step the wildcat took he sank down in our grandmother. He penetrated her up to his ankles. One arm too, was in the earth.[53] Then he took a second step.[54] As he extended his other arm he felt it penetrate snow, penetrate He-whom-we-call-our-nephew.[55] Then he took a third step and extended his right (?) leg. Again up to his elbows he penetrated our grandmother. Fully open and spent she had become.[56] Then he took a fourth step. He-whom-we-call-our-Nephew, the snow, had become fine and powdered as he penetrated our grandmother up to his elbow.[57]

The wildcat was now approaching the entrance. On its right side stood a male snake, on its left a female. He seized hold of both and shook them repeatedly and down into our grandmother, down to her very depths, he pushed them. Never thereafter would these entrance-posts be loose. Firm, forever, they would remain.

He threw back the entrance-flap and there, within the center of the lodge, half of the light, half of our life remained.[58] He pulled out the entrance-flap and with it there went the other half of the light, the other half of our life.[59]

The sky-walkers could be seen flying away, one by one, carrying something in their mouths. The earth-walkers could be seen, treading their way, one by one, carrying something in their mouths . . .

O, ancestors, O ancestors, I greet you, I greet you! (song) . . .

As each member files out, the entrance-flap opens and closes. When the last one has emerged, it flaps back and remains closed. The lodge is dark.

334

NOTES

1. In the sense that he had the same parts of the body that we have, not that he looked like us.

2. I do not know why this hero who is mentioned in no other version of the origin myth was included by Blowsnake.

3. Hare is supposed here to be actually indistinguishable from us, in contradistinction to the other four culture heroes.

4. To set him off completely from the other heroes and spirits who were formed and molded by Earthmaker. In the Winnebago theology of the Medicine Rite there are four types of spirits: Hare, created by Earthmaker's thoughts; the good spirits and the three other culture heroes, Trickster, Turtle and Bladder, formed by Earthmaker's own hands; the children and descendants of such spirits and, lastly, the evil spirits who are quite independent of Earthmaker. Let me point out that this is not the theology of the ordinary Winnebago but the esoteric doctrine of the Medicine Rite and, inconsistently, of the rituals in general.

5. This particular turn may represent Christian influence. However the virgin birth of Hare is a very old theme of Winnebago mythology.

6. Human beings are, of course, Hare's uncles and aunts because his mother was their sister.

7. The light that, according to the esoteric doctrine, all spirits radiate because of the life-giving powers stored within them. Light and life are here interchangeable. However, in addition, Hare is the symbol of light, of the dawn, of snow and of whiteness in general not only among the Winnebago but among many other tribes as well.

8. This is the first mention of the main theme of the Medicine Rite, the quest for immortality. That it should be associated with Hare is not accidental, because, in the exoteric Hare cycle, it is through his misconduct that immortality is lost for man, a theme that is retained even here in the greatly transformed Origin Myth (cf. page 22).

9. In the exoteric Hare cycle Earth is the sister of all the evil spirits Hare is destroying and protests, at times, violently against his actions. The theme is retained here in order to motivate Earth's resistance to granting man immortality.

10. The same motif, not to look back, is found in the exoteric cycle but not in connection with so high a purpose.

11. The circle of fire, that is, the possibility of attaining to old age, is represented as broken by Hare's disobedience, and Hare and Earth immediately reunite the two ends of the encircling fire. This fire is one of the obstacles that the ghost must surmount in his journey to spiritland. Cf. the myth on page 259.

12. These are the great spirits, the four cardinal points, the Island-Anchorers of the Medicine Rite. This episode does not appear in all versions of the origin myth nor does it belong there. It belongs to one of the various myths relating to the origin of death. The myth to which it properly belongs has been incorporated into our ceremony. Cf. pages 320 ff. It has been introduced here to still further emphasize the irrevocability of death. Not even the Island-Anchorers, the spirits who hold our island-earth in place and the basic spirits of the Medicine Rite, can do anything about it!

13. The way a mourner would behave. This mourning motif is a very clever utilization of an incident that belongs to an entirely different story where it functions in a far more vital fashion than it does here. In this story Hare is weeping because of the death of his younger brother who has been treacherously slain by evil spirits. His shrieks and cries are so tremendous that the universe is shaken to its very foundations and all the spirits, evil and good, are terrified and try desperately to appease him. All that is left of this is Hare's formal mourning and the very beautiful passage preceding it where the death of all things inanimate and animate is symbolized. Only a real poet could have done this.

14. To He-who-wears-human-heads-as-earrings is assigned the role of bringing Hare to Earthmaker because he is the last one dispatched. It is very interesting to see how the person who introduced this hero into the Origin Myth uses him here. He is actually one of the Thunderbird Spirits and so our remodeler calmly takes a well-known pertinent episode from another myth and fits it beautifully, in true Medicine Rite fashion, into the situation. All that was necessary was to bring Hare back with him. But since this is the esoteric and highly symbolic atmosphere of the Medicine Rite, our poet-re-modeler apparently found it impossible to transport a person immersed in life's evils to the purified air of Earthmaker. He must first be cleansed and freed from the contaminations and adhesions of the earth. This is accomplished by the shaking of the war club, a well-known motif associated, more specifically, with the journey of the ghost to spiritland.

15. This is the first of many metaphors for old age and the four ages of man which run through the whole ceremony like a main theme.

16. In the version of the Origin Myth given in the Rite itself there is no suggestion that specific clans were associated with the four seats of honor.

17. The stereotyped metaphor for the four ages of a man.

18. The stereotyped metaphor for the four ages of a woman.

19. Tanned buckskins and tobacco are the standard offerings to the spirits. Tanned buckskins are, however, never offered at the Medicine Rite today. It is conceivable that they were at one time.

20. The deities of the four cardinal points, often identified with the four winds.

21. Ritualistic term for bird.

22. Purports to be the historical account of the founding of the Medicine Rite.

23. The six standard commandments taught a young man.

24. There are certain female relatives with whom you are allowed to take liberties, specifically your cross cousins and your sisters-in-law. In other words do not treat all women as though they belonged to this group.

25. The Winnebago name for Red Banks, Green Bay, Wisconsin, the legendary origin place of the tribe and the place where they were first encountered by the French. That the Winnebago knew the Medicine Rite in its present form when they were living there is quite impossible. If we can accept this story as historically accurate, it must be the older form of the ceremony that is referred to here. The story that follows has definitely no place in the present Rite.

26. The ritual term for the occupants of the four seats of honor, the east, north, west and south.

27. This is the stereotyped description of how a blessing is received from a waterspirit.

28. The waterspirit, in contradistinction to all other spirits, offers his own body to the faster. The faster, himself, determines whether the medicines he compounds from the waterspirit's body shall be used for good or evil purposes. They are practically always used for evil purposes and the waterspirit is primarily a symbol of evil although actually his blessings are neutral.

336

Whiteness and red armpits are always associated with sacredness, the last with the added connotation of awesome power.

29. The anklets, bells and iron decorations, are the insignia of the evil shaman and medicine man.

30. What follows is a typical description of how medicines or any sacred objects are purchased.

The black hawk is the Iowa and his power to transform himself into this animal indicates that he is an evil medicine man. The pouches mentioned were the type used only in shamanistic practices. That the Iowa medicine man presses his guest to take the pouch has many significant overtones. The Iowa wishes his guest to take it because it is the more powerful of the two and because, as a competing shaman, he has no objection to the other over-reaching himself. However, it is also intended as a gracious compliment to the courage and the power of his visitor. Keramanic'aka, we see, is sorely tempted but finally realizes that it is too dangerous and takes the pouch made of the woman's scalp. Putting a person to such a test is a typical incident in the vision quest. It is the persistent preaching of the Winnebago to every faster, not to let his ambition and greed override his sense of proportion and fitness lest what is good and life-giving be converted into its opposite.

There is an explanation of some of the incidents in this story that has to be purchased separately from the particular individual who knows it. The pouch made of the woman's scalp, for instance, was that of the daughter-in-law of the Iowa, Tcacex'inga. She was a very beautiful woman and had red hair. Tcacex'inga asked his son for her. He gave her to his father, whereupon the latter killed her, buried her body, but kept her scalp from which he then made a medicine pouch. It is this sacred and highly prized possession that Keramanic'aka receives.

31. The ritualistic term for reincarnation is skin-shedding.

32. The story that follows unquestionably refers to the introduction of the birdskin pouches among the Winnebago. It is highly improbable, however, that they were introduced in this fashion. What we have here is a somewhat strange transformation of what is, to all intents and purposes, the stereotyped transfer of power from one medicine man to another. To explain what must have certainly appeared to the Winnebago, the sacrilegious claims of Nimaxguawa, it should be remembered that the speaker is not a Winnebago. His claims of power can thus be allowed to emphasize the tremendous nature of the gift received.

The whole story hardly belongs in content or implications to the Medicine Rite of today. I suspect, however, that Blowsnake had not purchased the knowledge necessary for its true understanding and that this is the reason for some of the inexplicable elements in it.

32. A sister's son always accompanied his uncle on the warpath as a kind of esquire. For a man to embark on the warpath without him was the height of daring and courage. For him not to be killed and actually return with the highest war honors represented military achievement *in excelsis.*

34. Not only as an expression of grief but as a method of appealing to the spirits, of helping him to forget his sorrow and of proving to the members of the Medicine Rite that he was qualified to recommend a person for membership in the Rite.

35. The term Creation-Lodge almost always refers to the lodge in which the first performance of the Rite took place.

36. Ritualistic term for those present and to whom special invitations were not extended.

37. Ritualistic term for tobacco, drum, speeches, songs, etc., in short, any object or action by means of which appeals are made to the spirits and thankfulness for their help is expressed.

38. That is, the relatives of a Rite member who has died.

39. Ritualistic name for the drum.
40. Ritualistic circumlocution for sleep.
41. Ritualistic name for drum.
42. That is, obtained blessings from all the spirits.
43. One of the few clear-cut survivals of the shamanistic aspects of the Rite members.
44. That is, be a member of the Rite.
45. Ritualistic term for those who have received special invitations.
46. Ritualistic term for gifts, food, etc.
47. That is, witches.
48. That is, his ties with the Rite.
49. Ritualistic term for fire and the fireplace.
50. That is, the tobacco.
51. Because so many are taking part in the performance and so many offerings of tobacco are being made.
52. That is, in the customary Winnebago fashion.
53. That is, just out of the desire to kill, for such a man would not suffer pain as would a husband and a father if those he loved were killed.
54. A privilege belonging to full-fledged Rite members.
55. That is, 'with whom we shall participate at the main ceremony.'
56. That is, the ground oak leaves that are mixed with the tobacco.
57. As a sign of their profound grief they neglect even to brush and comb their hair and because they do not wish to eat food full of hairs and dandruff, they stop eating entirely.
58. Stereotyped metaphor for death.
59. That is, someone will take the place of the deceased in the Rite or, if he has not been a member, to honor his memory.
60. Apparently, another name for the Medicine Rite.
61. That is, they also ascended it. For an explanation of this passage, cf. page 263.
62. That is, 'don't watch other people to see whether they are doing things correctly.'
63. Probably the most expensive of all the privileges in the Rite. Only old members of long standing possessed it.
64. That is, 'don't be too ambitious lest you come to grief.'
65. That is, they were present at the first performance of the Rite.
66. That is, get to the roots of things.
67. This is another version of the story on page 93. Cf. also p. 336, note 30.

PART TWO

Preparatory Note. I was never permitted to see the Vapor-Bath ritual, here called the Ritual of Purification, and had, therefore, to rely entirely upon the account given by Blowsnake. Because of its complicated symbolism it happens to be the most difficult to describe. In addition, I never felt quite satisfied that Blowsnake really knew all the symbolism. For that reason a certain amount of unclearness has crept into some of the details of the account which the reader will perhaps detect. The main difficulty, however, in attempting to adequately describe, for an alien audience, a ceremony like this one, is its very nature. It is really quite impossible to visualize what took place there

338

without a fairly complete knowledge of Winnebago culture which, naturally, no white man possesses. A full commentary would help considerably but lack of space does not permit it being given here.

1. Ritualistic term for invitation stick.

2. That is, the invitation sticks.

3. From a branch of the tree, sacred to Earthmaker, the oak, the invitation sticks are made. East, North, West and South have theirs stained with blue clay to represent light and life. Those of Ghost are rubbed with red to indicate that he is taking the place of a dead person.

4. Grandfather here refers to the heat of the stone and the latter is given its symbolic and ritualistic name, sacred woman. To paint and envelop oneself with our grandfather, means to let the steam arising from the heated stone of the vapor-bath lodge cover you.

5. That is, 'do you also enter the vapor-bath lodge.'

6. To cut across the lodge in this fashion is not only the most expensive of all privileges but also one of the most sacred and daring of actions.

7. East and South, the beginning of the Road and the end of the Road, are the positions invested with most prestige. North and West are in the middle and are felt to be somewhat inferior.

8. That is, the pole of the vapor-bath lodge.

9. The shells shot into individuals in the Medicine Rite are frequently called arrows, probably referring to the fact that in the old form of the shooting rite (cf. page 75) they were used instead of shells.

10. That is, shoot life into him with the shells.

11. The story that follows refers, of course, to the origin of the stone of the vapor-bath.

12. That is, the various colored clays.

13. As he pulls down the trees he pulls down and destroys evil as well. As he walks, the trees automatically bend toward him because of his power and holiness.

14. Their fear symbolizes not only the physical reluctance of entering the vapor-bath but, far more, the awesome terror of this most sacred experience that they are to encounter. The address to the spirit in the second paragraph following, summarizes these contradictory attitudes and emotions.

15. Foreshadowing the heat he will soon have.

16. Ritualistic term for fire. 'Not good to oppose' means that he overwhelms, burns up, etc. those who do.

17. He, that is, the stone, became hot.

18. In spite of his proximity to the fire and his being red hot his clothing remains untouched. Clothing here signifies the powers he possessed. The light flashing blue from his headdress is life.

19. The boys are the poles of the vapor-bath lodge.

20. The bear is the lodge covering. That is why he is depicted as being as large as the lodge itself.

21. The poles, that is, the boys, are now being bent over to form the framework of the lodge. As they are thus bent they symbolize the stooping of old age. Thus the very framework of the vapor-bath lodge symbolizes the whole gamut of life, from youth to old age.

When he is finished he, the bear, sits there facing the east, extending his claws out and looking white. His teeth are white and he is chattering. His lips are red. Thus he is a typical awe-inspiring spirit with the supreme symbols of sacredness and overwhelming power, the white body, the red lips, just as the waterspirit with his white body and round red armpits. The imagery here is also supposed to indicate how the vapor-bath lodge is really enclosed within the body of a spirit, a spirit of fierce demeanor and threatening claws and teeth. Into this animal-spirit those who are to take the vapor-bath must enter. They must be terrified and yet strong enough in purpose to overcome it.

22. Blowsnake has here incorporated what should have been an explanation into the body of the text.

23. That is, the sticks. These sticks are symbolical of both those surrounding the fireplace and the ones that carry the stones.

24. That is, invisible as Turtle for he has become transformed into water. But see the following note.

25. The following passage, because of its multiple symbolisms, has a detailed traditional commentary, which I shall give in full. It runs as follows:

Although it would have been impossible for an ordinary person to have done it, when Turtle made himself invisible, he went below the earth to get some holy water from one of the waterspirits who was likewise one of the Island-Anchorers that Earthmaker had pierced through the earth so that the Medicine Rite lodge might be strengthened by the addition of the power of the waterspirit Island-Anchorer. Turtle then transformed himself into this water and fell upon the breast of the sacred woman and white daylight arose. From this Turtle received a mark in the shape of a cross on his breast. (By cross here is meant the two crossed lines whose four points and crossing point are the symbol of the cardinal points and the nadir.)

A short supplementary commentary runs as follows: Turtle brought the stones and the water. Then he put the stone to his breast and lay down on his back. As he did so daylight burst through his navel and when he got up, the marks of daylight appeared as a cross on his back.

All this multiple and involved imagery and symbolism, expressed in concrete terms, signifies that when the water is poured on the heated stone within the vapor-bath lodge, white clouds of steam arise.

A long commentary could be given on this passage but this, of course, cannot be done here.

26. Because of the steam which is white physically and white (sacred and life-dealing), symbolically.

27. That is, she took some grass fibers and braided them into a handle for the ladle used in sprinkling water. The blue color refers both to the grass fibers and to life.

28. That is, the sprinkler.

29. East takes the tied-hair of our grandmother, that is, the sprinkler, touches Turtle, that is, the water, and sprinkles it on the stone.

30. This is the proper position for shooting. For a description, in proper detail, of the shooting ritual pages 232 ff.

31. Each seat was originally covered with an animal skin, this one with a bear skin. Frequently it was referred to as the bear or the bear's lair. 'To be wrapped in a dark haired skin' is a metaphorical way of referring to the seat.

32. Again the seat is meant.

33. 'Frail from holiness' means that he had deprived himself of sleep and food for a long time in his attempt to obtain blessings from the spirits. It is used particularly in connection with the vision-quest at puberty.

34. In taking the vapor-bath they had obtained life and, when they were through, they saw that the stone had become old and that the lodge-poles had become old and they realized that old age would come to them just as it had come to all these objects.

35. The bear here is the lodge covering. He is taking it off.

36. That is, having swallowed the shell and died, he will become alive again.

37. He is here identifying himself so completely with the Island-Anchorer he is impersonating that he uses the phraseology these spirits employed when Hare came to them for information. Cf. page 23.

38. That is, the food prepared with the water heated by the stone of the vapor-bath.

PART THREE

1. This simply refers to the fact that the night had evidently been windy and the lodge was full of smoke.

2. Literally, the phrase means 'to go on the warpath, to meet or conquer obstacles.' Actually, it refers to the placing of the otterskin pouch near the one who is to be shot.

3. That is, the former owner of the otterskin pouch is dead.

4. That is, to give up mourning.

5. That is, the substitute for the one who has died and who is now occupying his place in the Medicine Rite.

6. An expression of ritualistic modesty. He means that he possesses no knowledge that would demand his speaking or singing.

7. The seat personified as a bear.

8. That is, the shell.

9. The holiest part of the animal-spirit.

10. That is, the desire for revenge, the unwillingness to accept the situation, the thoughts of suicide, etc.

11. That is, to fast and torture oneself. In the early days, cutting off finger joints and offering them to the spirits was an accepted thing.

12. Refers to the fact that South and Ghost really occupy the same seat according to the older view.

13. That is, the speeches and songs of the impersonators of the Island-Anchorers. The Island-Anchorers are the winds.

14. That is, the Medicine Rite.

15. Whispering to people where many are present is considered by the Winnebago as ill-bred. He is apologizing for it. What the whispering is about is explained a few lines below.

16. Their function is to keep track of the shells, for there must be none missing at the end, not only because they are private possessions, but because they are too dangerous to be around loose.

17. That is, the main ceremony, which begins the following day.

18. That is, it would be ineffective there. He may possibly be alluding here to the shamanistic shooting of missiles still practiced by some members and which was uncompromisingly condemned by the Medicine Rite.

19. That is, because it can kill and bring to life again.

20. Ritualistic expression, meaning to tire a person and make him sleepy, by going through a lot of meaningless motions.

21. These privileges are given in detail on page 343, note 13.

22. That is, this is no place to do things on one's own or to begin experimenting.

23. That is, he is still mourning, paying no attention to the fire, and neglecting things in general.

1. That is, when they have been shot, have died and, then, recover consciousness again. What is here emphasized is the nature of coming to consciousness of (Earthmaker) out of nothingness. When, in the sentence that follows immediately, he speaks about (Earthmaker) having 'pity upon himself,' the narrator has had him pass to the age of puberty and begun to fast, for this is the stereotyped expression for fasting.

2. He is anticipating the world and the creatures he is about to create.

3. To make a thing round is to endow it with life and holiness. What has been created here is the world in general and the four directions, as well as the light that could make them visible. No Biblical influence is here involved.

4. Pleasing because he (Earthmaker) is now having his first real experience.

5. Where things first come into existence.

6. The earth is flat and, being a small island in a vast expanse of water, would have bobbed up and down in uncontrolled fashion, if it had remained round. It, of course, still did and the problem becomes how to make it remain quiet.

7. That is, snow, in the exoteric sense; extremely sacred life and power, in the esoteric sense.

8. In the esoteric sense because it is south, in the esoteric sense because, like Hare, he was the last of the four directions to be created and the last, in Winnebago mythology, is always the most important.

9. Esoteric and ritualistic term for stones, rocks.

10. That is, split and spread over the whole world. Light means life at the same time.

11. This clearly is a European influence.

12. That is, by the use of the shell in the otterskin pouch, man is to die and become alive again and be taught to lead a virtuous life.

13. This is another account of how the world was created and belongs to a myth common to the Ojibwa, Menominee, Fox and Algonkin Indians in general. The Winnebago have a version of it but this has probably been borrowed from one of these tribes.

14. The four positions are called ritualistically and esoterically, the plates from which you eat, i.e., derive spiritual life and sustenance.

15. That is, when he bit the fish, the light would run into the gap made.

16. That is, the food which he drew forth. However it also means nourishment in every sense of that term.
    The following sentence 'imprinted them with additional light and life' means that the plate was marked with spots of food.

17. This is a stereotyped metaphor from the vocabulary of a shaman.

18. Cf. notes 17 and 18.

19. Otter is now represented as experimenting with the object, the shell, very much as the trickster and the culture-heroes do in one of their adventures.

20. That is, it would always strike into the very core of life.

21. Otter has now proceeded from the gross, material and earthbound things, a tree and a rock, to a less material and heavenly object. His next shot is to be at the most mysterious and most powerful of all things in the world, fire.

22. That is, the fire.

23. The essence of things on earth.

24. In the myth that follows, because of the importance and the great length of the traditional commentary, I have incorporated this commentary into the text itself.

342

25. This was the generally given apology for what must have seemed to many individuals about to be initiated, a fraud. However, see Blowsnake's reaction, page 5.

26. This is the threat, physical and spiritual, held over the heads of members who divulged the secrets of the ritual.

27. Winnebago proverb, meaning either death has no terrors for me or the very fact that you ask me to betray the secrets of the ritual has killed me.

PART FIVE

1. He is the drum.

2. So tremendous was the force of the drum falling that the very foundations of the world were shaken.

3. Apparently the phrase 'by the force of his thoughts' simply signifies the extreme of power and sacredness.

4. That is, the poles in the centre of the lodge became firm and fixed. The man is the drum.

5. This is the translation given to me. The word translated 'conscience' here is the regular term for mind, will-power, etc.

6. This is taken from the 'official' set of instructions given a young boy.

7. Four was the sacred number of the Winnebago. This prohibition had not been enforced for many years before 1909.

8. This is the tree of life. Cf. the reference to it in the *Journey to Spiritland*, page 263.

9. This black hawk is symbolical for the shell.

10. Probably means at some performance of the Rite when, after death, he becomes reincarnated and returns to earth.

11. Refers to the fact that the givers of this performance, from their own pockets, paid for something to place on the ground for the shell to fall on as a sign of respect to it.

12. The technical name for that part of the ritual where they go around ejaculating 'yahi-hi, etc.'

13. When a man first becomes initiated he can do very little except participate in the general activities of the Rite. He has practically no privilege except the right to possess an otterskin pouch and a shell. Today, at least in 1909, he was allowed to shoot a person. In the old days he could not even do that. The privileges which play so important a part in the Rite had to be purchased individually and generally were so expensive that a man was well in his forties before he possessed them. These privileges are practically all shamanistic in nature and probably stem from a time when the present Medicine Rite was in its formative period. The privileges in the approximate order of their relative importance are as follows:

    1. The right to go directly from one's seat to the fireplace instead of first circling the lodge. Possessed by very few of even the oldest members.

    2. To kick up the ground with your feet before shooting.

    3. To shoot two or more people at the same time.

    4. To manipulate the otterskin pouch in such a way that sounds emerge from it.

    5. To tie bells to the ankles and have them jingle when you dance.

    6. To attach metal plates to the front of your moccasins.

    7. To drum.

    8. To stretch out your arms full-length before shooting.

14. For the eagleskin pouch.

15. For the sparrowhawk-skin pouch.

16. For the squirrel-skin pouch.

17. For the weaselskin pouch.

18. For the beaverskin pouch.

19. For the otterskin pouch.

20. That is, ate in them.

21. This refers to the belief that when you are eating an animal you must always leave enough over so that the animal can restore himself to life again.

22. This was the exact word used. It is essentially a bit of ritualistic modesty implying that, at best, the members are really indulging in play.

23. That is, by rolling together the clouds, Earthmaker produced something which turned into a shell as he threw it below. There, the otter, the least of all animals, seized it in his mouth.

24. That is, it deprived him of consciousness just as the shell does a man when he is shot.

25. That is, he had been killed and returned to the possibilities of a still greater life.

26. The fire.

27. He is the gourd.

28. Trickster.

29. That is, possessed of little power.

30. In order to contrast the important mission he was to accomplish and his utter powerlessness and inadequacy.

31. Turtle is the prototype *ad absurdum* of the warrior and shaman.

32. He is preparing himself, in contradistinction to Trickster and Turtle, for his mission.

33. That is, he has now passed the age where he has to be taken care of and has a place of his own.

34. This word can be analyzed into he-who-appears-to-be-but-is-not. My interpreter accepted this as correct but I doubt that this is anything but a folk etymology. *Herecgunina* is, in all probability, the Christian devil.

35. The lodges in a Winnebago village used to be arranged in a long, curved (?) line.

36. That is, his sorrow and anger. Compare this with the manner in which the same incident is handled in the other version of the Origin Myth, pages 21 ff.

37. That is, the ground was levelled.

38. That is, the sinews with which to tie the vertical sticks.

39. That is, the sinews with which to tie the side sticks.

40. This is a comment of the informant.

41. That is, the bearskin that formerly covered the ground on this side.

42. That is, the deerskin that formerly covered the ground on this side.

43. That is, dying or failing to achieve their purpose.

44. This is a well-known myth and is really concerned with the exoteric account of the origin of death. It is rather strange that it should have found its way into the Medicine Rite.

45. Corn blossoms.

46. Corn stalks.

47. Corn.

48. The oak leaves that are ground and mixed with tobacco.

344

49. Probably a reference to one of the messengers sent out originally to invite the spirits to the Creation-Lodge.

50. The gourd.

51. That is, the gourd.

52. This privilege was highly prized and, apparently, some members indulged in it without having purchased the right to do so from the proper person. They are here being warned about the iniquity of such an action and the dangers inhering in it.

53. He was so powerful that every time he took a step he penetrated the earth up to his arms and his ankles. Summer is here meant.

54. That is, his second step was in snow.

55. Hare and snow are synonymous.

56. That is, autumn.

57. Spring.
This succession of summer, winter, autumn and spring is not supposed so much to refer to the regular succession of seasons as to the fact that there would be such seasons.

58. Concretely, this means that he has thrown off the lodge covering.

59. Just as the removal of the lodge covering is symbolical for the return of the upper spirits to their home, so the pulling out of the entrance-flap is symbolical of the return of the earth animals to their home. This thought is further stressed by the magnificent final paragraph.

MYTHOS

The Princeton/Bollingen Series in World Mythology